# LAW'S QUANDARY

*Steven D. Smith*

# Law's Quandary

**HARVARD UNIVERSITY PRESS**
Cambridge, Massachusetts, and London, England

Copyright © 2004 by the President and Fellows of Harvard College
All rights reserved
Printed in the United States of America

First Harvard University Press paperback edition, 2007

*Library of Congress Cataloging-in-Publication Data*

Smith, Steven D. (Steven Douglas), 1952–
    Law's quandary / Steven D. Smith.
        p. cm.
    Includes bibliographical references and index.
    ISBN-13: 978-0-674-01533-3 (cloth : paper)
    ISBN-10: 0-674-01533-9 (cloth : alk. paper)
    ISBN-13: 978-0-674-02573-8 (pbk.)
    ISBN-10: 0-674-02573-3 (pbk.)
    1. Law—Philosophy. I. Title.
    K230.S627L39 2004
    340'.1—dc22        2004052296

*To Doug Smith,*
*my father and tacit mentor,*
*who wouldn't have needed any of this*

# Contents

# *Preface*

A preface typically tries to say what a book is about; sometimes it also serves to express acknowledgments. In my case, these purposes converge.

What is the book about? Well, I suppose I could describe it as an inquiry into the recurring complaint that provides the title for the first chapter—the complaint that accuses the vast, solemn outpourings of lawyers and judges of being "just words." But that sort of preview would be opaque—and potentially embarrassing. ("You actually wrote a book—a whole book—about whether law is just a lot of words? Have you no sense of irony? Nothing more worthwhile to do with your time?") Desperate to give the book greater dignity, I might overcorrect and say that it's about the metaphysics of law, or about how our understanding of law has deteriorated due to our wanton neglect (or, rather, our systematic suppression) of its ontological dimensions. But that sort of theme, baldly stated and standing alone, would be merely misleading and also, in the current climate of opinion, alienating. Who today has any use for "metaphysics" or "ontology"? Who has any clear notion of what, if anything, those terms even mean?

So for now, I can better express what this book is trying to do more obliquely, by offering two sets of acknowledgments. The first is to several generations of mentors who lived and wrote just a little before my time and, probably, yours. (I once met Lon Fuller, actually, but he was well past his prime.) A half-century or a century ago, it was possible to write about jurisprudence in a way that even the most celebrated legal thinkers of our own era—Ronald Dworkin, for example, or Richard Posner—no longer manage, and probably no longer aspire to. I have in mind three particular works: Oliver Wendell Holmes's essay "The Path of the Law," Karl Llewellyn's *The Bramble Bush*, and Lon Fuller's *The Law in Quest of Itself*. Given the choice between any of these writings and, say, a good novel, I suppose that even hardened professors of jurisprudence would choose the novel. So would I, probably. Even so, these writings manage to convey arresting insights in a way that is accessible, enjoyable, and even enriching in a general sense.

These writings are not "academic" in either the honorific or pejorative sense of the term. Perhaps because the writings began as public lectures, their authors present themselves as actual *persons;* they do not hide behind the numbing, homogenized, pseudo-objectivism that academic conventions often insist on. Their diction can be idiosyncratic, can sometimes even border on barbarous (especially in Llewellyn's case). In discussing a thinker or theory, they may resort to simplifying caricatures—caricatures that distort but that can also illumine the essence of a thinker or theory in a way that more ponderous description cannot.

Most importantly, Holmes, Llewellyn, and Fuller work on the assumption—one that today might seem close to preposterous—that, as Fuller puts it, "[jurisprudential q]uestions . . . affect the fundamental bent of our lives." Thus, Llewellyn explains that his lectures seek to be at once a primer on law—useful for beginning law students—and an expression of "some of the more passionate convictions which motivate his living." And in the last sentence of "Path," Holmes describes (with perhaps a touch of grandiloquence) his aspiration to "connect [the] subject with the universe and catch an echo of the divine."

To put the point a bit differently, these writings of the early twentieth century have a kind of multiple *openness*—openness to readers both specialists and laypersons, openness in revealing the authors' personal commitments and not merely their professional positions and, even more important, openness to the connections between law and the larger issues of life.

With few exceptions, such openness is scarcely discernible in even the best jurisprudential writing in recent decades. Indeed, I suspect that most legal scholars today would be embarrassed if these qualities were detectable in their work—as if they had been caught in the performance of some private function. Jurisprudential thinking in this respect has followed a familiar course. In many disciplines, it seems, periods of zestful, insightful innocence give way to periods . . . not so much of decline, exactly, as of professional virtuosity. Of scholasticism. Eminences of the later period—the virtuosos, the scholastics—may look back on their predecessors with a mixture of respect and condescension: they may view those predecessors as gifted novices. In this spirit, contemporary legal philosophizing is no doubt more sophisticated—more methodical, more technically proficient—than Holmes's, Llewellyn's, and Fuller's writings were. And yet . . . these jurisprudential virtuosos and their productions may prompt the same reaction that *Paradise Lost* provoked in Samuel Johnson: it is "one of those books which the reader admires, lays down and forgets to take up again. Its perusal is a duty rather than a pleasure."

Here is an instance: I recall how, the first time I taught a jurisprudence class at the University of Colorado, I assigned the students to read H. L. A. Hart's *The Concept of Law.* I later asked the class what they had thought of the book. One student (who seemed bright but, obviously, not duly acculturated) spat out his answer as if reacting to a piece of rotten meat. "I think it's pathetic," he said, "that an intelligent person would spend his life writing stuff as obscure and pointless, and *dead,* as this." Taken aback, I explained that Hart's book is widely regarded as a classic and a model of clear thinking and writing. What I said about the book was—is—true. Still, I have to admit that I can understand—maybe even sympathize with—the student's reaction. And if this stinging criticism can be made of Hart—well, there is an *a fortiori* lurking in the vicinity. So it is hardly surprising if, as I am told, student interest in jurisprudence is on the wane. Nor is the decline limited to students; it includes professors—even, I strongly suspect, professors of jurisprudence.

So then, is it possible to resist the flow of history, and thus to write about law with the same sort of openness sometimes achieved in an earlier period? To talk about law in a way that speaks to both specialists and the laity, and that "connects the subject to the universe and catches an echo of the divine"? I'm not sure, but this book is an effort to do that. So I have tried to take "Path" and *Bramble Bush* and *Quest*—not *The Concept of Law* and its ever more meticulously ponderous successors—as models. (I have fallen short, of course, in a whole variety of ways and for a whole variety of reasons.)

I should note one crucial qualification to what I have just been saying. Although I have taken Holmes and Llewellyn and Fuller as mentors in what you might call their "open" or "human" orientation to the subject, I have not followed their substantive teachings on the nature of law. On the contrary. On the level of jurisprudential substance, these predecessors are more nearly opponents than mentors, or perhaps mentors from whom I—and, I believe, *we*—need to break away. Holmes and his successors operated in an era that was determined to purge itself of "metaphysics" (whatever that is). And they thought that in doing this they were acknowledging, and advancing, a sort of inexorable movement of history. Holmes and Llewellyn were zealous for the movement; Fuller acquiesced in it. Everything these men and their contemporaries say about law is tinged with, if not permeated by, this anti-metaphysical animus.

A similar attitude still dominates the legal academy—and still, in my view, paralyzes our efforts to understand law. But the older assumptions about the inevitable course of history have by now been largely falsified, and it may be possible to take a fresh look at the world—and at law, and at how law relates to and reflects the world. Possible and also urgently *necessary*, because the "Path" that Holmes pointed to and that generations of his dutiful followers have trod, have trod, have trod has led to a jurisprudential dead end. That is why, I believe, the quality of openness sometimes apparent in our predecessors is now more opportune than the currently prevailing virtuosity that seeks mainly to restate, analyze, criticize, and extend their various claims with methodical care and ever greater sophistication. We need to emulate our distinguished predecessors' *qualities of mind* precisely so that we can get beyond their *substantive philosophies*.

This observation leads to a second, briefer set of acknowledgments, which I owe to a remarkable group of former colleagues at the University of Colorado. When I moved to Colorado in 1987, Bob Nagel was already there, and the next year Pierre Schlag arrived, and later Paul Campos and Richard Delgado and Jean Stefancic and Rebecca French and Curt Bradley joined the collection. ("Family" would emphatically not be the right word.) "Crits" all—in a catholic and nonpolitical sense of the term. (I hope that none of them is offended by the description.) Though these people differed tremendously from each other in their philosophies, politics, interests, temperaments, and life situations, they were all intellectually engaged and also iconoclastic in one way or another that made for endless and interesting conversations. Perhaps the Colorado environment—its mountains, its frontier innocence and remoteness from the sophisticated centers of high civilization, maybe even its peculiar politics incongruously situating "the People's Republic of Boulder" in the state that became famous for the anti-gay rights "Amendment 2"—contributed to the distinctive atmosphere. In any case, it seemed possible there to raise questions—*really* to raise them, all sorts of questions, about law and the Supreme Court and the legal academy and the modern Western worldview—that somehow could not be taken as seriously at other more self-consciously respectable institutions where I have studied or taught.

That freedom did not lead to uniform conclusions, of course. Quite the reverse. For example, I am sure that Pierre Schlag influenced me (or "corrupted" me, as a conservative friend wistfully told me) far more than I influenced him, such that many of my views (including many expressed in this book) by now probably owe much to Pierre even when I am no longer conscious of the debt. But in the end our outlooks were fundamentally different. Pierre seemed constitutionally incapable of viewing what I will simply call "faith" as a live option; and so for him critical openness was always a path to despair. (Or at least to what in my view amounted to despair; but Pierre did not see it this way.) For me, conversely, and for better or worse, it seems that faith was and is inescapable, even though it is an ongoing and at times frustrating struggle—for me as for many others—to articulate the basis and content of that faith. Nor can this struggle be divorced from the effort to understand law: hence this book.

These collegial differences made the exchanges all the more valuable, for me at least. In any case, this book is an expression of years of such discussions with Bob, Pierre, Paul, Richard, Jean, Rebecca, and Curt, to all of whom I am deeply indebted. We have all moved on; but the book seemed worth doing, among other reasons, as a sort of memoir of a decade of cordially combative conversations.

Others have helped me with the book in more direct and usual ways. A number of friends and associates generously read and commented on all or part of the book: Brian Bix, George Wright, Chris Eberle, Larry Solum, Gail Heriot, Paul Campos, John Garvey, David Brink, Richard Delgado, Laurie Claus, Emily Sherwin, Mike Ramsey, Patrick Brennan, Mike Rappaport, Sai Prakash, Tom Smith, Dan Rodriguez, Rick Garnett, Chris Wonnell, Richard Posner, and Maimon Schwarzchild. Larry Alexander and Michael Perry deserve my special thanks for giving both substantial comments and also encouragement and moral support along the way; such friends are one of life's larger blessings. Another good friend, Joe Vining, returned the manuscript with a barrage of marginal comments that, alas, I was unable on the whole to assimilate adequately into the book; but the comments were so perceptive and provocative that I almost wish they could have been printed along with the book. I also benefited from questions and challenges in presentations of parts of the book to the law faculties at Arizona State University, Emory University, and the University of San Diego. Much of the book was written while I was on the faculty of Notre Dame Law School, and I appreciate the support of the dean and faculty there. As always, I especially appreciate the moral support of my wife, Merina, and my children. And I owe a small debt of gratitude to the Peace Corps: thanks to its administrative ineptitude my daughter Rachel, who knows more philosophy than I do, was unexpectedly able to spend several months with us in South Bend, and thus to read and comment on an early draft before traveling to her assignment in Uzbekistan. And Rosemary Getty provided invaluable assistance in preparing the manuscript for submission.

Although none of the chapters here have previously been published, I have in places borrowed and adapted passages and sections of three articles with the permission of the original journals: "Believing Like a Lawyer," 40 *B.C. L. Rev.* 1041 (1999); Copyright © 1999 Boston College Law School; "Expressivist Jurisprudence and the Depletion of Meaning," 60 *Md. L. Rev.* 506 (2001), used with the permission of the Maryland Law Review; "Nonsense and Natural Law," 4 *S. Cal. Interdisc. L.J.* 583 (1995), used with the permission of the Southern California Interdisciplinary Law Journal.

I also thank the Princeton University Press for permission to quote from Joseph Vining, *From Newton's Sleep* (1994).

# LAW'S QUANDARY

# PART I

# Law and Metaphysics?

Jurisprudentially speaking, the twentieth century was a tremendously fertile—and tremendously futile—era. In a lecture given on the eve of the new century and destined to become the most celebrated and cited law review article ever published, Oliver Wendell Holmes foresaw exciting, even revolutionary developments in law and legal thought. In the not so distant future, he predicted, law would leave behind the sterile parsing of precedents, the haggling over rules and doctrines and, above all, the reverently moralistic application of legal tradition that from medieval times had composed the lawyer's daily duties. Instead, the practice of law was destined to become, and soon, a more rational and scientific enterprise—one that would make heavy use of statistics and economics and "theory." These changes were "the inevitable next step, mind, like matter, simply obeying a law of spontaneous growth."[1]

His descendants routinely pay tribute to Holmes's prescience. His "article is a prophecy," Richard Posner enthuses, "and it is coming true."[2] "A century later," Mary Ann Glendon remarks (though not as happily), "lawyers all over the world are marching to the measure of [Holmes's] thought."[3] The conspicuous growth of law and economics is perhaps only the most obvious fulfillment of Holmes's predictions.

Curiously, though, from a different and perhaps more discerning perspective, it seems that nothing much has changed: the radical advances in law anticipated by Holmes and repeatedly proclaimed by his followers look to be a thing of the surface. The ways in which lawyers and judges (and even most legal scholars) actually practice and talk about law are not so different than they were a century ago—or even five centuries ago. Thus, the distinguished historian and law professor Norman Cantor asserts that "[a] London barrister of 1540, quick-frozen and revived in New York today, would need only a

1

year's brush-up course at NYU School of Law to begin civil practice as a partner in a midtown or Wall Street corporate-law firm."[4] In his less sanguine
moments, Judge Posner (who comes as close as anyone to being a reincar-
nation of Holmes, or at least of Holmes's more cerebral side) admits as much.
"The traditional conception of law is as orthodox today," he laments, "as it
was a century ago."[5]

Few lawyers or judges today, Posner concedes, would admit to embracing
the formalistic legal methods and assumptions that Holmes deprecated. "Yet
most lawyers, judges, and law professors," he observes glumly, "still believe
that demonstrably correct rather than merely plausible or reasonable answers to most legal questions, even very difficult and contentious ones, can
be found—and it is imperative that they be found—by reasoning from authoritative texts, either legislative enactments (including constitutions) or
judicial decisions, and therefore without recourse to the theories, data, insights, or empirical methods of the social sciences."[6]

How to account for this gaping discrepancy between what was *supposed to*
happen and what by and large *has* happened (or, more accurately, has *not*
happened)? Some observers point to attitudinal and institutional factors.
Perhaps lawyers are traditionalist and conservative by nature—or maybe
just intellectually lazy? Or law schools have not adapted to the modern
world by teaching future lawyers the empirical and theoretical skills needed
to implement the newer visions of law. Other critics may attribute the fail-
ures of modern law to other sorts of factors—Weberian bureaucratic rationality, or capitalist ideology, or the cartel structure of the profession, or
an absence of the courage to face up to fears of "illegitimacy" or even "ni-
hilism."

This book is devoted to advancing a very different (though not necessarily
incompatible) sort of explanation. The malaise of modern law and legal
thought, I hope to show, is a manifestation of what is at bottom a *metaphysical* predicament. And the way out of the malaise—if there is one (a question
about which I have no confident opinion)—will require us to "take metaphysics seriously," so to speak.

This claim will surely be met with incredulity, so I hasten to point out that
I am not the only observer of the law to offer some such diagnosis. I will try
to enlist a few allies (including some less than eager ones) as the discussion
proceeds. Still, there is no denying that this is not the usual explanation. Indeed, the dominant view has been exactly to the contrary. It would not be
much of a stretch, as we will see in Chapter 4, to say that the central effort of
legal thinkers from Holmes through the Legal Realists through the modern

proponents of "policy science" has been precisely to improve law by ridding it of the curse of metaphysics.[7]

In this vein, although Morris and Felix Cohen devoted a chapter in their jurisprudence reader to "Law and Metaphysics" (which they defined, in rather docile terms, as "the bringing to consciousness of what is assumed in all legal argument"), they also anticipated skepticism—a skepticism that Felix Cohen's own writings surely helped to fuel. So the Cohens acknowledged that metaphysics is often viewed as "the effort of a blind man in a dark room to find a black cat that isn't there."[8] This aversion to metaphysics has become almost axiomatic in many quarters. Brian Bix observes that mainstream legal thinkers like H. L. A. Hart have seen the "primary purpose [of jurisprudence] as a kind of therapy: a way of overcoming the temptation to ask metaphysical questions ('what is Law?' or 'do norms exist')."[9]

Indeed, law has sometimes seemed an attractive field precisely because in its nitty gritty practicality it has appeared to offer a refuge from metaphysical questions. Many lawyers and law professors (like many people generally) are constitutionally averse to philosophy, and Michael Moore suggests that even "many philosophers became *legal and political* philosophers in part to avoid metaphysical questions."[10] Moore himself is an exception; he is among the handful of legal theorists—totaling, maybe, a half-dozen or so?—who occupy themselves with metaphysical issues. But at the conclusion of a lengthy, learned article on the subject even he seems to concede that his analysis has little or no practical payoff. The metaphysics of law, rather, is just an abstruse subject that a few unusually constituted people happen to find interesting: God knows why. (This is just a figure of speech, reflective of my own perversity: Moore peremptorily assures us in the article, with no hint of doubt or qualification, that God does not exist.)[11]

The preceding paragraphs mislead, though, if they suggest that contempt for metaphysics is limited to the field of law. Charles Larmore notes more generally that "'metaphysics,' . . . today functions mostly as a term of abuse."[12] When it occasionally comes up in actual conversation, the term is nearly always dismissive: "metaphysical" conjures up a hazy, generally unappealing image of things musty, abstruse, unfathomable—"academic" in the pejorative sense that connotes sterile quibbling about matters that have no possible relevance to actual life and that consist mainly of abstract word puzzles. (Except, that is, when "metaphysics" is taken as a code word for the paranormal or exotic, as in the shelf label for a large section of literature in a New Age bookstore I recall visiting in San Francisco.) Voltaire's famous portrayal in *Candide* of the metaphysician Dr. Pangloss sponsors a different but equally unalluring image—of a pathetic and borderline-delusional thinker who concocts airy and fantastic theories to escape from the messiness and unpleasantness of the real world.

These unfavorable impressions will not likely be corrected—they may in fact be reinforced—if you browse through a philosophy book dealing with the subject. You will encounter alien terms like "possibilia," "substitutivity," and "exemplifications," used in connection with arguments about such less than urgent (to most of us) questions as whether and in what sense numbers are "real," or whether possible worlds that do not achieve actualization can somehow be said to exist.[13] Indeed, many leading philosophers over the last couple of centuries have themselves called for an end to metaphysical speculation, arguing that the enterprise is futile or worse. A leading contemporary philosopher, William Alston, holds a more favorable view, but he concedes that the sort of work that modern metaphysicians have turned out makes them "sensitive to charges of engaging in parlor games during working hours."[14]

How then can a subject as removed and presumptively useless, if not actually pernicious, as metaphysics be the source of—or a possible remedy for—any difficulties in law, legal discourse, or legal theory?

It is a hard question. I cannot try to answer it all at once: this is, after all, the task of the book itself. But two preliminary qualifications may calm at least some suspicions. First, my concern here is not with the whole range of issues that get put under the heading of "metaphysics" but, more specifically, with the subcategory sometimes called "ontology," which is the subset of the discipline that addresses the question of "what there is"—of "the primary constituents of this or any possible world, the very alphabet of being."[15] Second, I myself am a law professor, not a metaphysician (or even a philosopher), and I can boast of only brief skirmishes with academic metaphysics. The argument in this book turns not so much on the rarified questions that academic philosophers spend their lives pondering as on what we might call "practical metaphysics."

That term may seem oxymoronic. So the chapters in this first part attempt to explain how law might present, at its core, questions that are at once thoroughly practical and deeply metaphysical, and how neglect of those questions might render our talk about law a form of highly refined "nonsense." (Which, of course, is just what law-talk looks like to many critics, both within and outside the legal profession.)

# CHAPTER 1

# *Just Words?*

Lawyers (and judges, and law professors) are targets of derision on a variety of grounds; but some of the most familiar criticisms disparage the way they—I suppose I should say *we*—talk, or the words we use. One criticism castigates lawyers for using *too many* words. I still recall the crestfallen look on the face of Sud, the stolid old farmer who was my boss for three fruitfully destructive summers at the Bonneville County (Idaho) Weed Control, when a fellow worker told him I wouldn't be back the next year because I was going off to law school. "You're . . . gonna be one of them . . ."—he groped for words—". . . them *talkin'* bastards?" A related criticism attacks lawyers (and judges, and law professors) for using the *wrong* words—for using a vocabulary that is obscure, or dishonest, or not cogent.

Almost imperceptibly, these criticisms shade into a subtly different one. The complaint is that lawyerly discourse is empty. It is *just* words, or *merely* words, or *nothing but* words.

This last is a long-standing charge, but it is also enigmatic. What else would a discourse be if not words? What exactly are the critics complaining about? If we could answer that question, we might gain a valuable insight into the nature of law—and into the deficiencies of modern thinking *about* law.

## Troubling Judgments

We might start with a recent article by Deborah Rhode, former president of the Association of American Law Schools, in which these intermingled objections are presented. Rhode's specific subject is not law-talk in general but rather legal scholarship. She begins by suggesting that a good deal of legal scholarship (including, she endearingly admits, some of her own) deserves the description once given of Warren Harding's speeches: "an army of pompous phrases moving over the landscape in search of an idea." The work is "bloated," characterized by an "offputting length and style." In fact, there is a consensus that "too much work is trivial, ephemeral, unoriginal, insular, pretentious or simply irrelevant."[1] This harsh description is not peculiar to Rhode: she cites Richard Posner's judgment that a great deal of legal scholarship is "trivial, ephemeral, and soon forgotten," Dan Farber's description of the "intellectual aridity" of legal scholarship, and Robert Gordon's opinion that much legal scholarship is "horribly pretentious and vacuous."[2]

It is little wonder, therefore, that most law review articles go wholly uncited. The authors of these involuntarily diffident articles may console themselves—ourselves—with the thought that surely someone, somewhere, is reading our articles, but just not citing them. Sadly, the reverse is probably even more likely: "What seems substantially more plausible"—Rhode shows no pity—"is that many of the 30,000 other articles were cited but not in fact read by commentators seeking scholarly embellishment."[3] (I promise that I did read Rhode's article—or at least skimmed it.)

The picture is dismal: broad, winding rivers—meandering into oceans—of *words*, but very little real substance. Too many words; too little content.

Rhode is talking about legal scholarship, though: perhaps the discourse of actual lawyers and judges is different? Judicial opinions, obviously, cannot be said to be "*just* words" in the same sense that scholarship can (as a losing litigant becomes painfully aware when the sheriff executes on her car or her bank account, or when the warden locks him in jail). Nonetheless, it is doubtful (to put the point charitably) whether the actual contents of judicial opinions—the words themselves—are more cogent or robust than the contents of legal scholarship. Most legal scholarship employs pretty much the same vocabulary that judicial opinions do anyway—hopes and fears to the contrary notwithstanding, Rhode reports, most legal scholarship is still mainly "doctrinal" in nature[4]—so it would be surprising if that vocabulary were vacuous when used by scholars but rich with content and connection when uttered by lawyers and judges. Indeed, the common view has been just the reverse—that judicial opinions are *less* substantial, more merely conclusory, than legal scholarship. Insofar as some legal scholarship (law and economics scholarship, for example) adopts a more distinctive discourse, that distinctiveness largely reflects an effort to avoid the perceived emptiness of conventional law-talk.

Reading in the primary materials will do little to dispel this gloomy perception. Thus, noting that Supreme Court opinions seem "increasingly arid, formalistic, and lacking in intellectual value," Dan Farber observes that these opinions "almost seem designed to wear the reader into submission as much as actually to persuade."[5] With reference to an opinion by Justice Potter Stewart that he takes to be typical of modern judicial decisions, Alexander Aleinikoff echoes the familiar charge: "Although Stewart's opinion uses all the right words, in the end they are simply that: *just words.*"[6] Michael Paulsen, in describing Supreme Court opinions as "arid, technical, unhelpful, boring, . . . unintelligible," "formulaic gobbledygook," uses adjectives only slightly less severe than those he deploys against legal scholarship (which he finds to be "incomprehensible, pretentious, pompous, turgid, revolting, jargonistic gibberish").[7]

So whether uttered by law professors or judges, it seems that law-talk is vulnerable to the same charge: it is profuse, but vacuous. *Just words.*

I have been quoting recent indictments, but in fact the criticism is a venerable one. The youthful Karl Llewellyn attacked lawyers' tendency to use "*words* that masquerade as things." A good deal of legal discourse "is in terms of *words,*" Llewellyn complained: "it centers on *words;* it has the utmost difficulty in getting beyond *words.*"[8] A few years before, Herman Oliphant had criticized legal scholars for "erect[ing] . . . a law of ruling cases composed of *word patterns* largely detached from life."[9] And two decades earlier, Roscoe Pound had said much the same thing: lawyerly argumentation, Pound thought, was pretty much just "empty words."[10]

So the criticism is a recurring one. But as noted, the criticism also presents a puzzle. No one could seriously contend, after all, that *law*—or the legal system—is "just words." Law encompasses too many muscular or at least corporeal things—lawyers and judges and litigants and sheriffs, courthouses and jails, robes and gavels—that are plainly *not* "just words." So it seems the criticism must be targeting not law or the legal system as a whole, but rather *legal discourse,* or law-talk. Thus qualified, the criticism may seem to lose its sting. How severe a charge is it to say that a form of discourse is "just words"? What else could it be?

What do the critics—the people who complain that law-talk is "just words"—want anyway? Pictures to go with the text, maybe? Fistfights to go with the legal arguments? In ordinary contexts we sometimes say that someone (a salesperson, a sweet-talking Don Juan) is guilty of uttering "just words" when she is being dishonest, or when he doesn't really mean what he says. ("You're the only one I've ever loved.") But it is hard to transfer this criticism intact to, say, legal scholarship. ("Sure, Professor Zilch *says* equal protection doctrine supports intermediate scrutiny for benign racial preferences. He says it, but does he really *mean* it?") So the old criticism—it's all "just words"—seems to circle back against itself: the criticism itself comes to look like "just words."

Still, it would be rash to dismiss too easily an objection that is so recurrent and so seemingly earnest. So we should look at the charge more closely. What might the complaint be asserting? What is it, exactly, that is bothering these critics?

## Ontological Inventories

Start with a commonsensical proposition: our language, and the particular statements we make, implicitly presuppose that the things we name "exist," or are "real," in some sense or another. Suppose you say "My grandfather owns a cattle ranch in the West": you implicitly assume that there is someone who is your grandfather, some thing or things that are cattle, and someplace that is the West. Otherwise, your statement would have no meaning; it would be so much gibberish (much in the way that Lewis Carroll's famous poem beginning "'Twas brillig and the slithy toves did gyre and gimble in the wabe" is gibberish to most of us, at least until we translate the line or supply imaginative referents for "toves" and "wabe" and "brillig"). We might say that our language, and our uses of language, manifest an implicit ontology— a sort of inventory of the kinds of things that we take to be real in some sense or other, and that can be signified or referred to with words.

Philosophers sometimes describe this aspect of our talk in terms of ontological "commitment." Thus, W. V. O. Quine explained that "[w]e commit ourselves to an ontology containing numbers when we say that there are prime numbers larger than a million; we commit ourselves to an ontology containing centaurs when we say there are centaurs; and we commit ourselves to an ontology containing Pegasus when we say Pegasus is."[11] Lacking such commitment, our talk would be empty—*just words*. Indeed, our talk would be "just words" in a way that seems at least distantly related to the similarly phrased criticisms we make of the salesperson or scheming seducer who, we say, lacks genuine commitment and therefore utters "just words."

So, is this what the criticism of law-talk as "just words" intends to say— that legal discourse uses words not backed up by any real and sincere ontological commitment? Before pursuing the question, we need to notice some crucial features of our ontological inventories. In the first place, our inventories are typically complex, containing sections for things that exist in quite different senses. My inventory and yours probably include sections covering not only physical objects (like pens or rocks) but also "fictional" entities (like Pegasus or Paul Bunyan), as well as intangible things (like ideas or theories). In addition, some things ("red," "fat") are usually thought to exist not "on their own," so to speak, but rather as attributes or properties of other things ("apple," "lady"), or as movements or activities of those things ("rot," "sing"). In this paragraph alone there are probably mysteries enough to occupy a professional metaphysician for an entire career; but for now, for us, the humble point is just that notions such as "exists" or "is real" need not be understood in a crude or naively materialistic way.

Moreover, ontological inventories differ from person to person and culture to culture, and even from hour to hour: the ontological inventory you carry into church (if you are the sort of person who goes to church) may be quite different from the one you employ on returning to your work as a lawyer or professor or scientist. One list may have a category of entries ("angels," for example, or perhaps "spirit") that does not appear in a different inventory, or that appears under a different heading—of "fictional" rather than "substantial" entities, perhaps.

Some important differences grow out of a further feature of these lists that needs to be noted: it seems most apt to think of ontological inventories as listing only the basic kinds of items and qualities that exist, not as an enumeration of every blessed thing that happens to show up somewhere in the cosmos. In formulating our ontologies, Quine explained, "[t]he rule of simplicity is indeed our guiding maxim."[12] So an ontological inventory need not contain entries for every individual instance of something (*my* red pen, *your* red pen, *her* red pen); nor will it list things that are best understood as compounds of other, more basic things (like red pens, or skyscrapers, or the U.S. Supreme Court). Different ontologies will vary in what they take to be basic; these differences are sometimes debated using terms like "realism" and "nominalism" or, in other contexts, "reductionism," "anti-reductionism," and "holism."

A helpful analogy here is the Periodic Table that most of us were required to study in high school chemistry. The Periodic Table, we will recall, lists basic elements—substances not reducible (at least in the ordinary processes of nature) into other, simpler substances. The table does not list separate instances of each element; nor does it itemize compounds made up of more than one element. So the Periodic Table contains a square for "carbon"—but not for the particular piece of badly overdone hamburger that you forgot about and later scraped off the grill. Neither are there any entries for "salt," or "water," or "air," because these substances are not today thought to be properly basic. In this way, all of the supposed elements famously identified by the earliest scientists-philosophers (earth, air, fire, and water) have been banished from the modern Periodic Table, to be replaced by more elemental stuff—hydrogren, helium, oxygen, uranium, and the like.

I have already suggested that every use of language—or at least every nonfacetious use—presupposes *some* ontological inventory. "Ontological statements follow immediately from all manner of casual statements of commonplace fact,"[13] Quine remarked. Consequently, metaphysics is not the preserve of a small coterie of especially brilliant (or perhaps kooky) philosophers. On the contrary: all of us have, of necessity, a metaphysics or, to use the metaphor I have been employing, an ontological inventory. In that sense, metaphysics is not only practical; it is inevitable, like it or not, for all of us.

And it is important. "One's ontology," Quine emphasized, "is basic to the conceptual scheme by which he interprets all experiences, even commonplace ones."[14] Quine's assertion is reminiscent of Holmes's remark that "although practical men generally prefer to leave their major premise inarticulate, yet even for practical purposes theory generally turns out the most important thing in the end."[15] You cannot intelligibly go beyond what is authorized by your ontology; so if you adopt or inherit an impoverished ontology, you will be consigned (at least in your own understanding) to an impoverished world.

So we would be ill advised to leave metaphysics entirely to specialists, whose purposes may differ from ours (or who may have forgotten the practical reasons why the questions ever arose in the first place). In this vein, I think the occasional suggestion that law and philosophy will be a more valuable and productive enterprise when it is supervised and executed by people with Ph.D.s is exactly wrong; it is a recipe for desiccation and irrelevance.[16]

Metaphysics is also practical in a different sense. The actual contents of our ontological inventories will not be given by philosophers, or by metaphysicians. We do not get our lists of "what there is" from Aristotle or Heidegger, but rather from other, more accessible sources—usually, as the next chapter will suggest, from everyday experience, or from science, or from religion, or from some mixture of these.

To say that everyone has an ontological inventory, however, is not to say that everything we say or think is automatically in complete harmony with the inventories we hold (or think we hold). If that were so, then we would never find ourselves in the kind of metaphysical quandary that I think underlies modern frustrations in understanding law (among many other things). Nor could we ever commit the crime—or enjoy the pleasure—of uttering "just words." But we are not so fortunate—or so confined.

## Words without Meaning?

An astute judge and philosopher, Francis Bacon, noticed a familiar problem that might be described (at least as a first formulation, later to be revised) as a sort of mismatch between our language and our ontology. Sometimes, Bacon observed, our language contains "names of things which do not exist (for as there are things left unnamed through lack of observation, so likewise are there names which result from fantastic suppositions and *to which nothing in reality corresponds*)."[17]

At least on first hearing, Bacon's observation seems to resonate with our experience. A "Dilbert" cartoon conveys a similar idea. In the first square, a goateed character exclaims, "Dilbert, my man, you're stayin' real and keepin' to the core." Dilbert asks, "Is that good?" and the fellow with the goatee answers, "I don't even know what it means." In the final square, Dilbert wonders, "Why do you say things that have no meaning?"—to which the response is "DU-U-U-DE!" We might say of such utterances—utterances that "have no meaning," as Dilbert puts it—that they are "just words." Or we might say that they are "nonsense." Suppose you walk into a Taco Bell and order a Whopper: in that small, bean-based universe your request is "just words," or "nonsense," because Whoppers do not appear on the Taco Bell ontological inventory.

Of course, we know by experience that such nonsense can take more pretentious and sophisticated forms. Thus, we may criticize the impressively convoluted or brilliantly evasive talk of a scholar or politician by saying that it is "all just words." And we occasionally find ourselves actual participants in conversations that beg for a similar judgment. The diction may be impressive, the grammar and syntax impeccable. As with a catechism recited by habit or rote, there may be recognizable patterns of assertion and response. We even have the ability to enter into those conversational patterns. ("If she says *X*, I'm supposed to say *Y*—or, perhaps, with a knowing nod and in an ironic tone, Z.") Even so, we are at least vaguely uncomfortable. "I really don't know what we're talking about," we might confess in a moment of candor. So we hope no one presses us to explain what we mean by some portentous pronouncement, because the truth is that we couldn't. It's all "just words." Or, in a special and somewhat technical sense, "nonsense"— not in the sense of "stupid" or "wildly implausible," but rather in the more literal sense of "without meaning." Non-sense.

Perhaps not everyone has had this experience, though I suspect that most of us have—perhaps in a social context, or in a religious or academic setting. We may have succeeded in playing along with a conversation, or answering an exam question, or laughing at a joke, even though we knew we weren't really "getting it," or that we were "faking it." I may be unusual, but I doubt very much that I am utterly unique in this respect: and I can give personal testimony that I have this sort of experience regularly. (Though not in the course of writing this book, of course.)

A quick example may be helpful. Recently I agreed to participate in a "Roundtable" in which several lawyers, a theologian, a lobbyist, and a minister discussed what was at the time the hot topic of government-sponsored "faith-based initiatives." Some members of the panel insisted that something they repeatedly and confidently referred to as "the law"—or "the Constitution," or "the First Amendment"—prohibits the government from supporting religiously sponsored social service programs. Other panelists claimed that "the law" does no such thing; in some circumstances, it might even *require* such support. For me the whole experience was a bit disconcerting, because at bottom I really had no idea what these claims might mean.

Yes, I keep a nice little copy of the Constitution handy at all times—not (like Justice Black) in my pocket, but at least in my desk or on my shelf. I've read the words—many times. And I've also written words about the First Amendment—thousands upon thousands of words, in fact, gradually adding up after lo these many years to a couple of books and a dozen or so articles. So the talk at the roundtable discussion was not exactly a foreign language. In a pinch I can speak this language myself. I even know when someone has said the wrong thing. ("No! Given your position, you're supposed to talk about 'substantive neutrality' at this point.")

So what exactly is my problem? It's that I really can't understand what sort of thing "the law" is—or what "the First Amendment," or "the Constitution" are—such that they are capable of prohibiting, or requiring, or remaining neutral with respect to faith-based initiatives. Someone asks, in all seriousness, "Do you believe 'the law' guarantees religious organizations the right to participate in government subsidy programs on a nondiscriminatory basis?" I'm expected to say, "Yes, because . . ." or "No, because . . ." And I blush to admit that sometimes I do break down and say one of those things. But what I really want to say is this: "What could that question possibly mean? What *is* this thing—'the law'—that you keep referring to? *What are we talking about?*"

In short, I can mouth the words. But—for me, at least—that is pretty much what they are: just words.

These days, few law professors seem to share or sympathize with my plight. In this respect (as in others, probably), I was born too late. If I had lived in the first half of the last century, for example, I could more easily have found people able to feel my pain. I have in mind the so-called logical positivists, who argued that all meaningful statements fall into one of two categories—empirical statements ("It's raining outside") and analytic or tautological propositions ("Bachelors are unmarried men")—and that any statement not embraced in one of these categories is nonsense.[18] In this way, whole fields of thought—theology, for example, or a good deal of moral philosophy, and pretty much all of metaphysics—could be peremptorily dismissed as "transcendental nonsense." A group of legal thinkers took up the argument and concluded that numerous familiar legal terms—"tort," "crime," "corporation," "property," "rights *in rem*"—were meaningless or nonsensical: Felix Cohen's article "Transcendental Nonsense and the Functional Approach" was perhaps the most famous articulation of this view.[19]

These people would be able to commiserate, I think, with my embarrassment at the "Roundtable." But, sadly, their commiseration would be promiscuous, because they would also extend their supportive sympathy to lots of people—to critics and scoffers of various sorts—who don't deserve it (in the way I think I *do* deserve it). Later on, that is, it came to be understood that both the logical positivists and the Legal Realists who followed them got carried away in their zeal to dismiss—or to condemn as nonsense—large areas of human thought and discourse. Thus, Jeremy Waldron observes that "[t]he logical positivism with which [Felix] Cohen buttressed his critique [of legal conceptualism] looks rather passe almost sixty-five years later."[20]

The basic problem is that, as noted, ontological inventories are complex; they recognize that things can exist in a variety of ways. Any simple and severe test of meaningfulness, such as the logical positivists' verification test (which condemned nonanalytical statements as nonsensical unless they were empirically testable) tends to overlook this complexity and thereby fall into naivete—pleasingly disguised, ironically, as tough-minded rigor. Moreover, as later philosophers observed, the verification test fails to satisfy its own requirement for meaningfulness: it is itself neither analytic nor empirically verifiable. Thus, logical positivism is itself nonsense by its own standards.[21]

A natural reaction to the self-negating overextensions of logical positivism might lead us to think that statements cannot be meaningless or nonsensical after all. Won't all of our terms necessarily refer to "real" things, even if these things can only be located in the category of "concepts" or "beliefs"? Indeed, to say that something is "just words" is already to locate it in a section of our ontological inventories—the section for "words," perhaps, or "language games."

John Searle hints at some such conclusion when he asserts that "it is a very deep mistake to suppose that the crucial question for ontology is, 'What sorts of things exist in the world?', as opposed to, 'What must be the case in the world in order that our empirical statements be true?'"[22] If we're talking about something, then it *must* exist—otherwise, how could we talk about it?—so the only question is *how.* Right? So long as we stick to Searle's second question and scrupulously avoid the first one, it is hard to see how any of our statements could be adjudged to be metaphysical nonsense. (Unless, that is, we imitate Lewis Carroll and deliberately set out to gibber, slithily wabing and wimbling, like a pack of gimbling toves ugluk hocus rub-a-dub-dub # % * !?}/.)

## Nonsense After All?

But Searle, as we will see later, is not scrupulous in following his own counsel; nor should he be. If the logical positivists erred in the direction of a misguided rigor that condemns too much of our talk and culture to the category of "nonsense," the more accommodating approach errs in the opposite direction of excessive laxity, and thereby forfeits a valuable critical tool. That approach also defies experience (not to mention the imposing joint authority of Francis Bacon and Dilbert) because in fact, as noted above, we *do* at times hear or speak what we understand to be nonsense—"just words"—in something resembling the logical positivists' sense. Let it be conceded that everything we name in our language necessarily exists *in some sense:* a term may still be used that does not refer to anything that exists *in the sense a speaker supposes,* or *in the way the thing would need to exist in order to justify some action or practice.*

Thus, in response to the argument that Pegasus necessarily exists at least as "an idea in men's minds," Quine sensibly remarked that "[w]e may for sake of argument concede that there is an entity . . . which is the mental Pegasus-idea; but this mental entity is not what people are talking about when they deny Pegasus."[23] Or suppose I invite you on a safari to hunt unicorns, and you answer, "That's nonsense. There are no unicorns." If I respond that you are metaphysically naive and that unicorns *do* exist—you can find them in the category of "legendary beasts"—I will have missed the point. And we could fairly describe these kinds of misconceived utterances—about Pegasus or unicorns—as nonsensical.

In the same way, I suspect that disappointed children who are comforted with explanations of how Santa Claus really does exist in a metaphorical or ethereal sense (perhaps as a symbol of the spirit of generosity) know perfectly well that they are being subjected to a bald equivocation. Subtleties will not salvage the reality of *their* Santa Claus. At least, I don't recall that, after hearing our second grade teacher's sensitive explanation along these lines, any of us responded: "Gee, now I understand. Santa is so much more truly present—so much *more* real, really—than we had supposed. How simple-minded we were to have felt upset."

So it seems that nonsense is possible after all. But how might this qualified form of nonsense happen? Why would someone (or how *could* anyone) utter things that make no sense, even in terms of that person's own ontological inventory?

One possibility is already suggested by my facetious example of the person who walks into a Taco Bell and, perhaps forgetting where she is, asks for a "Whopper." To be more serious, suppose that a person has changed her beliefs and hence her ontological inventory, so that she no longer believes in the existence of things (angels, perhaps, or ghosts, or God) that she formerly accepted as real. Or, more precisely, she no longer believes that such things exist in the same sense as before: they have been transferred on her inventory from the "substantial entities" to the "fictional entities" section. But occasionally, perhaps from old habit or cultural pressure, she may revert to talking as if such things were real in the previous, more robust sense. In these cases, there is a disjunction between this person's talk and her current ontological inventory—a disjunction we could describe by saying that, measured by her own ontology, her statements are "nonsense."

This scenario suggests larger possibilities. After all, if this sort of disjunction can happen to an individual, might it not also happen to a group, or to a whole society? Think of it this way: language and language patterns are in a perpetual if barely perceptible process of change, and consciously held beliefs about what sorts of things exist (and in what senses) are also constantly changing. But it would be well-nigh miraculous if these patterns of change coincided perfectly. So we should hardly be surprised if the ontological inventories implicit in the way people in a given society talk sometimes do not cohere with the ontologies that people in the society would own up to if pressed. We might describe such incongruities in terms of a sort of "ontological gap" dividing the society's *explicit or owned* ontological commitments from the ontological assumptions that are *implicit or presupposed* in practices and ways of talking. And we might naturally describe the kind of talk that goes on in that gap as . . . "nonsense." Meaning, once again, non-sense.

These reflections suggest that we are free after all to be meaningful or not. The logical positivists' overreaching has not deprived us of that freedom: nonsense is still a live possibility for us.

But the failure of logical positivism *is* decisive in one important respect: it suggests that there will be no simple test—no verification criterion or its equivalent—for separating the nonsensical from the meaningful. So then how are we to tell when we, or other people, are speaking nonsense?

## The Socratic Audit

So far as I can see, the answer (if there is one) is that we might try to do a careful, reflective audit of our practices, our ways of talking, and our consciously held beliefs about what is real to see if these square with each other. It would be impracticable, no doubt, to attempt such an inquiry for *everything* we say, or even for very much of it; but, following the example of the IRS, we might try conducting such an audit for selected statements (perhaps where we have some reason to be suspicious). So for any statement we make, we might ask if we can give an account of how the things we name or describe in the statement exist in terms of the kinds of things recognized in our ontological inventories.

This inquiry will present no easy challenge, in part because, as noted, those inventories will include only basic elements, while most of the things we talk about will be complicated compounds or aggregates. The parallel to the Periodic Table is again helpful. At this instant, as I look straight ahead, I see a variety of objects (a keyboard, some paper, a wooden table, the screen on a computer monitor, and so forth), and not a single one of these objects owns a square on the Periodic Table. All are compounds—or compounds compounded. Even so, at least in principle a scientist would be able to analyze these objects into elements that *are* on the table. In the same way, we routinely talk not only of material objects like desks and chairs but also of much more interesting and complex things: society and law and moral responsibility. Such talk might be nonsensical, at least sometimes. My suggestion, however, is that such statements will be meaningful insofar as we can, if pressed, give a satisfactory account explaining how these things are "real" in terms of the entries on our ontological inventories.

So the inquiry suggested here—the "no nonsense" inquiry, so to speak—cannot be a merely mechanical or checklist exercise. And there is perhaps no way to be absolutely confident about the conclusions of the inquiry. Nonsense might sneak past even a careful audit; conversely, a judgment of "nonsense" might simply evidence a failure of effort or imagination in devising an account that would adequately connect something we have believed in to our ontological inventories.

But although the inquiry will be a delicate and fallible one, we are fortunate to have a good example of how such an audit might be conducted. Indeed, it could be argued that philosophy began with just such a series of inquiries. And, fortuitously for my purpose, the model auditor also happens to be someone whom law professors have traditionally taken as a sort of exemplar or patron saint. I refer, of course, to Socrates.

These classic ontological audits are written up in what are often classified as the earliest and most Socratic dialogues of Plato—the so-called aporetic dialogues.[24] Typically, these dialogues revolve around such questions as "What is courage?" or "What is temperance?" or "What is piety?"[25] When Socrates professes not to know the answer to a question, his interlocutors (usually sophists or citizens of Athens) are astonished; they are sure that they can easily supply an answer. And indeed, they *are* familiar with the conventional usage of the terms; and they are able to put that usage into practice by, for example, giving instances of what is conventionally regarded as courage or temperance or piety. Standing up to the foe in battle is an instance of courage; performing the required rituals an instance of piety. Beyond reciting specific instances, an accomplished sophist, such as Protagoras, can give eloquent speeches on the general subject—speeches that leave his listeners "spellbound."[26] So what then is Socrates's problem?

The problem is that under his examination, these answers are found to be deficient. So the dialogues end in a quandary of "aporia," or perplexity, with even Socrates reasserting that he does not know the answer to the question.

These dialogues have generated a huge array of interpretations. For present purposes, however, two points are significant. First, it is plausible to understand Socrates as engaged not in a *semantic* project, but rather in an *ontological* inquiry.[27] Socrates is not quibbling over words, as his detractors contend; he is not asking merely for a synonym or a definition or even a correct proposition.[28] Instead, Socrates wants his interlocutors to "give an account" of the quality or entity in question.[29]

But why is Socrates so intent on having an "account"? And what exactly is an "account" anyway? Terry Penner has helpfully suggested that when Socrates asks about justice or temperance or virtue, he wants to know *the thing itself.*[30] Thus, for Socrates, "[w]e must know the reference of 'virtue,' not just the meaning."[31] Such knowledge would be expressed through an account that would not merely tell how a term is defined or used, but would explain the actual nature of whatever it is in reality that the term refers to. Socrates wants to know, in other words, whether and in what sense courage or temperance or piety are *real.*[32]

The second pertinent observation is that in pursuing his ontological inquiry, the Socrates of the early dialogues does not offer his own ontology, as Plato is thought to have done with his theory of Forms. Instead, as Gregory Vlastos has argued, Socrates tries to determine whether an account of ethical terms can be given within the conventional ontology of his own culture.[33] For that reason, perhaps, the Socratic inquiry does not typically employ any highly technical vocabulary, or any concepts that only people with Ph.D.s would understand. Instead, Socrates makes constant use of analogies to everyday objects, practices, and trades with which his conversation partners are intimately familiar. We know what gymnastics or medicine are, Socrates suggests. We know what it is to build a house, or breed a horse, or play a flute. We know what the eyes, ears, and nose are, and how they are situated in the face. We can give an account of these things. But can we explain with comparable vividness or clarity what courage or piety are, or in what sense these things are real?

In the most Socratic dialogues, this investigation typically ends in failure and perplexity. Neither Socrates nor his initially confident conversation partners can give a satisfactory account of the quality in question. Greek ethical discourse fails the test of meaningfulness, in short, on its own terms: for all of its pretension it is little more than "the forced and artificial chiming of word and phrase."[34]

So although the sophists and the Athenians confidently deploy terms like "justice," "courage," and "virtue," they cannot intelligibly connect these qualities to anything that they themselves regard as real. They are, as Socrates tells Callicles, "playing with words but revealing nothing."[35] And if Socrates were to imitate their practice, he explains, he would be "babbl[ing] . . . or pretend[ing] to say something when I'm not saying anything."[36] It would be "just words."

By this interpretation, in sum, the conclusion of the Socratic examination is that within the Greeks' own worldview, Greek ethical discourse is nonsense. It may be nonsense that is elegant and erudite in its own way. It may be nonsense with consequences (as Socrates's eventual martyrdom would attest). But it is nonsense nonetheless. For Socrates and his contemporaries, this was *their* quandary.

## Law and the Socratic Inquiry

So what might *our* quandary be? Today, of course, we still talk about courage, virtue, and piety. (Or at least we talk about the first two of these.) And I suspect that our talk would leave a revivified Socrates with no shortage of work. But those moral qualities are not the subject of this book. Rather, we are primarily interested in terms or notions that are more integral to the discourse of law.

In law, lawyers (and many nonlawyers) can manipulate the conventional terms and patterns of discourse. We use that discourse to argue confidently for conclusions on the issues of the day. There is (or isn't) a right to abortion. The law does (or doesn't) give a remedy for the infliction of emotional distress. Faith-based initiatives are (or aren't) prohibited (or required) by the Constitution. Some of the most skilled among us—a Dworkin or a Tribe, perhaps—can even use legal discourse in performances that may leave a particular audience "spellbound," as Protagoras did in Socrates's day. There is no denying—and I hope not to be taken as denying—that we do these things.

But can we actually give an account connecting that discourse to reality—that is, to our ontological catalogues that set forth what we believe to be real? Or might these lawyers and scholars be, like Callicles, "playing with words but revealing nothing?" That is the central question to which this book is addressed.

More specifically, I propose to summarize in the following chapter the principal ontological inventories that seem to have some currency today in the American legal culture (and probably, though I make no claims in this respect, in Western legal systems generally). Then I want to ask whether, using these ontologies, we can give a satisfactory account of the law, and of the discourse of law. Not to leave readers in suspense, I think we *can* give an adequate account for much of law—for the humbler aspects of law—but not for its more ambitious or pretentious parts. We can give an account that is good enough to vindicate much of what is contained in the practical law books (of the "Write Your Own Will" variety) that you can find on the shelves in the "Law" section at Barnes and Noble, but not for much of what you will find in the opinions of the U.S. Supreme Court or the academic law reviews.

If that is true, then a good deal of what appellate judges and law professors write—including much of what you will be expected to write if you happen to be a young law professor seeking tenure—is nonsense. It is important, lofty nonsense, no doubt, backed up in many cases by promotion committees or even by federal marshals. But it is nonsense nonetheless.

This conclusion might seem utterly unsurprising to ordinary citizens. ("You're saying that lawyers talk nonsense? *Duh!*") But the conclusion may be a bit less welcome to the kind of person who might actually be tempted to read through a book about jurisprudence. It is hard to accept cheerfully the proposition that all of your high-toned talk—talk that is used to resolve portentous issues like whether public universities can adopt affirmative action programs or whether states can criminalize abortion or whether George W. Bush acquired the office of president legitimately—is nonsense. So there is good reason to resist the thesis. Realistically, it is a thesis that probably *could not* be widely accepted by an academic audience. I understand this, and can only ask readers to consider the argument carefully and see if it is persuasive.

But even if the argument *is* persuasive, I can also offer, tentatively, two potentially mitigating observations. First, supposing the main argument is persuasive, it might still be that even the more pretentious parts of our law can escape the judgment of "nonsense," though in a convoluted and not entirely congenial way. Legal discourse (or at least some of it) might make sense, that is, by reference to a different kind of ontology—one we purport no longer to hold (or at least that we refrain from invoking in academic contexts) but that arguably still flourishes on the sly and that we seemingly cannot quite bring ourselves to give up (perhaps because—who knows?—we may at some level actually believe it). It might be—I'm honestly not sure—

that we can avoid the judgment of "nonsense" by owning up to a set of beliefs that we hold at some level of consciousness.

Second, nonsense (as I have explained it) is far from being the most horrible evil that could befall us, and talking nonsense is hardly the most vicious sin we could commit. "Nonsense" describes a sort of intellectual dereliction, or a miscarriage of cognition and articulation; but it does not necessarily signify an inability to function. This is a further puzzle sometimes considered in the Socratic dialogues. How is it, for example, that someone who can give no coherent explanation of what courage even is can nonetheless be courageous? Still, the phenomenon seems undeniable.

So "nonsense" need not be debilitating. Recognizing and confessing it might even be therapeutic—confession, they say, is good for the soul—even if it does not lead directly to a remedy. Socrates seemed to think so, at any rate. And in a similar vein, Thomas Nagel suggests that "[c]ertain forms of perplexity" about the perennial human problems can "embody more insight than any of the supposed solutions to those problems."[37]

So there is more than one twist—and more than one possible moral—to the story. Even as I write this introductory chapter, I am far from confident, frankly, about what that moral ought to be. Maybe the picture will be clearer by the end of the book, which of course I will reach before you do. I'm not sure, and in any case I wouldn't give away the ending just yet even if I knew it. What *can* be said at this point is that we need to brace ourselves for disappointment. It should not be too surprising if we end up where the Socratic dialogues do—that is, in the quandary of aporia, or of (a potentially fruitful) perplexity.

# CHAPTER 2

# *Ontological Dynasties*

Our Socratic inquiry aims to investigate whether law—or law-talk—is meaningful, or whether instead it is "nonsense" in the sense discussed in Chapter 1. Before pursuing that question, though, we need to survey the ontological supply yard, so to speak, to get an overview of what materials are in stock. Once we have surveyed the available resources, we will be ready to launch our inquiry. In the following chapters, that is, we will be able to ask whether the metaphysical materials on hand are sufficient to permit us to construct a satisfactory account of law.

## Three Ontological Families

Here in the West, early in the twenty-first century, it seems that there are three principal ontological inventories—or perhaps, to shift metaphors, three sprawling ontological families—that offer their resources to us. Families need an identifying name, so we can call these ontological families "everyday experience," "science," and "religion." Each family encompasses numerous members that vary markedly while still exhibiting important family resemblances: here we will only be able to notice the principal distinguishing features. It is crucial to note, moreover, that these families are sometimes standoffish—but not always: they intermarry and intermix, sometimes enthusiastically, sometimes with reluctance and mutual suspicion. So nearly all of us will have ties to more than one of these families: at times we will join in one family gathering, while at other times we will find ourselves hanging out with the ontological in-laws.

### *The Ontology of Everyday Experience*

"Everyday experience" refers, of course, to the setting where nearly all of us spend nearly all of our time, engaged in the mundane activities of going to work, driving the car, walking the dog, chatting (or arguing) with friends and colleagues and parents and children, going to bed and setting the alarm to rouse us for another round of everyday experience a few hours later. And everyday experience has, of necessity, its ontological inventories. The boundaries between the everyday ontology and other ontologies are not neatly marked. But by "everyday ontology," I refer to the sorts of things that nearly all of us accept as the basic building blocks of reality when we are simply going through life without reflecting deliberately or directly on questions of metaphysics.

No doubt different people would arrange or describe this inventory in different ways. But for our purposes the basic categories of things that are treated as real for everyday use can be adequately described, I think, under four main headings: we believe in the existence of (1) *persons* and (2) *objects* that exist in (3) *time* and (4) *space*. These realities provide the framework within which you and I live, and think, and talk. I (a person) converse (a property or capacity of persons) with my wife (a person). I do this now (time), here in the living room (a place in space). You (a person) drive (a capacity of persons interacting with cars, which are complex objects, moving in time and space) to the store (a sort of complex object, or collections of objects, located in a particular place in space) to buy (an activity engaged in by persons, often using coins, which are objects) a head of lettuce (an object). And so forth. Our everyday life is composed of persons and objects (with their manifold properties and capacities) interacting in infinitely complex ways in time and space.

This four-category framework sponsors not only descriptive statements ("The book is on the desk") but also more normative claims and arguments. One of the most pervasive moral arguments, for instance, uses the everyday framework to assert the error of placing a person in the wrong ontological category—of treating a person "as an object," as we say. Moral criticisms asserting the wrongfulness of coercion or manipulation of others have their root in this sort of claim.

The opposite error—of treating an object as if it had the qualities of a person—is condemned as well, though usually not so much as a moral failing as a kind of irrational superstition. Astrology presents a familiar instance: the stars are unconscious objects, we think, and hence cannot provide intelligent counsel to mortals in the way a person can. I suggest in Chapter 5 that a good deal of talk about linguistic meaning and "textualist" legal interpretation might be a manifestation of the same kind of error.

If we reflect, it may seem remarkable that this seemingly simple ontology could support the vast complexities of everyday experience; and perhaps it cannot. John Searle, commenting on "the metaphysics of ordinary social relations," gives an illustration:

> I go into a café in Paris and sit in a chair at a table. The waiter comes and I utter a fragment of a French sentence. I say, *"un demi, Munich, à pression, s'il vous plaît."* The waiter brings the beer and I drink it. I leave some money on the table and leave. An innocent scene, but its metaphysical complexity is truly staggering, and its complexity would have taken Kant's breath away if he had ever bothered to notice such things.

Searle goes on to note the "huge, invisible ontology" of legal relations and regulations that lurk in the background of this simple transaction. And even this description leaves out a multitude of features.

> Waiters can be competent or incompetent, honest or dishonest, rude or polite. Beer can be sour, flat, tasty, too warm, or simply delicious. Restaurants can be elegant, ugly, refined, vulgar, or out of fashion, and so on with the chairs and tables, the money, and the French phrases.

The ontological complexities, he concludes, are overwhelming.

> If, after leaving the restaurant, I then go to listen to a lecture or attend a party, the size of the metaphysical burden I am carrying only increases: and one sometimes wonders how anyone can bear it.[1]

It may be that the everyday ontology *cannot* equip us to bear that burden. But the everyday ontology manages to take us farther than we might have thought possible because its basic components—objects, and even more so persons—are thought to possess a huge variety of properties and capacities. Persons, for instance, have "minds"—the "official doctrine," Gilbert Ryle reports, is that "every human being has both a body and a mind . . . ordinarily harnessed together"[2]—and as a result persons have the mentalistic capacities to believe, think, act, decide, intend, feel, speak, and understand. Philosophers like Ryle have found this mind–body, "ghost in the machine" phenomenon immensely troubling. Their consternation suggests that they are already operating from a different ontology—the scientific ontology, most likely—and are trying gallantly to give an account of "persons" and their properties within that more pinched framework. In our day-to-day lives, though, we lose little sleep worrying about the mind–body problem. That is because within the everyday framework "persons" are one of the basic categories in their own right; and to be a person just *is* (ordinarily) to have qualities such as "mind" with its attendant capacities of thinking, believing, intending, and so forth.

For ordinary purposes, therefore, these properties of persons provide a rich resource for developing practical accounts of the reality of Searle's restaurant transactions and lectures, and of even more complex developments—politics, society, and economics. Likewise, the practice and discourse of law operate mostly within this ontology. For this reason it will serve as the framework for much of the discussion throughout this book—as it does throughout most of law, and most of life.

We cannot just stop here and complacently proceed to the next chapter, however, because the ontology of everyday experience has its shortcomings. For one thing, it has fuzzy areas. What about "moral" terms and notions, for example? We talk routinely about what someone "should" do, or what we all have a "duty" to do? Should these moral terms be regarded as properties of persons, or do they deserve a separate category? What about "causes"? And should nonhuman animals—dogs, cats, and dolphins—be placed in the category of "persons" or "objects"? They don't quite seem to fit in either category, but animals are surely real, so the framework shows strain at this point. Debates about "animal rights" reflect this difficulty.

More generally, the everyday ontology passes blithely by questions that philosophers (and, occasionally, the rest of us) find it difficult to ignore. For example, when I lightly said just now that persons and objects have "properties," what sort of thing was I talking about? What *are* properties? Are they just another type of object? Are they a whole new entry onto the ontological inventory? If we were philosophers, these questions might lead us into a discussion of the problem of "universals." And what about "things" that, paradoxically, "don't exist"—as in

> Yesterday upon the stair,
> I met a man who wasn't there.
> He wasn't there again today.
> My gosh, I wish he'd go away.

Did that "man who wasn't there" exist? If he didn't exist, then how is it that we're talking about him right now? And was the fat man who wasn't there the same man as the bald man who wasn't there? Do we need to add a category for, say, "unactualized possibles"?

As we go through our day-to-day lives, we typically find it convenient, and possible, to pay no attention to such questions. We get by just fine, thank you, with persons, objects, time, and space and their properties. We get along fine, that is, most of the time. Still, the everyday ontology is a bit insecure because there is always the possibility that something or someone may come along to provoke us to consider such mysteries; and then, rightly or wrongly, the everyday ontology may come to feel embarrassed and inadequate.

This observation points to a further complication, which is that we typically recognize that the everyday ontology is not . . . , well, not quite *true*, or at least not quite *ultimate*. Scientists, in one direction, and prophets or theologians or mystics or even poets in another, seem to be investigating realities that are more elemental than the persons and objects that figure in everyday experience. And although all of us inhabit the everyday ontology for the better portion of our lives, most of us will also admit that scientists or theologians, or both, probably come closer to describing what is *"really* real," so to speak, or what is fundamental. So we need to notice the other ontological families as well.

### The Ontology of (Popular) Science

Searle (a philosopher, not a scientist) argues that "[t]he truth is, for us, most of our metaphysics is derived from physics (including the other natural sciences)." Many questions in science, are debatable, Searle concedes, but not all of them: in particular, "two features of our conception of reality are not up for grabs": "They are not, so to speak, optional for us as citizens of the late twentieth and early twenty-first century. It is a condition of your being an educated person in our era that you are apprised of these two theories: the atomic theory of matter and the evolutionary theory of biology."[3]

Searle goes on to fill out, "very crudely," the "picture of reality" that follows from these ostensibly nonoptional theories.

> The world consists entirely of entities that we find it convenient, though not entirely accurate, to describe as particles. These particles exist in fields of force, and are organized into systems. The boundaries of systems are set by causal relations. Examples of systems are mountains, planets, $H_2O$ molecules, rivers, crystals, and babies. Some of these systems are living systems; and on our little earth, the living systems contain a lot of carbon-based molecules, and make a very heavy use of hydrogen, nitrogen, and oxygen. Types of living systems evolve through natural selection, and some of them

have evolved certain sorts of cellular structures, specifically, nervous systems capable of causing and sustaining consciousness. Consciousness is a biological, and therefore physical, though of course also mental feature of certain higher-level nervous systems, such as human brains and a large number of different types of animal brains.[4]

Whether scientists themselves would embrace Searle's description is a question we can leave to the scientists themselves. One sometimes has the sense that conscientious physicists squirm when laypersons use a word like "particles" (which to most of us conjures up images of tiny brass balls bouncing around in the cosmic pinball machine), and would prefer to think of a more elusive reality that can be described only in mathematical terms. Perhaps Searle's depiction resonates best with a worldview shaped more by Newton than by Einstein and Heisenberg. I am hardly competent to say. Nor do I think it matters much, because for present purposes the question is not so much what the world is *really* like, or even what *real* scientists would say it is like, but rather how the typical "educated person in our era," as Searle puts it, conceives of the world—at least when he tries to be guided by the influence of modern science (as he probably feels that, as an "educated person in our era," he should be).

As an answer to that question, Searle's description seems at least *prima facie* plausible. The influence of atomic physics and, even more so, evolutionary biology does seem pervasive among educated persons: the growing attraction of law professors to evolutionary psychology is only one piece of evidence. More generally, law's aspirations to the status of a "science" are legendary. So it is not surprising if legal thinkers often gravitate to the ontology of science while feeling skittish about entities that resist disclosing themselves to the empiricist methods of science. Richard Posner's nervousness about such "mental entities" as "intent, premeditation, 'free will'" as being "of distinctly dubious ontology" is a clear manifestation of this tendency.[5]

How does this ontology of (popular) science square with that of everyday experience? Two of the elements of the more commonsensical ontology—namely, time and space—seem largely undisturbed. True, we are told that scientists think of these elements in radically new and different ways—books on relativity theory, for instance, are boggling to commonsense notions of time—but we are also typically told that for most everyday purposes the older, more Newtonian ways of thinking still work well enough. Driving my car to the store to buy a cantaloupe, I do not need to worry about whether time will slow down as I accelerate, or whether space is curved—whatever that might mean. (Years ago, an elementary school friend and I, having read in a science book that Einstein had proved that a curve is the shortest route between two points, tried for a few days to exploit this newly acquired knowledge by riding our bikes to and from school in a sort of smooth, wavy pattern. Our commuting time was not reduced.)

The scientific ontology works at most slightly greater changes to the everyday element of "objects." Particles can be imagined as minuscule objects—as submicroscopic marbles, so to speak—so the category itself remains intact. To be sure, people occasionally find it unnerving to think that the solid oak table on which they set their plates is really composed of billions of tiny particles, and that it contains much more open space (between particles) than hard matter. Atomic physics may make it seem as if we live in, as Gilbert Ryle put it, a "bubble-world."[6] But the consternation wears off quickly, and we again find that for nearly all practical purposes we can use the ordinary ontology: the plate doesn't fall through the table. So the scientific and everyday ontologies seem nicely compatible at this point.

The more serious tension involves "persons." In the first place, and strictly speaking, the scientific view appears to dissolve "persons" as a discrete ontological category, as Searle's account explicitly indicates. A person is now conceived to be, basically, an exquisitely complex system of particles. Moreover, the status of the various properties attributed to persons in the everyday ontology—mind, will, belief, intention, and so forth—becomes problematic. Thus, Daniel Dennett asserts that "if there is to be progress in psychology, it will inevitably be, as [B. F.] Skinner suggests, in the direction of eliminating ultimate appeals to beliefs, desires, and other intentional items from our explanations."[7] This is a problem, obviously, with which scientists, philosophers, theologians—and, to some degree, nearly all of us—have struggled, and it raises important questions for law. To take one obvious example: Does the scientific worldview entail that human beings are in fact "determined" in their actions and decisions, and if so, what does that mean for criminal law, which has typically operated on the assumption that humans exercise volition in choosing whether to obey or violate the law?

For all their importance, these particular questions are not the subject of this book, but they affect our inquiry in an indirect way. Insofar as the scientific ontology has difficulty accounting for (and may even undermine) our everyday belief that people are *ontologically* distinctive, or that people have properties or possibilities such as free will, or a distinctive "human dignity," we might turn to a different ontology to ground those qualities. And historically, the leading alternative source of an ontological inventory that might serve such purposes has been . . . religion.

## The Ontology of Religion

More than with everyday experience or science, the sorts of reality-pictures offered by religion are diverse, varying greatly among religious perspectives that we might crudely designate with terms like "theistic," "pantheistic," and "existential." For present purposes, though, it is enough to say that religion, in the forms that have most directly influenced Western culture and hence Western jurisprudence, can appropriate the elements of the everyday and scientific ontological inventories; but religion also adds further categories of things regarded as real. More specifically, the Judeo-Christian tradition, which has borrowed or incorporated a good deal of Greek metaphysical speculation and vocabulary, has no difficulty acknowledging the reality of persons, objects (including atoms and particles), time, or space. However, religion also insists on the reality of "spiritual" substances or entities—especially including "souls" (variously understood) and, above all, God. Drawing on comparative religion, Huston Smith summarizes the recurring themes: "Ontologically, Spirit is more real than everything else. Causally, it occasions everything else. And axiologically, it excels everything else by being perfect."[8]

Because it includes everything that the other ontologies do and more, the religious metaphysic could be described as richer than the everyday or scientific inventories.[9] Richer, of course, need not mean better, or truer. Sometimes less is more. Indeed, one might say that the central purpose of metaphysical reflection is to produce a more scaled-down or impoverished picture of reality by stripping the manifold things in the world of their individuating characteristics and reducing them to their common essentials—by moving from "this tree," "that flower," and "this bug" to something like "matter," "substance," or, finally, "being." In this spirit, Michael Moore invokes "the Law of Ockham's Cleaver, a rough paraphrase of which is that one should not unnecessarily proliferate modes of existence."[10] Religion resists this reductive thrust. Just for that reason, and for better or worse, the religious metaphysic offers more resources—more ontological terms and categories—for developing accounts of the things we encounter in the world.

### Must We Choose? Family Feuds

I have suggested that the sprawling ontological families designated "everyday experience," "science," and "religion" offer the leading alternatives today. Does it follow that we may appeal to any of these families in order to give an account, for example, of "law" or "legal meaning," and thereby avoid uttering nonsense? Or must we choose among possible family allegiances?

The question is complicated. As noted, the families are not inevitably hostile or mutually exclusive. Most of us have ties to at least two of these families, or perhaps to all three, and we feel unembarrassed moving from family to family. Stopping at the hardware store to buy a hammer and nails, I am firmly in the grip of the everyday ontology. Later, asked by my grade-school son why water turns to ice when it gets cold, I move shamelessly if awkwardly into the scientific ontology and answer with an explanation featuring forces and particles—though I might, inadvertently or from ignorance or in an effort to communicate, add some touches that a scientist would find unseemly. ("As they get cold, the water molecules huddle more tightly together.") After my son is asleep, I may in a moment of devotion shift to the religious reality-picture. Of course, some religionists would be more wary of the scientific outlook, and vice versa. But most of us sense no loss of integrity as we move from one ontology to another.

This sort of cordial intermixing might lead us to conclude that all three families are entitled to equal concern and respect, and that we need not be ashamed to associate with them or to accept help from any of them if, for instance, some of our statements are challenged and we are faced with an (ontological) audit. In this spirit, Gilbert Ryle amiably observed that "as the painter in oils on one side of the mountain and the painter in water-colours on the other side of the mountain produce very different pictures, which may still be excellent pictures of the same mountain, so the nuclear physicist, the theologian, the historian, the lyric poet and the man in the street produce very different yet compatible and even complementary pictures of one and the same 'world.'"[11]

It is an attractive prospect—*too* attractive, I am afraid. Though the major ontological families are not simply and irreparably hostile to each other, there are, as with most prominent families occupying a common neighborhood, inescapable rivalries, jealousies, and ambitions.

Start with the ontology of everyday experience. By and large, I think, the everyday ontology has no totalitarian aspirations. Its hold on its natural do-main—practical, day-to-day living—seems secure enough; at the same time, its practical focus leaves it quite willing to concede that it is not a complete theoretical description of the ultimate nature of reality. For that reason, the ontology of everyday experience is not jealous of appeals to other ontological families. For the same reason, though, the ontology of everyday experience has a sort of inferiority complex (and this attitude may be warranted). For example, the everyday ontology for the most part need not conflict with that of science: we are content to say that the table *looks* solid and *is* solid for all practical purposes. Even so, we may sometimes add, under our breath, "But it isn't *really.*" And sometimes the "it isn't really" may have practical bite. If we become thoroughly convinced that science shows that humans do not have free will, for example—if it shows that free will is an illusion—then presumably we might begin to think of people differently, and perhaps to treat them differently, at least in some respects. We might for instance come to feel embarrassed about blaming people for characteristics or behaviors that we may believe to be physically determined. ("If his genes, or maybe Twinkies, really made him do it, . . .)

In short, we can and inevitably will appeal to the ontology of everyday ex-perience in a whole host of matters, including legal discourse, and we ordi-narily feel no need to translate our everyday accounts into other accounts—scientific ones, for example. Still, we feel uncomfortable when our descrip-tions in terms of the everyday ontology actually conflict with the accounts generated by other ontologies that we think are "more true" or more ulti-mate. In cases of conflict, the everyday ontology is inclined (at least in aca-demic contexts) to yield.

But yield to *which* of the other leading ontological families?

## Science versus Religion?

Here we come to an even messier complication—the legendary conflict be-tween science and religion—and our discussion in terms of ontological in-ventories may help us appreciate the nature of this conflict (and to antici-pate some of its implications for law). In the nineteenth century, science and religion were often understood to be in warfare with each other. In retro-spect, the controversy may seem to have been characterized by misinforma-tion, misconceptions, and reckless charges and countercharges.[12] Today the conflict persists in some quarters, but in other neighborhoods an opposite characterization has become fashionable: many thinkers associated with both science and religion proclaim that the two are benignly harmonious—"nonoverlapping magisteria," perhaps—and that conflict was and is unnecessary.[13] And at the level of *conclusions*, or *specific theories or teachings*, it is probably true that science and religion need not conflict: science does not prove that God does not exist, and religion need not (though of course some versions do) reject, for example, evolutionary development.

So, is the ostensible conflict between science and religion purely gratuitous? If we focus on their metaphysical suppositions and strategies, I think we can see why announcements of amity are premature. Consider how each of these outlooks attempts to supplement or perhaps reorient the ontology of ordinary experience. The scientific orientation seeks to reduce the size of the ontological inventory by collapsing as much as possible into the category of "objects" (understood, as Searle says, as "particles") and "forces." In short, science adopts a reductive strategy: soul is reduced to mind, mind to brains, brains to chemical processes, chemical processes to the materials and processes of physics. "There is," Thomas Nagel observes, "a tendency to seek an objective account of everything before admitting its reality."[14] Religion, by contrast, frequently adopts an opposite, expansionary strategy. Religion maintains and emphasizes the personal. It tries to augment the ontological inventory to include additional (and, to the eye of science, dubious and superfluous) categories that are spiritual in nature, and to invoke spiritual entities—such as the soul, or God—in its explanations and descriptions.

From the scientific point of view, such religious accounts will often lapse into nonsense, in the sense that they depend on commitments to ostensible realities that simply are not a part of the scientific ontological inventory. And from the religious point of view, conversely, the reductionist scientific accounts will often squeeze the very life and essence out of the matters in question. "Even the most noble expressions of the human experience are rendered banal, commonplace," Luigi Giussani complains. "And the entire phenomenon of love is reduced, with bitter ease, to a biological fact."[15]

These differences in turn reflect an even more fundamental disagreement between the orientations of science and religion regarding their suppositions about the ultimate nature of the world. In Plato's *Laws*, the central character (the Athenian) explains this fundamental divide in terms that, with adjustments, seem remarkably cogent more than two millenia later. One view, he says, holds that "fire and water, earth and air, are the most primitive origins of all things" and that "the soul is a later derivative from them." So the things we encounter in the world—including ourselves—are produced "not . . . by the agency of mind, or any god, or art, but . . . by nature and chance." This is the dominant view, the Athenian explains, "widely broadcast, as we may fairly say, throughout all mankind." Skillfully advocated by "men who impress the young as wise," this naturalistic view has led to "youthful epidemics of irreligion." Despite its prevalence, however, the Athenian opposes this view in favor of a contrary position that holds that "soul came first—. . . it was not fire, nor air, but soul which was there to begin with." So what people call "nature" is actually "secondary and derivative from art and mind."[16]

In short, the standard scientific and religious ontological strategies *are* adverse, even though many of their specific conclusions need not be. So it is little wonder that mutual incomprehension and instinctive suspicion often prevail. What one view accepts as "real" in a robust sense, the other must nudge into the "metaphorical" category of its ontological inventory; what one regards as basic, the other treats as derivative or perhaps epiphenomal. So even the appearance of agreement is largely verbal. And it should not be surprising if these radically different perspectives permeate the ontological outlooks that flow from them and thereby influence, powerfully if imperceptibly, the accounts given by their proponents of all manner of things—including law.

Whether or how science and religion may ultimately make a genuine peace is of course not the subject of this book. For our purposes what is important is only that, as things stand, tensions persist on the level of basic ontology. So in some contexts, and where the ontology of everyday experience requires supplementation, we may have to choose which family claims our highest allegiance.

### The Fortunes of Family Dynasties

So what choice should we make? Which of these ontological families has the strongest claim on us today? My immediate concern in asking the question is not with ultimate truth—with whether science or religion finally provides a more accurate or truthful understanding of the universe—but rather, and more modestly, with the epistemic conventions or "climate of opinion" in which we live today. In conducting our Socratic audits, or in asking whether statements (such as those we encounter in law-talk) are meaningful, which ontology should we refer to? Which of the competing ontological inventories—the scientific or the religious—better fits prevailing views of the world?

Framed in this less ambitious way, the question may seem almost rhetorical. We have already seen that, according to John Searle, an "educated person" today will adopt a metaphysics based on "science"—and in particular one heavily informed by atomic physics and Darwinian evolution. The implication is that the religious worldview is inadmissible for purposes of serious thought, and Searle elsewhere makes the point explicit. The scientific world view, he says, "is not an option. It is not simply up for grabs along with a lot of competing world views."

> Our problem is not that somehow we have failed to come up with a convincing proof of the existence of God or that the hypothesis of an afterlife remains in serious doubt, it is rather that in our deepest reflections we cannot take such opinions seriously. When we encounter people who claim to believe such things, we may envy them the comfort and security they claim to derive from these beliefs, but at bottom we remain convinced that either they have not heard the news or they are in the grip of faith.[17]

This is a common view, at least in the academy. Though a bit presumptuous, perhaps, Searle's "we" surely encompasses a broad group.[18] But the situation is a bit more complicated than Searle would have it. In the first place, there are plenty of people who disagree—and not just religionists. In a book on moral philosophy, Charles Larmore, a philosopher not notably friendly to religion—indeed, earlier in the same book he argues that the religious worldview is not viable, or at least not helpful—says that the scientific ontology, which he calls "naturalism," is "one of the great prejudices of our age." This position, he says, "faces . . . grave philosophical difficulties so serious and so obvious that only dogmatic precommitment can account for why they are rarely even acknowledged."[19]

Moreover, we can readily regard the view expressed by Searle as the natural product of an interpretation of history that has been almost axiomatic among many "educated persons"—or academicians, at least—for well over a century, but that has also proven in recent decades to be significantly mistaken. More specifically, leading thinkers for the last century or so have confidently anticipated—and have scrambled to be on the side of—what we might call "the triumph of scientific secularism." This triumph was to be the inevitable and now imminent culmination of a historical progression that was typically divided into three phases. Different thinkers described the

progression differently, though—was it "Magic–Religion–Science," as per
E. B. Tylor and James Frazer, or "Savagery–Barbarism–Civilization," as
Lewis Henry Morgan thought, or "Theological–Metaphysical–Positive," as
Auguste Comte taught?—and the first phase was in any case located in remote times and places. So for popular purposes the relevant phases were
two: the period of religious faith, and the emerging period of secular scientific knowledge.

This development was perceived to be foreordained and inexorable.[20] The
taken-for-granted "fact" of secularization made it inevitable that understandings (of biology, of history—and of law) based on religion must give
way to understandings based on science. To cling to religion was thus to condemn oneself to backwardness and inevitable extinction.

This outlook continues to be powerful, at least within the academy. But
the assumption of secularization is also anachronistic in several respects. In
the first place, the well-known work of Thomas Kuhn and related scholars
has not undermined science, perhaps, but it has produced a somewhat more
sophisticated and more temperate view of how science works and what
it can hope to accomplish.[21] More importantly, religion has not withered
away, even from the developed world, in the way it was supposed to. On the
contrary, evidence suggests that in most parts of the world including the
United States—Europe and Japan may be significant exceptions—religion is
flourishing.[22]

Perhaps religion *has* become discredited among the educated classes, but
even here the matter is complicated. Douglas Laycock summarizes the confusing situation. "I have heard several colleagues say that religious claims
are absurd, ridiculous, irrational, or unworthy of respect," Laycock reports.
"I have never heard a colleague, at any of the three law schools where I
have taught, make a religious claim in an academic context. When the student chapter of the Christian Legal Society at the University of Texas needed
a speaker, I knew of only three or four church-attending colleagues on a faculty of sixty-five, none in the evangelical mode the students were seeking."
But Laycock also points to contrary evidence. "James Lindgren has survey
data showing that a substantial majority of law professors profess conventional Christian or Jewish religious views. These numbers are much higher
than either he or I would have guessed based on personal experience in several law schools."[23]

So it is hard to say, but even many academics may retain religious beliefs
and commitments. What seems clear, though (and what reports like Searle's

and Laycock's attest to), is that academics have internalized a norm prescribing that religious beliefs are inadmissible *in academic explanations*. Historians may believe in God, but they do not explain historical events by reference to the workings of God in history (as was once common). Scientists may be religious believers, and they may even argue that science provides support for religious belief,[24] but they typically do not resort to religious explanations for specific natural phenomena in the way that even "Enlightened" thinkers like Jefferson once did. With respect to the legal academy, Laycock himself draws this conclusion: "One inference is that the believers feel obliged to be quiet about [their beliefs]" in an academic context.[25]

## Family Fortunes Today

In sum, the familiar ontological family of everyday experience provides an inventory for explaining the meaning of many of our statements. We will assume that ontology for much of our discussion. But an everyday account of a statement is only presumptively adequate, because the everyday ontology is also deferential: it is quick to step aside, particularly when a representative of science enters the room. The ontological family of science continues to superintend the academic scene.

The situation of the ontological family I am calling "religion," by contrast, is more complicated. Religion has not disappeared, as many prognosticators have long anticipated, but its position is a curious one. In a sense the family is still powerful; its influence pervades our society. But the family is also not quite respectable in certain circles. So it lives partially underground. Even academics may descend from it, or belong to it, and they may visit it or even join in with it in their private time; but much in the way that people may be embarrassed to mention a parent or relative who is in prison for shameful behavior, academics today tend to avoid mentioning or relying on these religious ties in academic gatherings.

If this assessment is right, then the implications for the Socratic inquiry—the "no nonsense" metaphysical audit that I have proposed—are curiously complicated. In Chapter 1 I suggested that a statement or an explanation might be regarded as nonsense if it employs notions that cannot be accounted for in terms of the ontological inventory that the speaker (or her society) are using. But what should we say about an ontological inventory that, it now appears, many speakers might tacitly embrace, but which they feel they should not employ or refer to for certain public purposes? Suppose a statement makes sense in terms of that illicit ontology but not by reference to the professed public ontology. Is such a statement nonsense or not?

The question will make our Socratic inquiry—our effort to see whether we can give an adequate account of law using current ontological assumptions—more difficult than it would otherwise be. More difficult, but perhaps also more illuminating.

# PART II

# (How) Is Law for Real?

"When we study law," Oliver Wendell Holmes contended in the first sentence of his famous "Path of the Law" essay, "we are not studying a mystery but a well known profession." Holmes's successors have been repeating the contention—repeating it insistently, aggressively—ever since. The contention is at least mildly enigmatic, because if it is right then it would seem scarcely to need saying. Why, after all, would we need to be warned, over and over, not to barter away a secure, accurate knowledge already in our possession in exchange for gratuitous obscurity? So the fact that the contention evidently *does* need saying—frequent, repeated saying—prompts us to wonder whether it might be hiding something—some "mystery," as Holmes put it—that is not reducible to the ways of "a well known profession." "Methinks," a suspicious observer might say to Holmes and his descendants, "you do protest too much."

"When we talk about courage (or piety, or temperance)," Socrates's interlocutors typically begin, "we address not a mystery but a well-understood virtue." Their impatient self-assurance turns out, in the course of the Socratic examination, to be unwarranted. Part 1 of this book explained how a similar Socratic examination might be called for in law. The chapters in this part attempt to initiate such an examination.

# CHAPTER 3

# Does "the Law" Exist?

Imagine that a visitor from an alien culture—or, if you like, an alien planet—comes to visit, and after a few weeks in this country she wanders by your law office, introduces herself ("Please, call me Tess"), and asks you to show her "the law." "People talk about it all the time," she says, "and it sounds like a remarkable thing. The crowning glory of your civilization, from the way people sometimes talk. So I'm just dying to see it. You're a lawyer. Please, could you show me 'the law'?"

You think for a moment, and then conduct Tess on a tour. After showing her around your own firm, where she witnesses a deposition in progress and a client counseling session (as well as armies of secretaries and paralegals scuttling from computers to copiers to fax machines), you take her to a courtroom, where she spends an hour watching a criminal trial or a "law and motions" session. Then you lead her back into chambers, where she sees judges and law clerks and secretaries at work. After a hasty lunch, the two of you sit in on a legislative session for a few minutes, and then visit a public defenders' office and then a law school, where you sit through a first-year contracts class. Then you tour the law library, with its seemingly endless shelves of stately volumes containing case reports, statutes, and law review articles. You spend the better part of an hour browsing through these. Afterward, exhausted but pleased with the thoroughness of your tour (and feeling modestly noble for having sacrificed so many billable hours in the service of hospitality), you ask your visitor, "So, Tess, what do you think?"

"It's all been very interesting," she says in a controlled tone. "Thank you so much for your time."

But you can sense the disappointment in her voice. "What's the matter?" you ask. "Isn't this what you wanted to see?"

"Well, I enjoyed it all immensely. Really. But . . . well, I was hoping you might show me 'the law.'"

41

Clearly, one of you has misunderstood something. Is Tess guilty of the misunderstanding? Or are you?

## Of Category Mistakes—and Countermistakes

Perhaps Tess has made what is sometimes called a "category mistake." In fact, I have based this fictional adventure on a very similar story told by Gilbert Ryle to illustrate that sort of mistake. Ryle imagines a foreigner who visits Oxford or Cambridge and asks to see "the University." After being shown various colleges, libraries, museums, and offices, the visitor asks "But where is the University?" The question reflects a misconception, Ryle says, and the visitor needs to be told that "the University is not another collateral institution, some ulterior counterpart to the colleges, laboratories, and offices which he has seen. The University is just the way in which all that he has already seen is organized. When they are seen and when their co-ordination is understood, the University has been seen."[1]

Ryle gives additional illustrations. One involves a child who watches a military parade and then, after the soldiers have marched past, asks to see "the division." Another features a foreign spectator who attends a cricket match and afterward asks to be shown "the famous element of team-spirit."[2]

In these contexts, the mistake Ryle identifies seems obvious enough: the visitor's question *does* reflect a misconception. But we can imagine other situations where a similar question would not be out of order and where, on the contrary, a critic who tried to dismiss the question, Ryle-fashion, would himself be guilty of the mistake. Suppose someone shows up at the University's astronomy department and says that she has always wanted to see Alpha Centauri. A graduate student is assigned to conduct this inquirer around the department, where she is shown astronomers peering into telescopes, professors giving lectures to students (sometimes referring to Alpha Centauri), researchers reading and writing books (some of which describe Alpha Centauri), and so forth. If at the end of the day the visitor says, "Thank you very much, but what I actually asked to see was Alpha Centauri," her complaint will be perfectly legitimate. And the tour guide would be confused if he responded, "You don't understand. When the things I've shown you have been seen and when their coordination is understood, Alpha Centauri has been seen."

In this case, it seems that there is a simple solution: someone should just take the curious visitor to a telescope, position it according to the proper co-ordinates, and say, "Look in there. See it? That's it—Alpha Centauri." In other cases, of course, the object of the visitor's interest might not be something that can so easily be shown to her. If the visitor were to approach the physics department and ask to see a quark or an electron, she might need to be instructed that although these things or their traces can be detected in complicated ways, they are not actually visible to human sight. Even so, the question would at least be intelligible, and it would be a mistake—a "category mistake," if you like—to suggest that when the visitor has been shown some laboratories with scientists peering into microscopes and some libraries with books about subatomic particles, she has actually seen an electron or a quark.

Some situations might straddle this division between Ryle's examples, in which the visitor's question reflects a category mistake, and my own counterexamples where the question seems perfectly sensible and a Ryle-type dismissal would be the mistake. (And in fact Ryle's "team-spirit" example seems to me a borderline case.) Suppose someone asks to see "romantic love" and is shown couples in various postures of amorous embrace. If the spectator then says, "Fascinating! But I still would like to see 'romantic love,'" the question seems a bit off: romantic love isn't something that can be *seen,* exactly, apart from such enactments of it. At the same time, it would not be quite accurate for a guide to say, "You don't understand. What you've seen *is* romantic love." After all, these physical performances are not in themselves romantic love. They might not even be manifestations of romantic love: the participants might be paid actors who have no feelings at all for each other. Conversely, romantic love can exist even between people who are forcibly separated from each other. But at the same time it would be an error to suggest that romantic love is a wholly independent entity, like Alpha Centauri or a quark or an electron, that exists on its own as a sort of "brute fact" whether or not any humans are in the picture. So it seems we would need to explain to an inquirer that romantic love is a subtle sort of many-splendored thing that involves persons and often is manifest in physical actions such as those she has been shown, but is not identical with such actions. The activities she has seen may come as close as any visible spectacle can to conveying the nature of romantic love, and they are also (we hope) an instantiation of romantic love; but she will still need to make a sort of empathic leap in order to apprehend romantic love itself.

What can we say, then, of these assorted examples? How do we know whether the question ("Show me a ____") represents a category mistake or, conversely, whether the Ryle-type dismissal ("You've already seen it. What you've been shown *is* a _____") is the mistake? I am tempted to say that there are practices or institutions (such as "the University") that are self-contained and self-justifying; and other practices and institutions (such as astronomy) that are dependent on or dedicated to realities (the stars) that are believed to exist independent of the practice or institution. But this distinction won't carry much weight. We can readily imagine someone visiting a university and asking to be shown something to which the university *is* dedicated—knowledge, maybe, or "enlightenment"—that could not be exhibited in the form of persons and buildings. So perhaps the best we can do—or at least the best I can do at the moment—is to say that when such questions arise we need to give close, reflective attention to the situation in order to judge whether the inquiry asks about something that exists independent of—or, conversely, that is fully contained in or reducible to—the visible workings of the institution or practice.

To be sure, such judgments will diverge. Suppose someone pleads, "Show me God," and then after being led through various worship services and catechism lessons and so forth repeats the request. An atheist might say, "Insofar as God is anything at all, what you've seen is it. That's all there is." A theist would give a very different sort of explanation. Such differences, of course, express differences in the respondents' ontological inventories: to the theist God "really exists," while to the atheist God is at best an imaginary or perhaps metaphorical character employed by certain religious associations and in certain religious rituals.

Which brings us back to Tess—our alien visitor who wants to be shown "the law," and who renews the request even after being conducted through courtrooms and judges' chambers and law school classrooms. Is her request sensible? Is it at least as intelligible as that of the person who is not satisfied that physical embracing *is* "romantic love"? Or is Tess guilty of the same kind of mistake committed by Ryle's visitor who wants to see "the University"? Does "the law" exist in the way the theist thinks God exists? Or only in the way the atheist thinks God exists (a view usually expressed by saying that God *doesn't* exist)?

## Does the Law Need "the Law"?

In investigating these questions, we need to distinguish between two things, the first of which surely exists while the second is more doubtful. There are the sorts of things that you showed your visitor on the tour—the lawyers, judges, and clerks; the courtrooms, chambers, and offices; the legal briefs and oral arguments. When we talk about the law, we may be referring to these sorts of things plain and simple—to Holmes's "well known profession."[3] Then there is—or *may* be, because this is what is in question—that independent, more ethereal (and perhaps merely imaginary) entity that your visitor wants you to show her: "the law."

It is not always clear which of these things we mean when we talk about law. It did not become clear until after your tour was over, for instance, that Tess wanted to see "the law," and not just the law-as-profession. So the distinction is elusive. But it is also vital to our inquiry, and it permits us to re-phrase the question ("Does 'the law' exist?") posed in the title to this chapter. We might put the question in this way: Does the law (or, if you will, the legal system) depend on, or presuppose, "the law"? Can you say to your visitor, following Ryle, that the law *is* "just the way in which all that [she] has already seen is organized"? That "[w]hen [these things] are seen and their co-ordination is understood, [everything that there is to the law] has been seen"? Or is some "ulterior counterpart" to the law—"the law"—real and necessary?

### The Classical Response

At this point, what we might call the "traditional" or "classical" account of law diverges sharply from more modern accounts of law. (In talking about classical and modern accounts of law, obviously, I will be invoking simplified composites.) The classical account at least appears to say that Tess's request is intelligible and that "the law" really does exist in some substantial sense—even if (like romantic love) it is not exactly a visible or tangible object to be inspected. So we are guilty of a category mistake if we respond with a Ryle-type dismissal. ("The things you've seen—the judges, lawyers, professors, lawbooks—*are* the law.") Modern accounts often say just the opposite. Law is not, as Holmes insisted, "a mystery but a well know profession": it is pretty much what Tess saw on her tour.

We can start with the older view. Our own legal system descends from (or still *is*) a "common law" system—a "Case System," as Karl Llewellyn put it[4]—which centrally features judicial decisions as the materials that law students study and that lawyers and judges argue with and about. In the classical view, however, these judicial decisions are not themselves "the law," exactly, but rather are "evidence" of something that precedes and transcends them—of "the law." And the intricacies of common law argumentation are calculated to get at that deeper or larger authority. In this vein, that great expositor of the common law, William Blackstone, explained that "the decisions of courts . . . are the *evidence* of what is common law."[5] A famous American case expressed what sounds like a similar view. "[I]t will hardly be contended," Justice Joseph Story wrote for the U.S. Supreme Court in *Swift v. Tyson*, "that the decisions of courts constitute laws. They are, at most, only *evidence* of what the laws are, and are not, of themselves, laws."[6]

It is not perfectly clear, of course, just what this "evidentiary" conception meant, or whether it meant the same thing to its various proponents. But it at least sounds as if Blackstone and Story believed in, as Holmes would later scornfully put it, "a transcendental body of law outside of any particular state but obligatory within it."[7] Unwilling to attribute preposterous opinions to learned men, later scholars sometimes charitably construe their statements in less metaphysically exotic terms.[8] But is this charity misdirected? Is belief in a "transcendental body of law" so preposterous? Or, rather, *was* such a belief preposterous, given the ontological inventories that men like Blackstone and Story were using?

Blackstone and Story were, after all, heirs of a worldview that assumed that God was real—*more* real than anything else, in fact, or *necessarily* rather than just *contingently* real—and had created the universe according to a providential plan. This view had important implications for the nature of law. Perhaps the most systematic working out of those implications had been performed centuries before Blackstone or Story—by Thomas Aquinas. In Aquinas's account, human or positive law emanates at one level from an earthly ruler or legislator.[9] So far, modern legal thinkers like Holmes should have no quarrel with the classical account. But more is needed for law, Aquinas maintained, than enactment by human legislators. More essentially, even human or positive law derives from the "eternal law," which is the divinely ordained order governing the universe,[10] and positive law gains its status *as law* by virtue of participating in that order. "Since then the eternal law is the plan of government in the Chief Governor," Aquinas explained, "all the plans of government in the inferior governors must be derived from the eternal law."[11] And it followed that "every human law has just so much of the nature of law as it is derived from the law of nature."[12] Aquinas added that "if in any point [the human law] deflects from the law of nature, it is no longer a law but a perversion of law."[13]

Sir John Fortescue, the great fifteenth-century theorist and chief justice of the King's Bench, cited Aquinas repeatedly in his treatise on English law and governance,[14] and so not surprisingly his conception of law as grounded in the divine scheme echoed Aquinas's. Fortescue declared that "all laws that are promulgated by man are decreed by God"; hence, "to learn the laws, even though human ones, is to learn laws that are sacred and decreed of God."[15] Indeed, Fortescue went on to observe that "because this law cannot work in you [the Prince] without grace, it is necessary to pray for that above all things."[16]

Over a century (and a religious revolution) later but in a similar vein, Edward Coke, that classic scholar and expositor of the common law, explained that a common law decision "agrees with the judicial law of god, on which our law is in every point founded."[17] And still another century and a half later Blackstone expressed a strikingly similar understanding.[18] "This law of nature," he explained, "being co-eval with mankind and dictated by God himself, is of course superior in obligation to any other. . . . [N]o human laws are of any validity, if contrary to this; and such of them as are valid derive all their force, and all their authority, mediately or immediately, from this original."[19]

A possible misconception, which leads to a familiar and dismissive caricature, must be guarded against here. The classical position as expounded by thinkers like Aquinas did not naively suppose that there is, say, a sort of ghostly Internal Revenue Code in all of its magnificent detail written in the heavens, and that the Code we find in our more terrestrial tax volumes is merely a mundane photocopy of the celestial original. A few legal rules, such as the prohibition of homicide, might be derived directly from—"read off of," as we say—the eternal law. But the overwhelming bulk of positive law consists of the detailed specification, or *determinatio*, of what the eternal law gives only in generalities. Such specifications are the product of judgments by human legislators, whose pronouncements have the status of law. Even so, the legal status of such pronouncements depends on their indirect derivation from the eternal law, and they should be understood and interpreted in accordance with that overarching reality.

The theistically oriented metaphysics positing God as a sort of transcendent Legislator and the hidden source even of human law was sometimes expressed in the statement that Christianity was part of the common law. Stuart Banner observes that, in 1676, when the great common law judge and scholar Matthew Hale made this pronouncement, he was merely making explicit what would widely have been regarded as self-evident.[20] And the association persisted in this country. Thus, in the nineteenth century, "[f]rom the United States Supreme Court to scattered local courts, from Kent and Story to dozens of writers no one remembers today, Christianity was generally accepted to be part of the common law."[21] Banner further explains—the point is crucial to our present discussion—that the proposition that Christianity was part of the common law was "not a doctrine so much as a meta-doctrine." This meta-doctrine helped support a "non-positivist" view of the common law "as having an existence independent of the statements of judges,"[22] and hence as something that was there to be "discovered," not made.[23]

Even from this classical perspective, to be sure, we would need to explain to our foreign visitor that "the law" itself is not a discrete object visible to human eyes; so we unfortunately cannot take her somewhere and just point to it. ("There it is. Isn't it spectacular?") Nonetheless, within this classical framework she is right to assume that the lawyers and judges and professors and law books she has seen are not themselves "the law" (just as the astronomers and telescopes and lectures are not Alpha Centauri). These activities are dedicated to "the law," which in some sense exists independently of them.

### The Modern Repudiation of "the Law"

Against the backdrop of a theistic metaphysics, this conception seems at least intelligible. Conversely, with the rejection of this metaphysics (an abandonment that, as noted in Chapter 2, pervades at least academic culture),[24] the classical conception becomes nonsensical, almost incomprehensible. The modern reaction to this perspective is nicely expressed in Holmes's repudiation of the notion of law as—we can almost hear the contempt in his voice—a "brooding omnipresence in the sky."[25] Among other things, the modern outlook makes the "evidentiary" account of the common law look like a piece of irrational superstition. Not surprisingly, therefore, Holmes emphatically rejected that account as "fallacy and illusion."[26] And in this respect, Holmes's view had the rare good fortune (for a proposition of jurisprudence and, in essence, of metaphysics) to be explicitly adopted by the Supreme Court in a landmark case that every first-year law student is required to study.[27] In a similar vein, Karl Llewellyn noted that the classical approach to precedent had reflected the fact that for centuries "law was felt as something ordained of god, or even as something inherently right in the order of nature"; but he peremptorily dismissed this view as "super-stitition."[28]

Having rejected the classical account because it was a sore thumb within a more modern conception of what could be accepted as real, thinkers like Holmes have needed to give a different account that *is* consistent with a modern ontology. In this vein, Holmes asserted that the law is nothing more than a set of predictions about what judges will do.[29] The basic ingredients of this account—judges making decisions, lawyers making predictions about judges' decisions—are firmly a part of the lawyer's familiar, workaday world.

To be sure, the limitations of this particular "prediction" account of law are by now notorious (though the account still receives an occasional quali-fied defense).[30] Imagine the judge who asks her law clerk to prepare a bench memorandum describing the law on a contested point: the judge is not likely to react cheerfully if the clerk, fresh from reading Holmes's "Path" es-say, turns in a memo that merely reads, "Your Honor, I think I know you pretty well by now, and I predict that you'll rule for the plaintiff. You asked me to describe the law on this issue: that's it."[31] Holmes himself was not con-tent with—and as a justice surely did not employ—this "prediction" account of the law. Among other difficulties, it would seem to render almost inco-herent the sort of opinion that Holmes became renowned for—that is, the dissenting opinion that purports to disagree with the majority not just about what the law *should be*, but about what the law *is*. The Great Dissenter would on these assumptions be an almost shockingly inept lawyer: How hard can it be, after all, to "predict what the judges will do" when the judges have al-ready voted and you were right there in the room when they did it?

Even so, we can surely sympathize with the motivation behind Holmes's prediction theory. At bottom, he was simply trying to replace an account of law that no longer made sense in terms of the ontological inventory that he and many of his contemporaries embraced with an account that *would* be in-telligible in terms of that ontology.

To put the point a bit differently, Holmes was trying to deflect inquiries about "the law" in the same way Ryle tried to deflect his hypothetical visi-tor's question about "the University." Holmes wanted to say, along with Ryle, that "once you've seen the judges and lawyers at work, you've already seen the law. All of that—the judges and lawyers and so forth—*is* the law. If you think there's anything more, you're making a category mistake."

So despite the deficiencies in Holmes's particular version of this response, legal thinkers throughout the twentieth century have offered basically similar, if far more elaborate versions of the same response. Legal Realists like Llewellyn expanded Holmes's account to include not only judges but other officials as well: "the center of law," Llewellyn said, "is not merely what the judge does, . . . but what *any* state official does, officially."[32] Other theorists have gone beyond what seems the almost physical behaviorism of these descriptions ("what any state official *does*") to include what we might call "verbal" behavior. Law is a "language game"; it is the way lawyers and judges talk.[33] In the classical account, law-talk is *about* "the law" (much in the way that astronomy-talk is about the stars, and a John Madden commentary is about a game of football). In this more modern account, legal discourse *is* the law. A modern approach, with its behaviorist and discursive variations and dimensions, can produce highly sophisticated accounts, such as the more sociological or institutional theories of H. L. A. Hart and Neil MacCormick.[34]

We will look more closely at some of these strategies in Chapter 4. For now, we can say that the common element is the effort to eliminate something that the modern ontologies grounded in everyday experience and science no longer give us leave to affirm—"the law"—and to account for law in terms of things we *can* acknowledge as real: lawyers and judges arguing and explaining and deciding. The imperative, as Felix Cohen put it, has been to "redefine supernatural concepts in natural terms."[35]

It may seem that there is nothing especially surprising or unprecedented about this transformation. It often happens that people quit believing in the substantial reality of something they formerly believed in—witches, or mermaids, or the universal ether—and then they revise their understandings and desist from practices that presuppose the reality of such things. If we believe in witches (in the early modern sense, or perhaps the Grimms' fairy tale sense), then we may take measures to detect and eradicate them; once we become convinced that witches of the warty-nosed variety do not exist, these measures will seem pointless and barbaric, and we will abandon them.

But the case of law is more interesting, because in fact we have *not* abandoned the practices that originated in a belief in law as, to use Holmes's derisive expression, a "brooding omnipresence in the sky." Not only have we maintained the practices; if closely inspected, our practices and our ways of talking and thinking about those practices strongly suggest that we still *do* believe that "the law" is real in some such sense (even though we will protest, when confronted, that we do *not* believe any such thing). That is the predicament of modern law and legal discourse: it seems that we cannot believe in "the law," and we also cannot live without quietly harboring something like this belief.

Let us consider, in the remainder of this chapter, the powerful evidence of a persisting belief in "the law." Since in our time we also commonly purport (at least for professional purposes) not to believe in the classical ontological inventory in which "the law" was grounded, our persistent belief in "the law" threatens to leave us in the position of committing nonsense—nonsense—on a massive scale. In Chapter 4 we will inspect the major modern attempts to escape that embarrassment.

## "The Law" After All?

Your visitor has been waiting patiently as you indulge in these reflections, and you suddenly look up and realize that you have not yet responded to her last remark about how she had hoped to see "the law." What to say? As it happens, I walk in on you at this point, and so you buy time by introducing us:

"Professor, I'd like you to meet—"

"You can call me Tess."

"For Theresa?"

"No, actually it's short for Socratessa. . . . We have some unusual names where I come from."

"Interesting. Well, glad to meet you, Tess."

You then tell me about your day with Tess, and about her desire to see "the law." We consult for a moment and then explain to Tess that although people may once have believed in "the law" as the sort of thing-in-itself her question supposes, we now realize that this was a misconception. Today we understand that this belief was "fallacy and illusion," as Holmes put it: law does not exist in any such sense. Rather, the law is constituted by the practices of judges, lawyers, legislators, and citizens—by the sorts of activities and institutions she has already observed.

That should be the end of the inquiry, shouldn't it? (And of this book as well?) Having spent a few weeks in our society and a few hours in our legal culture, though, Tess is suspicious of this explanation. "Oh, yes, you *do* believe in 'the law'!" she protests. "It's obvious that you do." And she insists that in offering this dismissive explanation, you and I are behaving like spurned lovers who protest through our tears that we don't care at all about the person who has rejected us, even though it is plain to any observer that we do. In turn, we explain to Tess—diplomatically, of course, because Tess is after all a foreign visitor—that she is mistaken. We are in a better position to know what we believe than she is, aren't we?

But Tess remains unconvinced, and promptly cites some verbal evidence to support her somewhat cheeky assessment. And in fact we acknowledge—with a chuckle, which to Tess sounds just a bit nervous—that of course lawyers (and many nonlawyers) constantly and routinely refer to "the law" *as if* it were some entity, or some thing that exists independently of us and possesses some more or less definite content that is somehow authoritative for us. We describe a situation or problem and then ask, "What's 'the law' on that?" Or we make assertions about "what 'the law' requires." At least to the uninitiated, our usage might suggest that such phrases allude to some elaborate, multivolume rule book, and that the questions call for someone to look up the answers in the same way that we look up unfamiliar words in a dictionary. Indeed, clients sometimes come to attorneys—and beginning law students sometimes come to law school—with some such "rule book" notion in mind. Experienced lawyers know better, of course. Alas, if only it were so simple—if only there *were* such a rule book stashed away somewhere. Even so, lawyers argue passionately and judges pontificate solemnly about what "the law" is or requires, even when (or especially when) there is admittedly no established rule—no statute or regulation or precedent "on point."[36]

Sometimes we refer reverently to "the rule of law"—or, more ambitiously and mysteriously, to "the rule of law, not of men." These familiar phrases might seem to treat "the law" as if it were some discrete and authoritative entity, or perhaps as a sort of quasi *person* who wields authority. The child's "*Mama says* you have to go to bed now" matures into "*'The law' says* you have to file your tax returns by April 15." Indeed, lawyer and psychologist Benjamin Sells has found that both lawyers and nonlawyers *do* readily picture "the law" as a person—sometimes, for example, as "an older man, gray-haired and distinguished looking" who wears a leather or camel coat, carries a briefcase, and drinks his coffee black without sugar.[37] Or our talk might imply that "the law" is some ethereal and impersonal object—perhaps (Sells is here describing the images of law that people in fact seem to carry around with them) "an outside and occupying force responsible for imposing and maintaining order."[38] Commenting on his research, Sells explains that "the Law can be imagined as if it has a life of its own. *The Law that lives in our imagination is far more influential than we might think.* Usually it operates unconsciously, affecting our ideology, our everyday practice, how we think about the Law's role in society, how we relate to concepts like order and obedience, and how we understand larger themes like truth and justice."[39]

Still, these usages can be dismissed as cases of figurative or metaphorical expression. Indeed, Holmes freely acknowledged all of this: he admitted that if you try to understand the common law from books, "[i]t is very hard to resist the impression that there is one august corpus, to understand which clearly is the only task of any Court concerned." It is as if there were "a transcendent body of law outside of any particular State but obligatory within it." But in fact there isn't any such thing, Holmes said, and we know it.[40] So when Tess, our visitor, cites such usage, you and I explain (now with just a hint of impatience) that she has taken our phrases too literally. Perhaps we *do* occasionally refer to "the law" as if it were some sort of person or autonomous force. In the same way, even hardened evolutionary biologists may talk poetically about "Mother Nature" and her "purposes." But they don't mean it, and neither do we. These are just figures of speech.

Still suspicious, though, Tess decides to linger a little longer in our legal culture. A few weeks later, having gathered additional evidence, she returns to challenge our dismissive explanation.[41]

### Precedent-Practice

Tess now knows, first of all, that a good deal of legal discourse consists of marshaling, citing, and distinguishing precedents. To a significant extent law school is devoted to training future lawyers in the intricacies of this precedent-oriented method of reasoning, or to what Llewellyn called "the case system game."[42] And legal briefs and judicial opinions are chock full of it. The practice of precedent occurs not only in areas thought to belong to the "common law" (where there is little or no written law *other than* precedent), but also in the exposition and implementation of statutes and constitutional provisions. If you want to understand the effective meaning of the Sherman Act, or the First Amendment, or the Eleventh Amendment, that is, you had better look at the cases: the text of the statute or amendment itself is likely to be of little help, and may only serve to mislead you.

Despite (or perhaps because of) the learning and technical sophistication it entails, however, this practice has often struck detached observers as curious—"weird or exotic," as Cass Sunstein acknowledges[43]—or even, more bluntly, as irrational or even wicked.[44] Jonathan Swift's derision was typical:

> It is a Maxim among these lawyers, that whatever hath been done before, may legally be done again: And therefore they take special Care to record all the Decisions formerly made against common Justice and the general Reason of Mankind. These, under the Name of *Precedents*, they produce as Authorities to justify the most iniquitous Opinions; and the Judges never fail to direct accordingly.[45]

Swift's description is exaggerated, but it raises a very good question: What exactly *is* the point of this elaborate practice of recording, collecting, arranging, reciting, and distinguishing past decisions as a basis for making present decisions?

In the classical account of law, as we have already seen, there was a standard answer to this question. Common law precedents were not themselves "the law," but rather were "evidence" of something lying above or beyond them—of the real law, ultimately deriving from God's providential plan— and the lawyerly techniques were devices for using that evidence to apprehend and give effect to this authoritative reality. Robert Gordon makes the point colorfully: quoting Richard Hooker's statement that law sits "in the bosom of God, her voice the harmony of the world," Gordon observes that pre-Holmesian lawyers "had, as they saw it, a direct line to God's mind through their knowledge of the principles of legal science."[46] And that "science" was manifested in the techniques of common law argumentation.

If the pre-Holmesian view were plausible, then the lawyerly reliance on precedent might make very good sense. But of course, we have long since rejected that evidentiary account of the common law practice.

Or have we? Tess thinks not. If judicial decisions are not evidence of "the law," she asks, then why *do* we honor them so lavishly in legal discourse? One answer is that precedents are authoritative not as evidence of anything else but because they themselves *are* the law. This answer seems most secure in the area of common law, where, as noted, there is little or no written law *except* the judicial decisions. And indeed, common law decisions today are routinely described as "judge-made law." It is law that is made by judges performing the function of legislators—of "interstitial" legislators, we sometimes say, to minimize the affront to traditional separation-of-powers notions.

But although we often *say* this, our common methods and techniques even of common law argumentation belie this description. In a variety of ways, our actual practices involving precedents seem more consistent with the classical evidentiary account than with the modern proposition that judicial decisions *are* law—law made by judges acting as legislators.

In the first place, we might wonder what part of a judicial decision is the law. All of it? Only some of it? And if so, which part? How do we know and extract what is law from what isn't? And if judicial decisions themselves *are* law, what is our excuse for treating any part of a decision as *not* law, or as something less than law?

As it happens, these questions have baffled lawyers and theorists. In discussing a prior case lawyers and judges plainly do not treat the case in its entirety as legally authoritative: they may say a judicial decision is law, but what they clearly mean, at most, is that some parts of the decision are law. So lawyers and judges purport to search for what they call the "holding" of the case; this is to be distinguished from other, nonobligating features, described as the "dicta," that may in fact make up nearly all of what is written in support of the decision.

Moreover, despite diligent efforts, jurists and theorists have found no consistent method or formula for sorting out these elements. The embarrassment can be appreciated by comparing the first and second editions of George Christie's textbook *Jurisprudence*. In the first edition, Christie devoted a substantial block of text and materials to the problem of figuring out exactly how to extract the holding, or *ratio decidendi*, from a precedent.[47] Even then, in 1973, Christie's materials were a bit anachronistic—they were composed mainly of readings that were already quite stale—and Christie acknowledged that "one may be forced to conclude that there is no really satisfactory theory of the concept." But he was unwilling to accept this conclusion because, as he cogently observed, without some account "it is no longer possible to base one's explanation of the binding nature of precedent upon the concept of the *ratio decidendi* of a case." Or, to put the point differently, we would have no way to figure out what in a precedent is actually *law*. "We therefore cannot avoid trying"—here Christie began to sound faintly desperate—"to make whatever sense we can of the concept."[48] By the time of the second edition, Christie had evidently given up trying to "make sense . . . of the concept": this entire section of the book was simply dropped.[49]

Thus, it is no secret that despite our insistence that judicial decisions *are* law, we have—or judges have—considerable discretion to decide what in a decision counts as law. Justice Scalia exaggerates perhaps, but only a little, when he remarks that "what constitutes the 'holding' of an earlier case is not well defined and can be adjusted to suit the occasion."[50]

And the discussion thus far actually understates the incongruity between the modern proposition that judicial decisions are law and our actual use of precedents. The problem is not just that *not everything* said by a court in presenting its decision is treated as law; it sometimes happens that *nothing* actually said in the decision is treated as explicitly stating the law. To put the point differently, later courts may treat a precedent as standing for a rule of law that was not actually stated anywhere in the decision at all. The result, as the eminent legal historian Brian Simpson observes in an essay reflecting on the nature of the common law, is that "if six pundits of the profession, however sound and distinguished, are asked to write down what they conceive the rule or rules governing the doctrine of *res ipsa loquitur,* the definition of murder or manslaughter, the principles governing frustration of contract or mistake as to the person, it is in the highest degree unlikely that they will fail to write down six different formulations."[51] Much the same might be said of a modern constitutional decision such as *Brown v. Board of Education.*[52] Scholars and jurists have interpreted the case to mean any number of things, of course, but the one thing you will *not* find if you search the opinion itself is the crucial ruling that the decision is most celebrated for—that is, the repudiation of the "separate but equal" doctrine.

The oddity of this whole practice may become apparent if we compare it to the direct application of statutes. Portions of a statute may be declared unconstitutional, of course, or treated as having been repealed by later statutes. And statutes (and even more so constitutional provisions) may become submerged in a sea of precedents that purport to be interpreting them but in reality displace them. Even so, courts typically do not consider themselves at liberty simply to disregard sections of a statute as "dicta." ("We think that in Section 4 of the statute Congress wasn't actually *legislating;* it was just sort of . . . , well, *talking.* That section is legislative 'dicta.'") In the same way, if judicial decisions were truly *law* in themselves, and not merely evidence of law, this technique of dismissing large sections of previous decisions should seem extraordinary. The practice is extraordinary and incongruous, that is, on the assumption that judicial decisions themselves *are* actually law "of themselves" (as Justice Story put it in denying that the decisions were any such thing).[53]

Even if agreement is reached about a particular case's "holding," moreover, there are further complications. The holding of any given case must be harmonized with the holdings of any number of other, often divergent cases to reveal the law, and once again there is no standardized method for achieving such harmony. *"[N]o case can have a meaning by itself!"* Karl Llewellyn emphasized. "Standing alone it gives you no guidance."[54] Later, in a magnificent study, Llewellyn counted thirty-two "impeccable" techniques for deflecting or confining or extending precedents, another twelve methods that he thought legitimate, an additional sixteen methods that are "correct but less usual," and four techniques that he regarded as "illegitimate" but that are nonetheless used.[55] In addition, holdings are sometimes explicitly rejected or overruled on the ground that they are out of line with some higher criterion—one that might most aptly be described as "the law."

So it is too simple, or too evasive regarding real complexities and mysteries, to say flatly, as the modern view likes to say, that judicial decisions *are* the law, or that common law is the product of judges acting as legislators. Modern jurisprudential wisdom notwithstanding, and decades after the ostensible demise of *Swift v. Tyson,* lawyers and judges still in practice treat prior decisions as if they were evidence of something more subtle and coy and unitary—of "the law."

One of the most perceptive legal thinkers of the twentieth century, Lon Fuller, nicely described this discrepancy. Fuller himself was in uneasy accord with modern thinking on the subject, and thus he maintained that common law decisions reflect judicial legislation—albeit legislation of an institutionally special kind.[56] But Fuller also acknowledged that judges typically do not talk or think of their decisions in this way: they claim to be "finding" law, not "making" it.[57] And he noted that not only the judges' talk but also their actual practice—the way they actually use precedents—is in fact more consistent with this description than with the "judicial legislation" characterization.

> [I]t is not too much to say that the judges are always ready to look behind the words of a precedent to what the previous court was trying to say, or to what it would have said if it could have foreseen the nature of the cases that were later to arise, or if its perception of the relevant factors in the case had been more acute. There is, then, a real sense in which the written words of the reported decisions are merely the gateway to *something lying behind them* that may be called, without any excess of poetic license, "unwritten law."[58]

Fuller noticed other features of common law adjudication that support this observation. One feature is the common practice of writing dissenting opinions.[59] A legislator who votes against a successful bill is said to disagree about what the law *should be,* but she normally will concede that the measure she has opposed *is* the law (once it is duly enacted). Dissenting judicial opinions, by contrast, typically assert that the majority has *misstated the law*—a characterization that would make little sense if the judges were in fact acting as legislators. And dissenting judges may hold to this view even in future cases: the position that gained majority support in the previous decision, and that continues to enjoy majority support, is nonetheless said to be a misstatement of "the law." What could this kind of talk mean if the judicial decision *is* law?

More recently, Connie Rosati makes a similar point:

> It is not uncommon to hear apparently legally knowledgeable critics insist that most judges have gotten the law wrong. The majority of judges likely hold, and a majority of justices in their time did hold, that the death penalty is not unconstitutional, yet this fact did not stop Justices William Brennan and Harry Blackmun from arguing otherwise. But if the law just is what the majority of judges say it is, or rather, what they would approve, then how are we to make sense of such a dispute? . . . Indeed, the practice of writing dissenting opinions becomes puzzling. If justices intend to follow the law, then once a majority of the Court has made its view clear, it would seem the dissenters ought simply to sign on to the opinion of the Court.[60]

Fuller was also impressed by the common practice of citing and relying on precedents from a variety of different jurisdictions. "Saskatchewan may cite a precedent from New South Wales," he noted. "Vermont may derive guidance from the law propounded by the judges of Arkansas, while the Queen's Bench may find a decision of the Supreme Court of the United States persuasive." Fuller acknowledged the most natural inference: "Judges who thus habitually borrow legal wisdom back and forth across political boundaries are apt to talk as if they were all working together in bringing to adequate expression a *preexisting thing called 'The Law.'*"[61]

### Enacted Law

In arguing that we still believe in "the law" (our own protestations to the contrary notwithstanding), our visitor Tess finds valuable supporting evidence in our practices of precedent-based reasoning. But of course precedent-practice does not dominate the field in the way it once did. Increasingly, legal discourse revolves around enacted law—statutes, regulations, constitutional provisions—and the prominence of this newer type of law means, according to Guido Calabresi, that the "legal world has totally changed."[62] (Though in fact enacted law is still typically mediated by and absorbed into the standard forms of precedent-practice.)

Enacted law is sometimes treated as being fundamentally different in character from common law,[63] where some might suppose that there is nothing but precedent; and enacted law clearly *is* different in a variety of ways. We can say just when a statute was adopted. It has a canonical form. It typically is not formally accompanied by elaborate justificatory opinions (or by officially presented dissenting opinions). And as already noted, judges and other interpreters typically would not feel free to dismiss whole sections of a statute in the way they pass off portions of a judicial decision as dicta.

These differences are real enough, but the important question for present purposes is whether statutes (by which I mean for now to include enacted law generally) are different from common law in a way that defeats the claim that I have been attributing to our hypothetical visitor Tess—the claim, that is, that although we say we no longer believe in "the law," our practices in fact manifest and presuppose such a belief. This is a complicated question that for the most part I will defer and take up again from a slightly different angle in Chapters 5 and 6. For now, though, two points are important.

First, the mere fact that statutes come into existence through enactment does not by itself demonstrate any inconsistency with what I earlier called the "traditional" or "classical" account of law. Though there may have been fewer statutes in their times, Aquinas and Blackstone were perfectly familiar with enacted law and saw no incongruity between this sort of law and their overall jurisprudence, with its supporting metaphysics. Indeed, Aquinas's very definition of law asserted the necessity of a legislator: as noted, he defined law as "an ordinance of reason for the common good, *made by him who has the care of the community.*"[64] And his explanation of human law featured a human legislator who would, among other things, exercise judgment in specifying numerous details that are not given directly in the eternal law. At the same time, Aquinas suggested that this legislator's enactments would derive their status *as law* from their participation in that eternal law.

So the mere fact of enacted law is perfectly compatible with the classical account of "the law." This observation leads to a second one. The differences between statutes and common law, though undeniable, also should not be overdrawn. In many pertinent respects, the judicial treatment of statutes is not so different from the approach taken to common law precedents. Recall, for example, the particular aspect of precedent-practice that led Lon Fuller to say that "reported decisions are merely the gateway to *something lying behind them*": it was the fact that "judges are always ready to look behind the words of a precedent to what the previous court was trying to say, to what it would have said if it could have foreseen the nature of the cases that were later to arise, or if its perception of the relevant factors in the case had been more acute."[65] If we substitute "the statute" for "the precedent" and "the legislature" for "the previous court" in this sentence, Fuller's observation remains largely intact: courts routinely employ analogous tactics with statutes. In place of the various techniques for using or distinguishing precedents, courts resort to a host of "canons of construction" to limit or extend, to shape and reshape, the meaning of statutes. And what is true of ordinary statutes holds many times over for that supreme example of enacted law—the Constitution—where the various textual phrases ("due process," "equal protection," "freedom of speech," "cruel and unusual punishment") quite plainly serve as little more than, as Fuller put it, "gateway[s] to something lying behind them."

We might put the point in this way: though statutes differ in various respects from common law, it is nevertheless wholly implausible to suppose that judges have discretion in common law areas but are merely mechanically carrying out textual commands in the application of statutes or the Constitution. For certain purposes we sometimes like to imagine that law does or should work in this way. But familiarity with the actual practice leaves no doubt that this is a gross misdescription. Whether we are interested in common law precedents or statutes, judicial and other interpreters are always looking behind and beyond the written words to something that is not fully contained in or exhausted by those words, and that gives those words both their authority and their meaning.

So we can say that statutes *are* the law. We can *say* this. And the description may fit our use of statutes better than it fits our use of judicial precedents (where in fact the description fits barely at all). Even so, if offered as a jurisprudential proposition, that description is simplistic and, standing by itself, misleading. As with common law precedents, our actual practices pervasively belie the simplistic account. And in some respects, an evidentiary account may actually come closer to fitting what we actually *do* with statutes.

We will return to consider the interpretation of enacted law in later chapters. For now, it is enough to say that our actual uses of statutes are at least nicely compatible with (even if they do not in themselves confirm) Tess's claim that we still, in fact, believe in "the law."

### The Remarkable Fact of Retroactivity

At this point, it seems that Tess can offer considerable evidence in support of her claim that even today we act as if we believe in "the law." But she has saved what may be her most telling argument for last. Probably the starkest evidence of our ongoing presupposition of an independently existing "law," she argues, lies in the common judicial practice of treating decisions—including, it is important to note, both common law decisions and decisions interpreting statutes—as retroactively applicable even to events occurring before the decisions were rendered.[66] The assumption has always been that it is appropriate to subject past actions to a newly announced judicial ruling—so that you or I can be sued for all we're worth for violating a legal rule that was unknown and unarticulated at the time we violated it—because the ruling merely announces or declares what "the law" *is* (in an ominously expansive sense in which "is" describes a sort of perpetual present reaching back into the indefinite past).

This practice is usually followed even in so-called cases of first impression and—most strikingly—even when a decision explicitly overrules a prior decision.[67] The new decision is said merely to declare "the law" that obligated parties all along—even though a previous judicial opinion mistakenly declared otherwise. In his lectures to Columbia law students Llewellyn described the familiar practice and assumption (albeit in a tone that was as dismissive as he could make it): "case law rules (though new) are applied as *if* they had always been the law; this derives from our convention that 'judges only declare and do not make the law.'"[68]

This practice of retroactive application, along with the "declaratory theory" of law that supports it, fits nicely with the classical assumption that "the law" exists independent of our particular interpretations of it. Indeed, within that framework, it is hardly apt to talk of retroactive application at all: if "the law" was already there, then it is not being retroactively applied.[69] Conversely, the practice and theory fit awkwardly at best with modern conceptions that deny the existence of any such law. Within a modern framework, retroactive application can be justified, if at all, only as an awkward pragmatic expedient.[70] Not surprisingly, "realist"-minded scholars and jurists have sometimes criticized this practice of retroactive application and have argued that decisions should be applied prospectively only.[71]

And for a time it appeared that a selective practice of prospective rulings might develop.[72] More recently, though, not only the traditional practice but also the classical rationale for that practice have firmly reasserted themselves. Thus, Justice Souter observes that retroactive application of decisions is "overwhelmingly the norm." Souter goes on to explain that this practice is grounded in the view that "the function of the courts [is] to decide cases before them based upon their best current understanding of the law"—a view that in turn reflects "the declaratory theory of the law, according to which the courts are understood only to *find the law, not to make it.*"[73] In the same case, Justice Scalia, writing for an unusual coalition including himself and Justices Marshall and Blackmun, goes even further; he maintains that retrospective application of decisions is constitutionally required because the courts' function is simply "'to say *what the law is.*'"[74]

The embarrassing incongruity between this position and modern notions of law is reflected in—let us put the point charitably—an enigmatic disclaimer that Scalia felt moved to add. "I am not so naive (nor do I think our forbears were) as to be unaware that judges in a real sense 'make' law," Scalia hastens to explain. "But they make it *as judges make it,* which is to say *as though* they were 'finding' it—or discerning what the law *is.*"[75] We do not in fact believe in the classical account of law, Scalia seems to suggest: that would be naive. We only act *as if* we believed in it.

But why should we act as if "the law" is there if we actually believe it isn't? At least on the face of the matter, this practice of retroactivity and the explanation given for it furnish strong *prima facie* evidence of an ongoing lawyerly commitment to "the law" that exists before, and thus independent of, the decisions that merely declare what is already in existence.

## A Suspicion of "Nonsense"

We should size up the case as it stands at this point. Since at least the time of Holmes, lawyers and legal thinkers have scoffed at the notion that "the law" exists in any substantial sense or that it is not reducible into our discourse and practices. Law is not a "brooding omnipresence in the sky." We have rejected any such conception of law not whimsically, but rather because we perceive, correctly, that our ontological inventories (or at least those that prevail in most public and academic settings) could not provide any intelligible account of, as Fuller put it, this "preexisting thing called 'The Law.'"

At the same time, our hypothetical visitor Tess has pointed to what looks like cogent evidence suggesting that we still *do* believe in "the law." It is not just that we constantly refer to or imagine "the law" as if it were a sort of person, as Benjamin Sells observes, or "an outside and occupying force." Those sorts of images and usages might be explained away as figures of speech. But the fact is that our actual practices seem pervasively to presuppose some such law: our practices at least potentially might make sense on the assumption that such a law exists, and they look puzzling or awkward or embarrassing *without* the assumption. Our routine practice of retroactively applying even novel or surprising decisions (or even decisions overruling past decisions) on the ground that the decisions are merely saying "what the law is" provides only the starkest evidence of this ongoing assumption.

Brian Simpson summarizes our current predicament:

> For lawyers, to quote E. P. Thompson, writing in 1975 of what he calls "the greatest of all legal fictions," "the law itself evolves, from case to case, by its own impartial logic, true only to its own integrity. . . ." There is, of course, a sense in which *nobody really believes this any more,* but it remains the case that much legal behaviour proceeds on the assumption that the law is like that. For example, all legal argument in court makes this assumption.[76]

This disjunction between what we *say* we believe (or, more accurately, what we say we do *not* believe) and what our discourse and practice seem to presuppose provokes the suspicion that conventional law-talk is a form of nonsense. To recall the description offered in Chapter 1, there is at least a strong *prima facie* case that modern legal discourse is operating in a sort of "ontological gap" that divides our explicit or owned ontological commitments (which preclude us from recognizing the reality of "the law") from the ontological assumptions not only implicit in but essential to our discourse and practice (which seem to presuppose the reality of "the law").

This assessment might help explain the malaise in legal scholarship, and law-talk generally, described at the outset of that chapter. It should hardly be surprising if a discourse that is essentially nonsensical—nonsensical, that is, relative to the society or culture in which that discourse is carried on—tends to become "just words," or "incomprehensible," as so many critics charge. Nor should we be surprised if, in an at least half-conscious effort to escape the embarrassment, that discourse often resorts to being "pompous," "turgid," and "jargonistic." We would hardly be the first generation in history to resort to bluster and obfuscation to hide the fact that we're not really sure what we're talking about (and not willing to acknowledge our ignorance).

But if the evidence of nonsense seems *prima facie* persuasive, the charge itself still provokes incredulity. How could an entire culture—that is, a legal culture composed of and by highly sophisticated, well-trained professionals—persist and even flourish for over a century on the basis of a discourse that is mere nonsense? (As noted, even Socrates worried about this kind of question. If no one understands what virtue is, how is it that some people seem to practice it?) Certainly the residents of that culture—those who are suspected of committing nonsense on a massive scale—cannot be expected to accede easily to this assessment.

And in fact, modern legal thinkers have offered a sustained if sometimes ambivalent resistance, employing a variety of defensive strategies. Indeed, the bulk of jurisprudential thought in the twentieth century consisted precisely of such strategies. We will consider those strategies in the next chapter.

# CHAPTER 4

# The Jurisprudence of Modernity

The twentieth century spawned a variety of important jurisprudential movements: a roughly chronological list might include sociological jurisprudence, Legal Realism, legal process, law and policy (especially including law and economics), law and society, law and philosophy, Critical Legal Studies, law and literature, feminist jurisprudence, Critical Race Theory, and Legal Pragmatism, to mention only some of the prominent movements that have been most influential in the United States. These movements arose in response to a variety of questions and problems. At the heart of much modern legal thought, however, has been the concern to address a central, ongoing challenge: the challenge of explaining how the law makes sense without "the law."

The principal responses to that challenge have shaped up along two main lines, both of which were foreshadowed in Holmes's essay "The Path of the Law." We can describe these as the "autonomy" strategy and the "law and" strategy. The first strategy maintains, basically, that the observable legal enterprise—Holmes's "well known profession" composed of lawyers and judges and legal practices and institutions—is sufficient unto itself. It does not need anything outside itself—neither "the law" nor any substitute or replacement for "the law"—to make sense. We can and should understand the legal enterprise on its own terms and with reference to its visible functioning—not importing any extraneous disciplines, and *a fortiori* not referring to any spooky metaphysical entities such as "the law."

The "law and" strategy disagrees, though only in part. Viewed as an autonomous institution, this response maintains, the law does *not* make sense: it is indeterminate, artificial, mindlessly arbitrary. The law needs supplementation. It is true, though, that this supplement can no longer be "the law." So something else must be brought in as a substitute. That substitute might be "policy," or "policy science." It might be moral philosophy. Or perhaps pragmatism, or judgment, or practical reason. In any case, the law is like the tango: it takes two. We will always need to think of "law and ___." Without whatever it is that fills in the blank, law soon lapses into nonsense.

So, can either of these strategies succeed in showing how the law makes sense without "the law"? I will argue in this chapter that they cannot. Indeed, the proponents of these strategies have themselves typically been of mixed mind. As we will see, it is often hard to tell whether modern legal thinkers are defending the law against suspicions of nonsense or rushing to join in the indictment.

## Law as Autonomous?

The autonomy strategy aims to give an account of law that is safe, in two senses. First, the account would avoid invoking any ontologically controversial entities, such as "the law," or God, or the providential plan that Blackstone alluded to and that Aquinas described as the "eternal law"; in this way the description of law would be metaphysically beyond reproach. Second, the account would limit its description to phenomena and activities that everyone would naturally associate with the legal system; in this way we could be confident that the description was of *law*, not something else.

In Chapter 3, we noticed leading versions of this strategy. Some versions have a *behavioral* and others a more *discursive* emphasis. In the first vein, Holmes famously defined law (though this was hardly a complete statement of his jurisprudence) as the prediction of what judges will do. Legal Realists like Karl Llewellyn extended this behavioral account to include *all* government officials. "The main thing," Llewellyn emphasized, "is what officials are going to *do*."[1] Richard Posner's "activity theory" of law is in the same vein.[2] Other theorists have focused not so much on the overt behavior of judges or other officials—on what officials *do*—as on the ways they *talk:* legal discourse *is* law.

In one sense, the behavioral and the discursive accounts might seem almost the opposite of each other. In a different sense, though, these accounts reflect a common strategy: both depict law as autonomous—as intelligible in its own right without the necessary supplementation either of "the law" or of outside disciplines. These descriptive accounts of law seem safe in the first sense because they invoke only the elements of what we earlier called the "ontology of everyday experience": judges (persons), lawyers (persons), all engaged in recognizable patterns of talking (a property or capacity of persons) with each other. We can add in, if we like, other persons (sheriffs, bailifs, jurors) as well as objects (robes, gavels, books, case reports, courtrooms). The crucial point is that there is no apparent reference to anything more metaphysically exotic or mysterious (like "the law"). The descriptive accounts are also safe in the second sense, because no one doubts that lawyers and judges (and legislators, and sheriffs), as well as legal briefs and judicial opinions, are part of the system we call "law."

### Obviating "the Law"?

The autonomy strategy may indeed generate accounts of law that make no direct, explicit reference to "the law." Moreover, such accounts can yield valuable insights into how the law works. But do those accounts show how the law *makes sense* without "the law"? Can the autonomy strategy actually rescue law from the suspicion of nonsense raised at the end of Chapter 3?

An analogy may be helpful here. Suppose that a candidate for high public office shows symptoms of a potentially dangerous heart problem, so that opponents argue that he is not physically qualified for the job. Needing to respond to these concerns, the candidate appoints doctors to issue a (truthful) medical report showing that his lungs, brain, kidneys, and digestive organs are in excellent working order. This sort of commendatory medical description may be perfectly accurate as far as it goes, but it is also fatally incomplete. If the candidate had been suspected of suffering from hereditary baldness or weak teeth, perhaps a report showing all of his vital organs in good condition *would* be responsive to health concerns. But the heart is an essential part of the person, and of his capacity to perform official duties, so simply leaving the heart out of a description does nothing to dispel the concern.

A positive description can serve to deflect suspicions, in short, but only if it accounts for everything that is vital to the subject that is being described. So, do modern, ontologically safe descriptions of law fully account for everything that is essential to our law and legal system? Or do they leave out vital elements? A close inspection will show, I think, that the accounts generated by the autonomy strategy are deficient because they either overlook or else distort the essential element of *legal discourse*. But this element is not only at the heart of law; it is also where law's metaphysical commitments are most clearly manifest. Consequently, the safe description strategies do nothing to "explain away" law's metaphysical commitments, but instead simply decline to notice those commitments; in doing so, they give a seriously deficient description of law.

## Behaviorist Descriptions: The "Law in Action"

This deficiency is easiest to see in a straightforward behaviorist account of law, such as the prediction theory associated with Holmes. To say that law consists of "the prophecies of what the courts will do in fact, and nothing more pretentious" is to give a description that is at once correct and grossly deficient; it is deficient, in part, because the description leaves out nearly everything that lawyers and judges do and say—including what they do and say when they are engaged in predicting what judges will do.

In this respect, the prediction theory is like a person who walks into a sports bar and overhears some fans discussing why the Yankees beat the Red Sox in the game that just ended. The fans argue about managerial decisions and strategies, or a crucial throwing error or base-running mistake, or a clutch hit in the late innings, or the Yankees' superb relief pitching. Suppose the newcomer interrupts to explain, in condescending tones: "You guys are way out in left field. The Yankees didn't win for any of those reasons. They won because they scored more runs." Not content with this limited point about a single game, our sage goes on with a magisterial flourish: "In fact, I can universalize the point: in baseball—take it from me—the winning team *always* wins because it scores more runs. Once you understand that, you know all you need to know about winning in baseball. Your cute little theories, your hunches and hypotheses about pitching, and hitting, and managing and all that minutia: *sometimes* they'll tell you something about why a team won. Sometimes they won't. But my theory—about scoring more runs—will *always* give you the true explanation."

We immediately recognize that this explanation of winning in baseball is unassailably correct—and profoundly obtuse. *Of course* a team wins a baseball game by scoring more runs. And of course lawyers try to predict what judges will do. Everyone knows these things. But the fans, and the lawyers and legal scholars, are trying to understand in more detailed and illuminating ways just *how* these functions are performed, or how the sought after outcomes are realized. And the more generalized description (winning results from scoring more runs; law is what judges do) simply fails to engage with the problem. Offering itself as a descriptive account, the description in fact ignores nearly everything that is central to the subject of its description.

In ignoring that subject matter, moreover, the descriptive jurisprudential strategy defaults with respect to the charge that the talk and practice of lawyers and judges presuppose an independent, metaphysically illicit law. The strategy thus leaves the "nonsense" suspicion unanswered. This default is not surprising, and may even be deliberate: proponents of descriptive accounts, such as Holmes, may resort to such accounts precisely because they suspect that conventional legal discourse *is* nonsense. Holmes's famous "Path" essay, in which he offered his prediction theory, is filled with criticism of conventional legal discourse suggestive of this conclusion. But if legal discourse is nonsense, and if this discourse is in fact central to the practice of law (including the lawyerly prediction of what judges will do), then this concession defeats any descriptive effort to rescue legal discourse from suspicions of nonsense.

These problems with a Holmesian prediction theory are not avoided, moreover, by introducing more complicated or sophisticated descriptions—or by expanding the field while retaining the behavioral focus. Suppose, for example, that instead of identifying law with what *judges* do, as Holmes prescribed, we equate law with what state *officials* generally do, as Llewellyn suggested. Exactly the same objections apply. Much of the subject matter—and in particular the elaborate, specialized discourse that the officials treat as regulative of what they do—is neglected. The expanded description is still like the generalized proposition that avoids intricacies and contested issues by asserting that victory in baseball results simply from outscoring one's opponent. Well, of course, but . . .

For similar reasons, the recurrent prescription that suggests that the malaise of legal scholarship might be cured if scholars would devote themselves to performing more careful empirical studies "describing how some court, agency, enforcement process, or legal transaction actually works"[3] seems naively sanguine. There is nothing wrong with doing such studies; they might be informative. But an empirical and institutional focus will not directly engage with the discourse—and the beliefs that animate that discourse—that motivates and guides the actors in those institutions.

We can put the point simply: discourse or argument (and indeed discourse of a highly specialized kind) is obviously central to the enterprise of law, so any reductionist account that tries to understand law purely in terms of behavior will to that extent be inadequate. Michael Moore explains that "to the extent anyone, Legal Realists included, reduces law to judicial behavior, he leaves out the essential reason-giving character of law."[4]

Just how legal discourse relates to legal behavior is a hard problem, to be sure, but the problem cannot be solved simply by ignoring one of its vital dimensions. There is a direct parallel here to the long-standing philosophical "mind–body" debate: How does the "subjective" element of *mind* relate to the more "objective" and observable behaviors of *body?* It is a vexing question, and so one tempting response is simply to ignore or dissolve one of the elements—mostly likely (in the modern climate of opinion, at least) mind. To do this, though, is to disengage from the problem, not to resolve it. Thus, Thomas Nagel notes that reductionist and behaviorist accounts of mind have been "fairly common among contemporary philosophers, but the only motive I can see for them is a desire to make the mind–body problem go away. None of them has any intrinsic plausibility."[5] Substitute "the problem of legal discourse" for "the mind–body problem" and Nagel's comment applies precisely to modern behaviorist and reductionist jurisprudences.

### Discursive Descriptions: Law as a "Language Game"?

It might seem that descriptive accounts of law that focus not so much on what judges (or other officials) *do* but rather on how they *talk*—that is, on their discourse—would avoid these vitiating errors. After all, discursive accounts do not ignore discourse as an aspect of law, do they? On the contrary, they make it their central feature and concern. Or at least, so it would seem.

In a more subtle way, though, even the discursive accounts fall into the same errors as the more behavioral accounts. In fact, perverse though it may seem, modern accounts that identify law with legal discourse, by virtue of that very identification, systematically distort and overlook law's distinctive discursive character.

Take as an example Dennis Patterson's argument equating law with legal discourse. "The essence of law is legal argument," Patterson declares; and again, "law *is* a practice of argument."[6] "The law" does not exist independent of the discourse: it *is* the discourse. Consequently, it is a mistake to suppose that legal discourse—with its talk of rights and duties and immunities and privileges,—is *about* anything independent of itself. Patterson endorses Philip Bobbitt's view that "legal propositions are not propositions about the world": they have meaning only within the self-contained world of legal discourse.[7]

Bobbitt's work carefully distinguishing and illustrating six "modalities" of constitutional argument[8] is exemplary for Patterson, who agrees with

Bobbitt that "there simply is nothing more for 'philosophy' to do than describe accurately the practice of constitutional argument, for that practice *is* constitutional law."[9] The same point holds for law in general. "The modalities [of legal discourse] are not true by virtue of something outside the practice of argument," Patterson maintains. "There is only the practice and nothing more."[10]

Far from neglecting legal discourse as a central component of law, as behavioral approaches tend to do, Patterson's (and Bobbitt's) approach might seem to give that component lavish attention. And in a sense it does: Bobbitt's analysis of constitutional law, for example, is a learned and perceptive study of the way constitutional discourse works. He nicely distinguishes among six different types or "modalities" of constitutional arguments—historical, textual, doctrinal, prudential, structural, and ethical arguments—and shows how these arguments work, and work together, in a variety of constitutional decisions.

In a more subtle sense, though, the discursive approach in fact repeats the behaviorist error of paying no attention to what the participants are saying or, indeed, to *how they are talking*. This objection is initially paradoxical, to be sure. But consider a case in which a student in a freshman English course becomes enamored of his teacher and, after much soul searching, writes her a passionate love letter declaring his devotion. Suppose the letter is returned, drenched in red ink and with copious marginal commentary—with metaphors explicated, syntax parsed, overall structure analyzed, literary antecedents and allusions annotated, and a final comment of "Splendid work! A+." In one sense, the teacher has read the letter; indeed, she has given it exquisite attention—we might almost say "loving attention"—far surpassing the care that most writings ever receive. In another sense, though, the teacher has wholly ignored what we might call "the love letter itself," or the "real" letter. The disenchanted student might be excused for complaining, "She completely misunderstood what I wrote," or even "She never even read what I really wrote at all."

More specifically, the teacher has failed (or perhaps self-consciously refused) to understand that the letter is not merely an exercise in literary creativity; it is meant to be *about* something that is independent of the letter—namely, the student's feelings for the teacher. The letter presupposes those feelings. Without them it makes no sense, serves no purpose. It becomes an exercise in futility. Thus, while purporting to take the letter very seriously, the teacher has not only failed (deliberately or inadvertently) to understand the character of the letter; she has in effect rendered it meaningless. It's "just words."

This may seem a facetious example. So consider a more serious one—and one that comes very close to the jurisprudential position advocated by theorists like Patterson and Bobbitt. Suppose that you, or your whole society, finds that you can no longer believe that God exists in the strong, old-fashioned way, as your parents and grandparents believed. Should you desist from religious exercises—saying grace before meals, for instance, or baptizing children—and refrain from using the old-time religious language? Perhaps the most obvious and honest answer is simply "Yes. Of course. Drop the charade." But in what is described as a Wittgensteinian or neo-Wittgensteinian vein, it is sometimes suggested that any such conclusion is unnecessary and even confused. Thus, advocating a position that closely parallels Patterson's account of law, Norman Malcolm argues that religion is simply a "language game": it is "a form of life; it is language embedded in action." Consequently, religion and God-talk do not depend on the actual, independent existence of any being who is God—a notion that Malcolm attempts summarily to deconstruct.[11] In this view, religious discourse refers to nothing outside itself and hence needs no external justification: believers are perfectly free to go on talking about God without naively supposing that "God exists" in any more substantial sense.

Though Malcolm ostensibly proffers this interpretation as a way of permitting religionists to continue in their way of life, John Hick points out that the neo-Wittgensteinian approach in fact "cuts the heart out of religious belief and practice." To be sure, religious talk *is* a special kind of language, and religionists often use terms in distinctive ways—"as pointers rather than as literal descriptions." So an observer who does not understand the nature of a religious discourse will not really understand the religion. Even so, "the pointers are undoubtedly intended to point to realities transcending metaphors and myths; and to suppress this intention is to do violence to religious speech and to empty the religious 'form of life' of its central and motivating conviction."[12] There would be no reason to engage in this elaborate form of discourse, in short, if it were *merely* a form of discourse. Indeed, it would seem unnatural to describe someone who participated in the discourse on Malcolm's understanding as a religious believer at all.

In a similar way, theorists like Patterson and Bobbitt seem to propose that lawyers think of law as legal discourse, and of legal discourse as a self-contained language game. But, as our visitor Tess argued at length in Chapter 3, the discourse itself belies this description: in a variety of ways it suggests that lawyers and judges experience it as a way of referring to something beyond the discourse—to some "preexisting thing called 'The Law,'" as Lon Fuller perceptively observed. In focusing on the discourse while declining to recognize or affirm what the discourse refers to, discourse theorists are like the baby who, when his mother points at a bird or a flower and says "Look!," stares intently at his mother's finger. In both cases, the observer has paid rapt attention to the pointer, but in entirely the wrong way, and has thereby failed to grasp the pointer's real nature and purpose.[13]

These observations admittedly fall short of destroying the account of law as a self-referential or self-contained discourse. An imaginative defender of that account could always say, I suppose, that law is a very peculiar kind of language game—one in which pretending that we are pointing to something outside the game is actually part of the game. So when our visitor Tess from the previous chapter marshals evidence indicating that the discourse presupposes "the law," the answer would be: "Of course. That's the kind of truly remarkable game this is. Your evidence actually confirms our account."

So far as I can see, there is no way to prove conclusively that law is not this sort of bizarre game of pretend. It is pertinent to note, though, that although humans love to play games, grownups usually do not play this sort of very peculiar game, and we would almost surely decline any invitation to join such a game. To be sure, we may spend a few hours playing "Risk" or "Diplomacy," but we do not seriously pretend, even while playing, that the armies and the battles exist outside the game. If we did actually manage to put ourselves in this frame of mind, the game would likely become quite different and, for most of us, considerably less enjoyable. Our ordinary game behavior and banter ("Ten of my divisions were just slaughtered in Irkutsk. Oh, well. Pass the pretzels, please.") would come to seem monstrous. We know what real armies are and what the "as if" armies in the game are (and if we did not believe in real armies it is unclear what sort of conception of the "as if" armies we could have). And we maintain the distinction. It is not pleasant to picture what would happen to someone who could not appreciate the distinction—whether in the actual army or the game.

The account of law offered by theorists like Patterson and Bobbitt self-consciously seeks to conflate the reality and the game, or to obliterate the distinction between the reality and the game. But on these assumptions legal discourse becomes quite senseless, just as a love letter loses its sense unless it is taken as an expression of love (which is not reducible to self-contained and self-referential words in the letter), or in the way God-talk is senseless without a God who exists beyond the talk itself.

Indeed, by this account law would be worse than nonsensical; it would be brutally perverse. That is because law, in its consequences, is most emphatically *not* a self-contained language game: it is an enterprise with dire real-world effects. Law takes place, in Robert Cover's memorable phrase, "in a field of pain and death."[14] If "legal propositions are not propositions about the world," as Patterson asserts, then it is hardly clear why those propositions should be allowed to regulate the world—often by inflicting "pain and death."

What sense would it make, after all, that a criminal defendant should be executed—or a substantial sum of money extracted from one person and conferred on another—just because an exercise in the "modalities" of a self-referential language game worked out in a particular way? To let actual controversies be decided on the basis of such a game seems much like making a game of "hangman" dictate the fate of an accused criminal, or like letting an antitrust suit against AT&T turn on the outcome of a game of "Monopoly." If law is this kind of game, it is, as Arthur Leff observed, "like a game of chess in which, when the King is mated, a real king dies."[15] We can imagine seeing such a game on an eerie episode of, say, *Alfred Hitchcock Presents* or *The X-Files*. But if we caught people actually setting up such a game, we would not honor them by giving them status and power in society (as we do with lawyers and judges). On the contrary, we would quickly move to have them committed.

## The "Law and" Strategy

In part for reasons like these, the autonomy strategy has not in fact been the dominant strategy in modern legal thought. Most thinkers have recognized that if law is to be seen as a meaningful and sensible activity, it is necessary to go beyond descriptions of the everyday behavior and talk of judges and lawyers. So, by and large, twentieth-century thinkers adopted the different strategy of arguing that there is actually much more to law and legal discourse than meets the eye. This "something more," however, is not "the law," as in the classical account, but rather something slightly more down to earth: it is "policy," perhaps (principally economics), or moral philosophy, or practical reason.

Most modern legal thinkers have had resort to some such supplement. In addition to explaining law in more ontologically secure terms, "law and" provided the principal remedy for the last century's obsessive nervousness about legal "indeterminacy." Though formal legal discourse viewed in isolation might indeed be indeterminate, that is (as the submission of briefs making legally respectable arguments for antithetical conclusions in most cases seems to demonstrate), the presence of the "something more" might serve to make law sufficiently determinate after all.

Hence, the twentieth century was more than anything else the century of "law-and." And for most legal thinkers, it was what followed the "and" that gave the law its solidity and sense.

### The Varieties of "Law and"

In considering these "law and" strategies, we should appreciate that they come in various forms, which often blend almost imperceptibly into each other. As already noted, the strategies differ in what they place after the "and": economics, or moral philosophy, or practical reason, or something else. But two further distinctions should be underscored at the outset.

First, a "law and" position can be offered either for *interpretive* and *apologetic* purposes or, conversely, for *reformist* purposes (or for some mixture of these). A devotee of law and economics may argue, for example, that by contrast to conventional legal reasoning, economic analysis is a rational or sensible way of making decisions. If this claim is offered for apologetic purposes and *as an interpretation* of law, the argument must go on to claim that, beneath the surface, economic calculations have all along exerted significant influence over judicial decisions—even over decisions presented in conventional legal terms without any obvious reliance on economic reasoning (which is to say, nearly all of them).[16] If this reinterpretation is persuasive, then it will follow that legal discourse is already meaningful and rational in a way that is not immediately apparent to the casual observer who takes the (on its own terms quite vacuous) official reasoning at face value. Conversely, the superiority of economic reasoning may be asserted for *reformist* rather than reinterpretive purposes: the argument now is that because economics provides a more rational way to make decisions than conventional legal discourse does, the law should be reformed in accordance with (or perhaps replaced by) economic analysis.[17]

Second, insofar as "law and" positions are offered for the first of these purposes—that is, as reinterpretations and for apologetic purposes—they can come in either of two versions, which we might call the "code" version and the "two-stage" version (though, as noted, these are not always neatly distinguished in practice). The code version asserts that conventional legal discourse itself is a veiled way of carrying on the preferred discourse. The vocabulary of "rights," "duties," "privileges," "immunities," and "reasonable care," as well as the parsing of precedents and statutes, add up to an oblique way of conducting economic analysis[18]—or moral philosophy, or practical reasoning. The two-stage version of an apologetic "law and" position does not make this claim, but rather suggests that legal decisions occur in two steps. At the first step, the decisionmaker uses the hidden but more rational and hence preferred discourse—economics, or moral philosophy, or whatever—to decide how a controversy should be resolved. At the second stage, the decisionmaker officially presents the conclusion in the language of conventional legal discourse—perhaps for cosmetic or public relations purposes.

By either version it might fairly be said, as Judge Posner asserts, that "the true grounds of legal decisions are concealed rather than illuminated by the characteristic rhetoric of opinions."[19] But in the code version, to understand a judicial decision you must read the court's opinion carefully but obliquely, realizing that the court will usually be speaking in a sort of cipher that needs to be translated. In the two-stage version, by contrast, there is little incentive to pay much attention to what courts say at all. Instead, you must cut through the explicit reasoning—"strip[] the . . . cases of their rhetoric"[20]—in order to understand the real bases of the decisions.[21] Grant Gilmore was describing this approach when he remarked, with his usual flair, that "[f]or two or three generations past it has been the merest truism, in much American legal writing, that the doctrine which may be found enshrined in case report and treatise is neither important nor relevant."[22] More recently, but in the same spirit, Jed Rubenfeld advocates "jettison[ing] the whole enterprise of taking constitutional doctrine seriously" because the doctrine is a manipulable cover for political purposes and hence "the only question worth asking is whether the agenda pursued by a particular Court" is attractive.[23]

## "Law and" and the Problem of Nonsense

For present purposes, we can cheerfully concede that "law and" theorizing over the last century has greatly enriched legal thought in some respects (which is not to deny that such theorizing may have impoverished legal thought in other respects). Our concern here, though, is whether the "law and" strategy effectively rescues law, or law-talk, from the charge that legal discourse is to a significant extent nonsense because it depends on metaphysical commitments that cannot be squared with the ontological inventories that prevail at least in the academic world. Can policy, or moral philosophy, or practical reason adequately substitute for "the law" of the classical account?

Put differently, do "law and" positions explain why legal discourse "makes sense" as a way of making or presenting important decisions without tacitly depending on classical assumptions about the existence of "the law"? I will argue that the strategy fails in that respect for two principal reasons. First, when offered as interpretation and for apologetic purposes, "law and" positions (whether in the code or two-stage versions) cannot plausibly account for the bulk of legal decisionmaking. These positions do not offer plausible interpretations of the way law actually works. We might put this point differently by saying that "law and" accounts are not really explaining *law* as we know it, or as we practice it and see it practiced.

Second, even if they were plausible interpretations of the way law works, "law and" positions would not provide convincing justifications for carrying on the enterprise of law either in elaborate and misleading codes or in a deceptive two-stage process. Indeed, the proponents of "law and" have typically conceded this point, or even insisted on it.

In sum, "law and" thinking may offer rich insights into law, but it does not persuasively defend law against the suspicion of nonsense. We can appreciate its shortcomings by considering the leading "law and" strategies more closely.

## Law and Policy

Like so many developments in twentieth-century law, the "law and" perspective was eloquently foreshadowed in Holmes's "Path of the Law" essay. Holmes maintained that although lawyers and judges talk *as if* legal conclusions follow from legal premises—as if the precedents or rules or doctrines *require* particular results—the apparent logic of judicial opinions is misleading. In most cases an equally plausible legal argument can be constructed to justify just the opposite conclusion. "You can give any conclusion a logical form. You can always imply a condition in a contract. But why do you imply it?" The apparently deductive quality of legal reasoning is largely illusory,[24] in short, and to accept that reasoning as the real basis of a decision is to fall victim to "the fallacy of logical form."[25] What really determines the outcomes in cases, Holmes thought, is not the parsing of precedents and rules and doctrines, but rather an underlying "judgment as to the relative worth and importance of competing legislative grounds," or "some opinion as to policy." Though often "inarticulate and unconscious," this sort of policy judgment is in reality "the very root and nerve of the whole proceeding."[26]

THE TRIUMPH OF POLICY   Over the next century, most legal thinkers accepted and sometimes elaborated on Holmes's general diagnosis (though their thinking was often reformist rather than apologetical—a divide that Holmes's own essay had straddled). Robert Summers has shown how "pragmatic instrumentalism" dominated American legal thought throughout most of the twentieth century.[27] Beginning about a decade after Holmes's essay, Roscoe Pound gained prominence by criticizing what he called "mechanical jurisprudence"—essentially the conventional and formalistic approach attacked by Holmes—and advocating a "sociological jurisprudence" in which courts would self-consciously balance social interests and promote social goals.[28] Two decades later, Pound engaged in some less than cordial debates with a younger generation of Legal Realists, but from a more detached perspective the contending positions appear to be minor variations in a common program. The Realists exhibited the same deep skepticism toward traditional legal methods. Many of them also favored a more policy-oriented law grounded in the learning of the social sciences.[29] The instrumentalist or policy view of law was again plainly manifest in the Law, Science, and Policy movement in the 1950s,[30] and later in the law and economics movement—perhaps the most influential development in legal thought in the second half of the century.

Only slightly revised or updated versions of the same law and social policy vision appear with regularity.[31] Indeed, the basic idea of law as social policy is by now pretty much axiomatic for scholars who have very different ideas both about what the content of social policies should be and about what means will be most efficacious for advancing those policies. "Since the legal realist movement," Edward Rubin observes, "most scholars have been convinced that law is a social instrumentality. . . . [I]t is a system whose components are derived from social policy, not from either a universal moral order or the collective wisdom of the ages."[32] Probably the leading contemporary proponent of the law and policy approach has been Richard Posner: an emphasis on making law more instrumentalist and less beholden to conventional legal discourse has been Posner's dominant theme from beginning to present.

CAN "POLICY" SUBSTITUTE FOR "THE LAW"?  Beyond keeping generations of law professors in business, law and policy thinking has produced a wealth of fresh insights into how the legal system works. Our question, though, is whether this approach can satisfactorily explain how the law makes sense without "the law." With respect to that question, however, law and policy seems ambivalent in its attitude, unsure about whether it should even try to defend conventional law-talk against suspicions of nonsense. Law and policy seems most candid, and most cogent, when offered for reformist purposes. But it encounters embarrassment when offered as an account of how law as we know it actually works. Thus, in its most plausible versions, law and policy reinforces the suspicion that law as it currently operates (and as it has operated for decades, or centuries) is largely nonsensical, at least under modern ontological assumptions.

We can start with a proposition that most proponents of law and policy would probably endorse: on its face, conventional legal discourse usually does not appear to be engaged in policy analysis in any systematic way. To be sure, conventional legal argumentation contains—and always has contained—a certain amount of policy talk. And perhaps there is a bit more policy in modern judicial decisions than there was a century ago. But even today that component of the discourse is secondary, and is greatly overshadowed by the conventional vocabulary of rights, duties, and precedents. Thus, while emphasizing that "[f]rom the formalist period to the present, the relative proportion of rule orientation has lessened in comparison to the play of instrumental reasoning," Brian Tamanaha acknowledges recent studies showing that more formalistic and conventional legal reasoning "is still more dominant."[33] Moreover, the courts have never even begun to attempt to address the conceptual questions or to formulate the methodology that might transform loose talk about policies or social interests into anything approaching a policy "science."[34]

But if the explicit discourse of judges and lawyers does not focus primarily on policy, then it seems that a law and policy position can offer itself as an *interpretation* of law as it actually functions only on one of two assumptions alluded to earlier: either standard law talk operates as a sort of code for the policy considerations that ought to inform decisions, or else courts in fact make decisions on the basis of a hidden review of such considerations but then present their decisions for official purposes in the entirely different language of "law." These assumptions have sometimes been defended. Yet there is a sort of quiet desperation in the defense, because on reflection both assumptions seem quite fantastic.

DO COURTS TALK IN CODE?    Consider the "code" version. How plausible is it—seriously?—to suppose that standard law-talk is serving as a workable code for, say, the very different kinds of economic calculations that appear in scholarly journals devoted to that perspective? Doing competent economic analysis is hard enough. To perform that analysis in the alien language of conventional legal discourse looks well-nigh impossible. How would judges learn and maintain this code across multiple jurisdictions and multiple generations? And *why* maintain the elaborate charade of talking always in code? It is revealing that the greatest modern champion of law and economics, Richard Posner, is a judge, and he is quite willing, on some occasions anyway, to discuss the economic bases of a decision without hiding behind a code.[35] This stance makes sense: if decisions are being made on the basis of economic analysis, why not talk in the straightforward economic terms that scholars and economists use and that are actually conducive to such analysis?

It is sometimes suggested that judges talk in code because even though policy analysis is in fact the rational way to make decisions, the general public is not ready to accept such analysis as "law" and is unwilling to allow courts to make decisions on that basis. The public still believes in archaic notions of "the law," perhaps, even though lawyers and judges understand that no such animal exists. But it seems doubtful that such a decisive gap separates the public's from the profession's metaphysical and jurisprudential assumptions.[36] Moreover, this explanation, while attempting to defend the legal system against the suspicion of talking nonsense, exposes the law to what is arguably an even more serious charge: the explanation in effect suggests that the law is a sort of large-scale conspiracy to defraud the public and to preserve for the legal profession power that the public would not be willing to grant if it understood what is really going on.

TWO-STAGE DECISIONMAKING?    Basically the same criticisms can be raised with regard to the two-stage versions of law and policy. How likely is

it that an enterprise could go on for generation after generation with decisions being made on the basis of one kind of reasoning while being publicly
debated and justified through a wholly different form of discourse? The
principal actors in this enterprise, recall, consist of hundreds of thousands of
lawyers and thousands of judges—in a variety of jurisdictions and of widely
varying backgrounds—who came to their positions in very different ways.
How likely is it that these disparate actors, while speaking a common legal
language in public, would in fact be making decisions in the privacy of their
chambers on the basis of wholly different considerations, such as economic
efficiency. And *why* would they carry on this bizarre, bifurcated charade (except perhaps to carry out the same sort of dubious conspiracy mentioned
earlier)?

If, on the other hand, the assumption is that these actors typically act
innocently on the basis of "unconscious and inarticulate" judgments, as
Holmes asserted and as followers like Posner have often claimed,[37] then we
are led to wonder what it even means to make policy calculations unconsciously and inarticulately. The suggestion turns ordinary assumptions
about rationality on their head. Since the time of Socrates and with support
from later thinkers like Freud, it has usually been supposed that we achieve
rationality by becoming more conscious and critical of our thought processes; the unruly swirl that goes on beneath the level of consciousness is
usually thought to be more under the sway of nonrational considerations.
This depiction seems plausible, but the suggestion that judges are "unconsciously and inarticulately" rational while consciously following a discourse
that makes little sense reverses the depiction. There is no apparent reason
for crediting that reversal.

CONFIRMING THE SUSPICION   Hence, the more plausible version of
law and policy is not the interpretive and apologetic version, but rather the
reformist version. Insofar as deliberate, careful policy analysis is the sensible
way to make public decisions (a possibility about which we can remain agnostic for present purposes), then law as it has functioned over past centuries and as it continues to function today is not sensible; that is because
law does not primarily work in this deliberate, policy-oriented way. Consequently, law needs to abandon its apparent servility to something that
doesn't exist—"the law"—to be reformed (or replaced) in accordance with
policy prescriptions.

And in fact, proponents of law and policy, though often presenting themselves as defenders of the law, have typically understood themselves to be advocating reform. In his "Path" essay, Holmes urged the abandonment of law's quaint moral vocabulary and the cultivation of a more explicit dependence on policy. The Legal Realists wrote in a similar spirit: legal decisions ought to be shaped not by the shuffling of precedents and doctrines but rather by a policy science built around the learning of social science. Jumping forward in time to the 1980s, in a colorful little book entitled *Reconstructing American Law*, Bruce Ackerman argued that conventional legal discourse is archaic, and he advocated a new "constructivist" legal discourse that would openly draw on social science and computer technology.[38] And of course Judge Posner increasingly describes "law" as it works today not as something that should be celebrated for its deep indwelling rationality, but rather as something that needs to be "overcome."[39]

In its reformist mode, law and policy does not defend law against the indictment of nonsense, but rather corroborates the charge. It is precisely because conventional legal discourse makes no sense as a way of making decisions, in this view, that it needs to be reformed or replaced by something more rational.

### Law and Philosophy

A different sort of "law and" position, and one that has often been taken as a sort of leading (and sometimes truculent)[40] competitor, prefers philosophy over policy as the modern substitute for "the law." "Law and philosophy" can be a label for different things. Sometimes it refers to the use of the techniques of analytical philosophy by law professors and philosophers to examine and clarify legal concepts and their interconnections. Here, however, I have in mind a different sort of position best typified by the work of Ronald Dworkin. In his early work, Dworkin called for a sort of marriage of constitutional law and moral philosophy.[41] Later, in a series of enormously influential writings,[42] he elaborated his proposal into a theory of law as an enterprise of interpretation carried on with the aid of philosophy.

In Dworkin's view, a judge or other interpreter starts with the standard legal materials—statutes, precedents, and so forth—and she is obligated to give those materials an interpretation that satisfies the conventional requirement of "fit." So an acceptable interpretation must "fit" the texts. But in many cases—and surely in the ones we argue about—more than one interpretation will meet this demand, Dworkin thinks. At that point the interpreter should choose the interpretation that best "justifies" the legal materials—or that makes the law "the best it can be"—by reference to the best available political and moral philosophy. Dworkin recognizes that real judges (by contrast to his mythical judge Hercules) might not have the training or ability to perform this philosophical task competently on their own, but they can be guided by philosophers: hence Dworkin's well-known statement that judges are only the "princes" in "Law's Empire," while the more exalted role of "seers and prophets" must belong to philosophers—"if they are willing." (Legal philosopher-prophets are not above engaging in a bit a deadpan humor.)[43]

As with law and policy, we can cheerfully concede that law and philosophy has contributed numerous insights to our understanding of law. But again, the question for us is whether moral philosophy is a satisfactory stand-in for "the law"—or whether law and philosophy in a Dworkinian vein furnishes a plausible defense to the indictment that conventional law-talk is an elaborate form of nonsense. And the answer seems to be that law and philosophy does not furnish such a defense. It fails for basically the same reasons that law and policy failed in this respect.

In the first place, law and philosophy does not give a plausible account of law as it actually works. If judges were proceeding as Dworkin says they should, judicial opinions would typically contain two principal sections of analysis. One section would focus on the relevant legal texts—the statutes, regulations, precedents—and would develop a list of possible interpretations that "fit" these materials. Another section would have a wholly different thrust: it would scrutinize this list of candidate interpretation to see which squares best with the best available political or moral philosophy (an inquiry that presumably would require an explanation of why Rawls's philosophy, say, is superior to Mills's, or Maritain's, or Nozick's, and so on). But in fact, actual judicial opinions are virtually always dominated by something like the first section—the analysis of rules and precedents for "fit"—and they virtually never have anything resembling the second section. On the contrary, it is the rare judicial opinion that makes any mention of philosophy, or that betrays any knowledge of or interest in anything that deserves to be dignified with the label of "political or moral philosophy."[44] Given that few judges or lawyers have any significant training in political or moral philosophy, this omission is hardly surprising.

Once again, it might be that judges are speaking in code—their legal vocabulary might have an esoteric and more philosophical meaning—or that they are following a two-stage process, doing philosophy on the sly in chambers but then concealing these philosophical deliberations in their official presentations. And once again, these suggestions seem extravagant. What evidence is there of such pervasive cunning? Why would judges carry on such a charade? And how could they manage to carry it on so successfully, so uniformly, and over such a long period of time?

Dworkin sometimes suggests that judges are indeed doing something like this—if not exactly philosophizing, they are at least interpreting on the basis of their own philosophical convictions—and that those judges who do not own up to doing so (which is to say, nearly all of them) are "guilty of a costly mendacity."[45] How could he know this? Mendacity is no mere *faux pas.* So Dworkin's is a serious accusation, not to be made lightly. How can he know that judges are in fact doing something dramatically different from what they say they are doing, and then disingenuously covering up what they have done?

Dworkin's response is that it is simply "inevitable," as he puts it, that judges will interpret in the way he suggests.[46] They can't help it. After all, judges *couldn't* actually make decisions on the basis of the conventional legal discourse that appears in their opinions, because that discourse standing by itself is too indeterminate to generate decisions. So they *must be* drawing on their more philosophical convictions.

But this argument is a stark *non sequitur.* The proposition that judges could not decide cases through conventional legal discourse alone, even if correct, leads to the conclusion that they are actually following the more philosophical "moral reading" approach only if those are the only alternatives. But it seems obvious that there are other possibilities. Judges might be doing policy analysis in the manner of Holmes and Posner. Or they might be "hunching," as Judge Joseph Hutcheson famously contended.[47] Or following the daily horoscope. Or flipping coins.

But we need not resort to such exotic hypotheses to see the fallacy in Dworkin's reasoning: his argument that judges necessarily resort to moral philosophy, even when (as is nearly always the case) they refuse to admit it, fails within the terms of his own account of interpretation. Let us concede, for example, that in a given case more than one interpretation can be said to "fit" the governing statute or legal provision. Even so, it seems highly unlikely that the *degree* of "fit" will be precisely the same for each of these possible constructions. I own several pairs of pants, acquired over the years—

some during lean periods and others in more prosperous times (corporally speaking). All of these pairs of pants "fit"—which is to say that I sometimes manage to get my lower half into them—but there is no doubt that some of them fit me much better than others do (as I am uncomfortably aware even as I write these words). The same could be said, presumably, of legal interpretations. So a judge might just try to determine which interpretation *fits best*, rather than being content with some minimal level of "fit"[48] and then launching off into the realms of political and moral philosophy. Indeed, this account of what judges do surely fits the actual explanations that judges give for their decisions better than Dworkin's two-criteria account does. In this way, Dworkin's own acknowledgment of the criterion of "fit" already suggests a cogent response to his claim that judges *must* resort to philosophy in interpreting law.[49]

But even if Dworkin's account accurately described the way law works, that account still provides little defense for the sort of conventional legal discourse that prevails (and that has prevailed for centuries). It provides no excuse, that is, for the "costly mendacity" by which judges ostensibly hide their real reasoning process behind a facade of conventional law-talk. Indeed, this is Dworkin's recurring complaint: the legal discourse practiced by most judges most of the time is a "pretense" in which "[t]he actual grounds of decision are hidden from both legitimate public inspection and valuable public debate."[50] While often appearing to offer a defense of law (against deconstructionist critics, for example),[51] Dworkin's position is more accurately viewed as reformist—even radically so. If judges are not already using moral and political philosophy to interpret law, they should start using it; and if they *are* already using moral and political philosophy (as Dworkin says they are), they should quit concealing this use behind the pretense of conventional legal discourse.

Either way, legal discourse as we know it—and as we practice it—is not exonerated from the charge of nonsense. On the contrary, Dworkin's claim that decisions *could not be* made in the way the discourse routinely indicates they *are* made is an emphatic if oblique condemnation of that discourse.

Standard law-talk, in short, makes constant reference to—and depends for its sense on—"the law," as we saw in Chapter 3. And moral philosophy, far from substituting for "the law" in this arrangement, is more like the stepmother who, once admitted to the household, is eager to send Hansel and Gretel (and perhaps their father too) off into the forest.

### The Impassable "Path of the Law"

Although both law and policy (as prescribed by Holmes and symbolized and represented today by Posner) and law and philosophy (exemplified in the work of Dworkin) sometimes present themselves as apologists for the existing legal regime, the preceding discussion suggests that both are more plausibly understood as reformist in nature. Far from providing a suitable substitute for "the law" or answering the accusation that law-talk as we know it with its apparent metaphysical commitments is nonsensical, these movements in their most plausible versions in effect endorse the accusation and urge that legal discourse be reformed or replaced by something more sensible.

Indeed, so sure have the proponents of these perspectives been of the senselessness of conventional law-talk that they have often been sure that this talk could not continue, and hence that reform was inevitable and imminent. And in this sanguine expectation they have been mistaken—over and over again. If Holmes was a prophet, as admirers like Posner often assert, he was a false prophet—and the father of a line of jurisprudential false prophets. Indeed, the twentieth century was in effect a graveyard for generation after generation of these happy, misguided predictions.

Thus, we have already noted that judicial opinions, though perhaps containing a bit more policy than they once did, are still primarily exercises in conventional legal discourse: they still engage in the same citing and distinguishing of precedents, the same search for the meanings or intentions or purposes of statutes, and the same effort to extract from this disparate mass of materials univocal statements of what "the law" is.[52] And the persistently conventional character of judicial opinions in turn both reflects and determines the character of legal pedagogy, and of lawyerly argumentation generally.

Consider legal education—the context where Holmes's "Path" campaign was launched and where, enjoying the luxury of fresh, bright minds not already mired in legal conventions, the campaign might be expected to achieve its greatest success. In Holmes's day, we are told, formal legal education following the "Harvard method" was largely devoted to the study of selected judicial opinions that were collected in casebooks.[53] Holmes's prescriptions called for radical transformations in this mode of study: law schools should greatly reduce their emphasis on history as reflected in past judicial decisions, and instead devote themselves to developing and inculcating policy science.[54] And so today, more than a century later, law students spend most of their time . . . studying selected judicial opinions collected in casebooks.

To be sure, many casebooks today include smatterings of "policy"—snippets from articles about law and economics, or questions raising considerations of efficient resource allocation. No doubt some teachers emphasize—and, if they are serious, supplement—these sparse policy materials. But it seems that most teachers touch on these policy materials lightly, if at all. Even more crucially, it is the rare course that is systematically organized around a policy perspective—and an even rarer course, if it exists at all in the laws schools, that actually tries to immerse students in the social science data and methodologies contemplated by the Holmesian revolution. The fact is that law students receive almost no training in the empirical skills that would be needed to implement the policy science vision.[55]

In short, both in its heavy use of case analysis and in its effort to extract the doctrinal content of the cases, law teaching is still highly reminiscent of the conventional methods that Holmes and his jurisprudential descendants derided. Norman Cantor observes that the social sciences have had only a marginal impact on legal education[56]: "The exclusive paradigm taught in American law schools remains that of the common law updated and democratized to a greater or lesser degree."[57] And a century and a year after Holmes's famous essay, Richard Posner acknowledged wistfully that "even today most law professors are analysts of cases and legal doctrines,"[58] while Deborah Rhode, then president of the Association of American Law Schools, complained that "classroom discussions are . . . too uninformed by insights from allied disciplines such as philosophy, sociology and economics."[59]

The teaching of tort law can serve as a concrete example. Holmes's essay commented specifically on what the policy orientation might mean for torts,[60] and indeed, perhaps as much as any subject area except antitrust, tort law has been a field for the development of economic analysis in academic writing. Moreover, in probably every law school in the country, students are required to take torts in the first year. Hence, tort law pedagogy would seem to be a promising area for promoting the Holmesian revolution. And in fact, a few teachers *do* try systematically to orient the torts course in a policy direction. (I know this to be true from personal experience: my torts teacher in law school was Guido Calabresi.)

More often, though, the doctrine-oriented, precedent-based approach prevails—with a pinch of law and economics or moral theory thrown in from time to time for seasoning. David Rosenberg, who teaches torts at Harvard Law School, explains:

> Constructed on Holmes's model, the course on tort law would concentrate on the systematic risks from business activity, and its general contribution to the curriculum would come from exploring the theories and policies of market regulation. Yet as they did when Holmes wrote, students spend most of their time today parsing the semantic logic of cases to derive, classify, and criticize rules. Few reliable empirical studies exist, and students are neither given the details of nor trained to evaluate critically the few studies that do. There is much talk about the deterrence and compensation functions of tort liability, but the actual costs and net benefits of such a system remain unknown. . . . Basic policy questions (at best presented in short, conclusory, casebook excerpts from scholarly literature) are raised as if they were merely another perspective rather than the shaping force and crucial matter at issue. Discussion of policy questions tends to be correspondingly superficial.[61]

If Rosenberg describes how tort law is taught at a leading national law school—at *Holmes's* law school—my observation based on experience at more humble schools is that there the consideration of systematic policy analysis is typically even more cursory. Thus, it seems that Rosenberg is right: "Legal education today falls far short of the mark Holmes set for the future."[62]

But if law students receive little instruction in systematic policy analysis, and instead learn little more than a thin policy vocabulary useful mostly for rhetorical purposes, it hardly seems likely that they will have the time or inclination to devote themselves to policy science after they have graduated and entered into the hectic life of lawyer or judge. Not surprisingly, it is precisely this rhetorical function that policy typically serves in lawyers' briefs and judges' opinions.[63] As revealed in these materials, few if any areas of law can offer anything remotely approaching a "science" for promoting public policy objectives through law. On the contrary, legal briefs and arguments are typically pretty much what they were in Holmes's day—labored efforts to cite and distinguish the relevant cases, doctrines, and statutes so as to extract a controlling rule of law that will allow the lawyer's client to prevail.

To a surprising degree, the same can be said of legal scholarship. Deborah Rhode points out that "the extent to which high theory and interdisciplin-

ary work have displaced traditional doctrinal analysis is overstated. . . . Doctrinal analysis . . . remains the method of choice for the vast majority of legal
scholars." Holmes and, later, the Legal Realists were confident that "a new,
empirically oriented era in scholarship was inevitable and imminent. But
that era never really dawned."[64] Brian Leiter observes that "in retrospect,
policy 'science' looks rather silly, a 'science' in name only."[65]

If policy science has only a marginal presence in current legal pedagogy
and scholarship, moral philosophy has, if possible, even less influence. Most
law students probably make at least a passing acquaintance with law and
economics in a torts or contracts or antitrust course; the same probably cannot be said of the neo-Kantian moral theory or Rawlsian political philosophy advocated by legal theorists like Dworkin. To be sure, most law schools
probably offer some sort of seminar—Constitutional Theory, perhaps, or Social Justice—that treats themes in modern moral theory, just as they may offer seminars in law and economics. But these courses are hardly the bread
and butter of the curriculum; most students probably go through law school
largely or wholly untouched. These students, of course, then go on to become the nation's lawyers and judges.

An inspection of legal education and legal practice thus suggests that
Holmes's prophecies are nowhere near "coming true," as disciples like
Posner sometimes wishfully assert.[66] Instead, we find a thin, spotty, mostly
rhetorical "policy" veneer that covers a reality in which legal argumentation
and justification work pretty much as they did a century (or perhaps five
centuries, or even eight centuries) ago[67]—that is, by muddling along on the
basis of precedents and rules and doctrines while presenting their conclusions as statements not of the judges' politics or philosophy, but rather of
that more elusive creature—"the law." And seventy years after Felix Cohen
described the "Restatement" project as "the last long-drawn-out gasp of a
dying tradition,"[68] the project continues to flourish—now in its third incarnation.

Jeremy Waldron succinctly captures our current situation:

Today, . . . almost sixty-five years after the publication of [Felix Cohen's]
"Transcendental Nonsense," it is noticeable that any steps we have taken
down this [more "realist" or "functionalist"] road have been taken without
giving up the conceptual terminology of traditional legal analysis. Opinions
may differ as to whether legal argument and judicial decisionmaking are

more realistic now, and more explicitly attuned to policy; but even among those who think they are, few would deny that the language of the law remains as technical and esoteric as it was in 1935.[69]

In short, Holmes's "Path" seems to have ended up in a jurisprudential cul-de-sac, in which theorists travel around and around in the same increasingly tedious circles while the staple discursive commerce of the law moves along other avenues. Holmes thought that radical changes in legal discourse were imminent. For a century, his descendants have thought the same thing; with embarrassing regularity they have solemnly or sometimes breathlessly proclaimed that conventional law is about to give way to a more rational, or more scientific, or more philosophical discourse. Scholarly careers have been made—and continue to be made—by in essence producing the second, and the third, and the tenth editions of the Restatement of Holmes. And in retrospect, the cogent observation was Grant Gilmore's from four decades ago: "The more things change, the French proverb reminds us, the more they are the same."[70]

But if conventional legal discourse is as unsatisfactory as not only radical critics but eminent mainstream figures like Holmes and Posner and Dworkin suggest, and if it is dependent on inadmissible metaphysical commitments to "the law" (as the previous chapter argued), then how and why does that discourse manage to survive, and indeed flourish?

### Law and (or as) Practical Reason?

Later in the book we will consider some more exotic possible answers to this question. But it seems pointless to look at exotic answers if a more common-sensical one is available, and in fact a commonsense answer *is* often suggested. (As it happens, the suggestions is one that severely tempts *me*, at least in my more complacent moods.) Legal discourse, the suggestion runs, is a form of practical reason.[71] As with other terms and positions we have considered, "practical reason" may mean different things to different people, but the most attractive version of this suggestion understands practical reason to include something like cultivated common sense, or pragmatic judgment, or perhaps the "Situation-sense" that Karl Llewellyn celebrated in his later work.[72]

Understood in this way, the law and practical reason position would suggest that legal discourse is not so much a special form of reasoning as simply a vocabulary that judges and lawyers use to fashion sensible solutions to practical controversies. Practical reason might thus incorporate the law and policy and law and philosophy positions in their least pretentious and hence most attractive forms: it could include pragmatic considerations of policy (without promising or pretending to draw on any "policy science") and moral and political convictions (without calling on judges to engage in or consciously incorporate any high-blown philosophizing).

The law as practical reason position, like other forms of "law and," can be offered either for apologetic or reformist purposes, and it can be considered in both a code and a two-stage version. For our purposes, the interesting possibility is the apologetic and code version of law as practical reason. That is because this version, if plausible, might actually help to explain how law as we know and practice it makes sense without "the law." And it might thereby offer a defense of standard law-talk against the charge of nonsense. By contrast, the reformist version, like other reformist "law and" positions, provides no such defense, but instead essentially reaffirms the criticism asserting that legal discourse *as it currently operates* is perverse or senseless and hence should be reformed to be less formalistic and more commonsensical. (This is in fact a very common view, I think—and one that ordinary citizens often express.)[73] The two-stage version, similarly, does little to defend *legal discourse* against the charge of nonsense. Instead, this version would in essence confess to the charge and then try to turn a vice into a virtue. It is because conventional law-talk is nonsensical, or "just words," perhaps, that it is so indeterminate; and it is because law-talk is so indeterminate that judges are able to give official, legalish justifications for just about any decision they might reach on other, hopefully more commonsensical grounds.[74]

So these versions of the practical reason position (that is, the reformist and the two-stage apologetic versions) do nothing to deflect the suspicion of nonsense, or to explain how law-talk makes sense without "the law." Conversely, if conventional law-talk itself could plausibly be viewed as a sort of serviceable code—or, better, an oblique vocabulary or common language—for presenting and reflecting on the pragmatic factors relevant to decisions, then that discourse might avoid the charge of nonsense. And the recurring references in law-talk to a metaphysically dubious "law" might be excused as merely figurative ways of importing the commonsense factors that are germane to the issues being addressed.

But can this code or common language version satisfactorily account for the actual discourse and practices of lawyers and judges?

THE INEFFICACY OF THE GENERIC CLAIM   The basic premise—namely, that legal discourse is a form of practical reasoning—seems unobjectionable. *Practical* reasoning is typically distinguished from *speculative* or *theoretical* reasoning in two principal ways. First, practical reasoning speaks to questions about how to act (or how to decide),[75] not merely to speculative questions about the truth or falsity of propositions. Second, practical reasoning lacks the demonstrative certainty of speculative reason.[76] By these criteria, legal discourse (assuming it qualifies as "reasoning" at all) would surely fall on the "practical" side of the line: it is primarily concerned with the appropriateness of human actions, not with the truth of abstract propositions, and it falls far short of the certainty of mathematical or logical demonstration.

But although law may properly be viewed as a form of practical reasoning, it is not just any form, but rather a form of practical reasoning that is highly distinctive, with its intricate and intimidating vocabulary, its attachment to and elaborate set of techniques for using precedent, its specialized appeals to "legislative intention" and statutory "purpose," its insistence that decisions be applied retroactively because they merely declare "what the law is." Law is a form of reasoning that often seems, as Cass Sunstein puts it, "weird or exotic . . . to nonlawyers or to people from other cultures"[77]—people who may themselves be skilled practitioners of practical reason in less exotic, more *prima facie* sensible forms. And it is these distinctive, or "weird or exotic," features that provoke the criticisms discussed above and that underlie suspicions of nonsense. Hence, placing law into the general category of "practical reason" does little to address such criticisms and suspicions.

Proponents of a law as practical reason view sometimes seem to be proposing a sort of tacit syllogism, which goes something like this: (a) practical reason is a sensible, legitimate, necessary human activity; (b) legal reasoning is a form of practical reason; therefore, (c) legal reasoning is a sensible, legitimate, necessary human activity. But the syllogism is faulty, because the question is not whether practical reason in general makes sense but whether *the particular form of practical reason operative in law* makes sense. After all, astrology and augury might also be described as forms of practical reasoning in this generic sense—these practices address practical questions about how to live, and they fall short of demonstrative certainty in their conclusions—but that characterization does not absolve them of being nonsense. In this respect, the claim that something is a form of practical reason—astrology, augury, law—is much like the plea, offered in response to an accusation of bank robbery, that "I was just earning a living." The plea harbors a syllogism much like the one noted above: earning a living is a legitimate and laudable activity; bank robbery is a way of earning a living; therefore . . . And the conclusion is equally fallacious in each instance.

THE PRACTICAL INEFFICACY OF LAW'S DISTINCTIVE DISCOURSE
So, *could* these distinctive legal features be understood in pragmatic, commonsensical terms, thereby "explaining away" the law's apparent commitment to that more formidable but dubious entity called "the law"? Possible explanations are familiar enough, but they fit awkwardly with the actual practices and vocabulary of legal discourse.

For example, precedents—and perhaps statutes or regulations—might convey factual information that would be helpful in crafting a sensible pragmatic decision. Emily Sherwin contends that precedents convey "a wealth of data for decision-making."[78] In addition, precedents might have given rise to expectations on the part of people who have relied on them; these expectations would themselves be factors that need to be considered in making a sound and fair decision.[79]

Precedents and enactments might also be viewed as expressions of wise counsel, from which judges might receive instruction or guidance. In this vein, Robin West contends that we ought to use the Constitution simply as a "source of insight" in the same way that we use "the writings of Aristotle, John Stuart Mill, John Rawls, and Roberto Unger."[80]

Can these pragmatic explanations fully account for the distinctive features of legal discourse, thereby making it unnecessary to suppose that the discourse is in fact seeking to ascertain the content of any more mysterious entity—of "the law"? No doubt conventional legal discourse *does* serve these purposes at least to a limited extent; it does manage to extract some useful information about the outside world from legal materials, to gauge and protect some expectations, and to elicit wisdom from past judges or legislators. Nonetheless, these pragmatic explanations hardly provide a complete or satisfying account of the rich intricacies of conventional legal discourse. On the contrary, they fit clumsily at best with actual legal practices.

Two criticisms embarrass the attempt to give a purely pragmatic account of these distinctive features of legal discourse. First, case law and enactments are in fact not very good ways of discovering or measuring these pragmatically relevant factors. For example, legal precedents typically make almost no attempt to convey the general societal or cultural information that a pragmatic decisionmaker might want; a standard almanac would usually be a far better source of this kind of data. Although (or rather *because*) Judge

Posner is all in favor of pragmatic decisionmaking, he observes that "the prior cases often constitute an impoverished repository of fact and policy for the decision of the present one."[81]

Indeed, reported cases are often very poor sources of information even about the facts of the cases themselves. "In the received theory of adjudication," Brian Simpson explains, "most contextual information about cases is simply irrelevant," and so it is filtered out of the reported decision.[82] And the filtered-out facts can be among the most important ones. Thus, Karl Llewellyn observed that "the facts which the judge has hidden from us consciously, or, as in most cases, unconsciously, are badly needed."[83] John Noonan's essay on the celebrated *Palsgraf* case shows, for instance, how virtually every piece of significant or interesting information about the parties, the accident, the context, the relevant enterprises, the judges, and the attorneys was methodically excluded from the judges' opinions.[84] And at least in this respect, *Palsgraf* was entirely typical.

In addition to filtering out needed information, moreover, case reports may supply *false* information. "Even if we leave on one side the fact that litigants normally tell lies," Simpson explains, "the picture of reality presented in a law report is more or less bound to be to some degree distorted. Indeed the incidents recorded in law reports may never, in any sense, have happened at all."[85]

Cases or statutes are also unreliable indicators of the extent or depth of expectations. In many instances it would be possible to obtain more accurate information regarding actual reliance or expectations (or the lack thereof) by direct investigation. Often such investigation might convincingly show that a party acted wholly without knowledge of a case or statute, and hence could not have harbored expectations on the basis of it. But in fact such investigation is virtually never undertaken. Indeed, *actual* knowledge of the law is for most purposes treated as irrelevant as a matter of law: that "ignorance of the law is no excuse" may well be the one piece of law that most people know.[86] Nor are case reports or statutes especially likely sources of wisdom. This is not to deny that these materials contain some insight or good counsel. But the person who is truly in search of wisdom (as opposed to something else, like "the law") would be better advised to go to her favorite columnist, or poet, or philosopher, or prophet—not to United States Reports or the West Digest system. Indeed, viewed as texts in moral philosophy, the Sherman Act, or the Robinson-Patman Act, or even the Constitution (if we really paid attention to its *text*, rather than the volumes of commentary and philosophizing that have over generations have been engrafted onto it), would be almost pitifully meager. A judge who wants guidance from the philosophical wisdom of an Aristotle or a John Stuart Mill would be well advised to read Aristotle or Mill—*not*, as Robin West suggests, the Equal Protection Clause.

A more general way of making this point is to notice that practical reason—and, more specifically, concerns about obtaining information, protecting expectations, and learning from the wisdom of others—are central to many enterprises, if not to *all* human activities. Not only lawyers and judges but also legislators, administrators, business executives, arbitrators, school teachers and principals, coaches, parents, and probably everyone else engages in practical reason with similar concerns in mind; consequently, all of these actors try to pay due attention to the decisions and pronouncements made in the past. But in no other field do these concerns generate the specific and extraordinary treatment of precedent and text that is so conspicuous in legal discourse. So without denying that legal discourse does to some extent perform these pragmatic functions, it still seems that more is needed to account for these peculiarly "legal" qualities.

A second difficulty with the wholly pragmatic account of conventional legal reasoning is that it takes the explicit reasoning less seriously than judges and lawyers themselves typically seem to take it. Judges and lawyers, that is, certainly *seem* to regard the formal legal reasoning as a deadly serious matter; in preparing briefs and arguing about an issue they may devote untold billable hours and hundreds of pages to amassing and explicating it. For some purposes, to be sure, judges and lawyers may also consult more pure and direct sources of information or wisdom—compilations of data or, very occasionally, philosophical works—but these sources are not treated as having actual legal "authority" in the way that precedents or statutes or other actual expressions of "the law" have. If philosophical insight were a governing criterion, Larry Alexander remarks, the moral judgment of the Harvard philosophy faculty might merit more deference than the opinion of a previous court; in our law these priorities are drastically reversed.[87] And judges and lawyers talk as if the conclusions reached through such explication of the more purely legal materials—the conclusions about the substantive content of "the law"—are authoritative and binding, not just a curious, backhanded way of conveying some more pragmatic decision about what seems sensible or fair.

Perhaps the clearest manifestation of this commitment to "the law," as discussed in Chapter 3, lies in the traditional approach to the question of retroactivity. As noted, courts typically treat a common law decision, even on a previously uncertain or hotly debated question, as governing even transactions that may have occurred well before the decision was rendered. In many cases, such retroactivity could hardly be justified on the assumption that in forming expectations people anticipated, or perhaps should have anticipated, what a court would ultimately say on the issue. Indeed, even when a court *overrules* a prior decision, the new decision is typically applied retroactively; this conventional approach serves not to protect expectations but rather to frustrate them. So it seems more plausible to suppose that the practice operates on the premise that courts nearly always give for it— namely, that courts are merely articulating *what "the law" is* (using "is," once again, in what we may call the perpetual present tense).

Nothing in the preceding discussion is meant to deny, of course, that a good deal of pragmatic or commonsensical judgment enters into legal decisionmaking. And that fact surely helps to make law more acceptable than it might otherwise be. But the practical reason position does not fare well as a general account of the distinctively legal features of legal discourse. On the contrary, it is more plausible to suppose that legal discourse is out to do . . . well, just what it says it is doing. Legal discourse is seeking to discover and declare something called "the law."

## The Abiding Suspicion

This conclusion brings us back to the problem with which the chapter began. As we have seen, it *seems* that legal discourse and practice depend, in a variety of ways, on a commitment to the substantial existence of "the law" in something like the "brooding omnipresence" sense ridiculed by Holmes. Modern jurisprudential thought can plausibly be viewed as a series of efforts to squirm out of that commitment. But the efforts have failed. Twentieth-century jurisprudence has enriched our understanding of law in a variety of ways (and it has distorted our understanding in a variety of ways as well). But neither the "autonomy" strategy nor the "law and" strategy has succeeded in explaining away commitments to "the law," or in explaining how the enterprise of law as we know it makes sense without those commitments.

On the contrary, the deeper theme running through modern legal thought, sometimes tacitly but often quite explicitly, is that the enterprise as traditionally conducted does *not* make sense—not, at least, on modern ontological assumptions—and is thus in need of (perhaps radical) reform. Thus far, it seems, the suspicion of low-talk as nonsense stands unrebutted.

# PART III

# The Metaphysics of
# Legal Meaning

If you have not already done so, forget the last chapter. Forget the last two chapters, in fact. The central question we have been asking through those chapters—basically, whether "the law" exists, or whether law makes sense without "the law"—is an unusual, perhaps uncouth question. Though I happen to think it is the most direct way to contemplate the quandary of modern law, I also realize that lawyers (and even more so legal scholars) may find the question irksome. So we are going to turn to a more conventional set of questions—questions that lawyers ask every day. These questions, beyond having a great deal of current practical importance in their own right, will eventually lead us around to approximately the same underlying issues that we have already been considering. But we will arrive at those issues through more familiar territory.

The central inquiry for this part of the book is: How does law mean? To be sure, lawyers do not ordinarily pose the issue of legal interpretation in quite this way. Instead, they usually ask what is the meaning of *this particular law*—this statute, or regulation, or doctrine, or precedent. But this "what does it mean?" question sometimes pushes lawyers to ask *where* a law means, as we might put it—or perhaps "*in* what" a law's meaning lies. Does the meaning of a statute reside in its text, for example, . . . or perhaps in the legislative intention behind the text, or in the minds of the judges who interpret the statute, or somewhere else? And from this "where" or "*in* what" inquiry it is only a short step to asking *how* a law means.

So these questions are old companions, as I have suggested, and there is also a set of standard answers to them. In the field of statutory construction, those standard answers have come to be grouped into three sprawling camps, often called "intentionalism," "textualism," and "purposivism."[1]

But upon examination, all of the standard answers suffer embarrassments. These embarrassments are well known, but as with social *faux pas* we routinely pretend not to notice them; and it might plausibly be argued that they *should be* ignored (at least by responsible people). Excessive reflection on these difficulties might tend to suggest that law *does not* or *cannot* mean after all. But that conclusion is plainly unacceptable—not just because it is unsettling or disappointing, but because the sort of reflection that leads to such conclusions seems demented. It is perfectly clear, after all, that law *does* mean. If it did not, the practice of law would be impossible. But for better or worse, the practice of law manifestly is not impossible: what *does* happen *can* happen.

So worrying overmuch about the difficulties of explaining "how law means" may seem like agonizing over Zeno's Paradox, or the conundrum about Hercules and the tortoise, and then inferring that since it is logically impossible actually to get anywhere anyway, we might as well stay in bed. Something is obviously wrong with the logic, because its conclusion is disproven every day by experience, over and over again. So most of us are sensibly content to leave such abstruse matters to people with surplus time and a fascination for paradoxes. "Just do it!" is our more practical slogan.

I feel the force of this objection. Even so, I think the question of "how law means" is worth pondering. My purpose in inviting us to reflect on the question is not to persuade anyone that law does not mean, or that the practice of interpreting law is impossible: those conclusions, I agree, would be merely goofy. Nor do I expect to settle the standard disputes about legal interpretation—the disputes that divide Justice Scalia from Justice Souter, say, or Ronald Dworkin from Robert Bork (though the discussion will sometimes collide with those debates). My principal objective, rather, is to consider from a different direction what we all constantly if implicitly presuppose when we make claims about what this statute or that constitutional provision "means." We can then ask whether those implicit presuppositions are ones we are willing to own up to.

The discussion will cover two chapters. My goal in Chapter 5 is modest, but not simple. Inspired by my former colleague Paul Campos, and prevailing wisdom to the contrary notwithstanding, I hope to persuade you that the search for the meaning of a legal text is *always*, of necessity and by its nature, the search for the (semantic) intentions of an author of some sort. This is not a merely practical claim but, more fundamentally, an ontological one. I add the qualifier "of some sort" so that you will not mistake this claim for an endorsement of the approach to statutory construction often called "intentionalism," or of the approach to constitutional interpretation often called "originalism." The claim, in other words, is not that meaning must be given by the intentions of what Umberto Eco calls the "empirical author"[2]—namely, the historical, flesh-and-blood legislators or enactors who wrote or voted for a law—but only that meaning is given by the intentions of *some* author.

Properly understood, this proposition is not really controversial, I believe; indeed, it might seem to belong in the "goes without saying" category. Why then devote a whole chapter to the point? The problem is that the proposition *appears to be* controversial, or even downright implausible, because of the way current debates have been framed. So in arguing for this proposition—that is, for the identity of "meaning" and "author's semantic intention"—I will also try to show that the proposition itself does not take sides among the familiar positions. Intentionalists, textualists, and purposivists all ought to accept the proposition; and they can do so without abandoning their basic positions and commitments.

Though not exactly taking sides, however, the equation of "meaning" with "authorial semantic intentions" does have implications for the standard debates. More specifically, this equation implies that the debates have been misleadingly formulated. They could be better framed not as debates about *whether* an author is needed—or about whether we ought to take our meanings from authors or from some other, nonauthorial source—but rather about *which* authorial candidate should be accepted as authoritative for legal meaning.

*That* question—the "*which* author?" question—will carry us into the Chapter 6. But we can note at the outset that judges and lawyers and especially scholars have powerful incentives to avoid the question, and thus to resist the claim that meanings depend on authors. That is because when the "*which* author?" question is openly posed, and when as a result the qualifications for "author of the law" are considered, it soon becomes apparent that none of the leading candidates comes close to possessing the requisite qualifications. The older, classical account of law *might* offer a way out of these difficulties—from our vantage point it is hard to be sure—but, as discussed, we are generally unwilling today to affirm that account: it does not square with prevailing ontological inventories. In this way, reflection on the routine matter of legal interpretation will lead us back, I predict, to our law's modern quandary.

# CHAPTER 5

# How Does Law Mean?

We can start with a familiar situation: lawyers are arguing over the meaning of a statute. Flipping through some advance sheets that happen to be on my desk at this moment, I see that the first case considers whether the term "creditor" as used in something called the Equal Credit Opportunity Act covers lawyers who delay in collecting fees from their clients. Or, to recur to what has somehow become the classic legal text for jurisprudential discussion: Does the word "vehicle" in an ordinance prohibiting vehicles in the park include skateboards, or ambulances, or the ambulance on a war memorial? In these and countless similar cases that lawyers handle every day, the argument is about *what* the statute (or ordinance, or regulation) means. Or, in constitutional cases, lawyers and judges argue over the meaning of "due process of law," or the words "the freedom of speech" in the First Amendment, or "cruel and unusual punishment" in the Eighth Amendment. Momentous consequences, sometimes involving millions or even billions of dollars and decisions on life or death, turn on the meanings that lawyers and judges find in, or assign to, these words.

We—not only lawyers but citizens generally—routinely find ourselves engaged in such debates. But can we say more than this about the nature of these arguments? What and where is that elusive entity—the "meaning"—on which so much hinges and over which lawyers do perpetual battle? What sort of thing are we talking about?

This chapter has a modest but essential purpose: I want to defend an answer to those questions that is simple and familiar (though not quite as simple and familiar as it might seem). The answer is that the meaning of a legal text is necessarily given by—indeed, is basically identical with—the semantic intentions of an author or authors *of some sort*. (I emphasize the "of some sort" because the qualification will become crucial.)

This proposition—namely, that legal meanings *must* be equated with authors' semantic intentions—is pivotal, I think, and any discussion of legal meaning that disregards it will be prone to fall into serious confusion; but it is also a proposition that today is widely regarded (in academic circles, at least) as untenable. Isn't it obvious, after all (even to those who think legislators' intentions *should* determine the meaning of legal texts), that it is at least *possible* to derive meaning from other sources? We can find meaning in linguistic conventions—can't we?—or in "dictionary meaning" or "the rules of the language," without referring to any author's "subjective intentions"? Or the meaning might be supplied by readers themselves, as the enthusiasts of "reader response" theories suggest. So my claim that legal meaning *must* be equated with authors' intentions seems to overreach: it is too strong to be plausible even to self-styled "intentionalists."

These are troublesome objections. So I want to respond to them by proceeding in this way. First, I need to lay out what I think is the most basic argument—not a merely legal or practical argument, but an ontological argument—for equating legal meaning with authors' intentions. Then I will consider the most common ostensible alternative suppliers of textual meaning—linguistic conventions (or the "rules of the language"), and readers or interpreters themselves—and will try to explain why, for all their importance, these cannot in fact serve as sources of meaning. That conclusion will help us see where the real issues and disagreements among approaches to legal interpretation lie, and how the common practice of dividing the contested terrain among intentionalist, textualist, and purposivist camps is likely to distort the real issues.

There are, to be sure, other common and powerful objections to "authors' intentions" approaches that I have not yet mentioned. One venerable criticism—the "dead hand of the past" objection—urges that we *should not* subject ourselves to the intentions of the human beings, often long since dead, who authored our legal texts. Another stock objection argues that at least for texts produced by large, disparate groups (like legislatures) we *cannot* be governed by authors' intentions: no such collective intentions exist, so any attempt to be governed by them is destined to fail. These are weighty criticisms—indeed, I am not sure that there is any satisfying answer to them—but for the most part I want to defer them to Chapter 6. They do not directly contradict the central claim of this chapter, but instead create the potential for a sort of tragic predicament, in which legal meaning *must be*—but also *should not* and even *cannot* be—given by authors' intentions. That is a predicament that we can worry about in due course: sufficient unto the day is the evil thereof.

## The Meaning of "Meaning"

At the outset, though, and even before introducing the basic argument, it will be helpful to notice a potential source of confusion. Even a moment's reflection will show, I think, that we use the verb "to mean" and the noun "meaning" in a variety of ways. For present purposes we must distinguish two different uses that if conflated (as they often are) can produce a pernicious confusion. We can illustrate these uses with typical statements:

> "When I said, 'I'll meet you at noon,' I *meant* 'approximately around noon'—give or take a few minutes; I didn't *mean* exactly at twelve o'clock sharp. You should have waited at the restaurant for a few minutes."
> "The fingerprints the police found on the gun *mean* that someone other than Jones was holding the murder weapon."

In the first of these statements, "mean" refers to what we might call "semantic meaning." Someone is using words to convey a thought or idea. And we call that thought or idea the "meaning" of the words used in this situation, or perhaps the "meaning" of the speaker: for the moment we can defer the question of whether it is more accurate in this context to say that the speaker or the words are what possess and provide the meaning. Lawyers, of course, are often concerned with questions of semantic meaning. Such questions are central, for example, in the interpretation of statutes or constitutional provisions—in the cases construing the Equal Credit Opportunity Act, for example, or the "no vehicles in the park" ordinance, or "due process" or "freedom of speech" or "cruel and unusual punishment."

If the first statement is an example of semantic meaning, let us say that the second statement illustrates "nonsemantic meaning." This usage of the term "mean" is also perfectly familiar. We say "mean" to denote an *evidentiary* relation ("The puddles on the lawn *mean* it rained last night"), or perhaps a *causal* connection ("The injury to his finger *means* that Zumboldt can't play in the piano competition.") Lawyers are sometimes concerned with nonsemantic meanings, as when they argue at trial over what a piece of "real evidence" (such as a gun or a footprint) means. But when lawyers argue over the proper interpretation of a statute or rule, they normally are concerned with semantic, not nonsemantic meaning. A particular statute may mean all sorts of things in nonsemantic, evidentiary or causal senses; it may mean that some Republicans in Congress bolted to vote with the Democrats, or that management is going to have an advantage over labor, or that the environment is going to suffer, or that the economy is likely to stabilize. But when a judge asks a lawyer about the meaning of the statute, these are not the sorts of meanings she normally has in mind.

Indeed, the nonsemantic senses of "mean" may seem so different from the semantic sense that we might almost suppose that we are using essentially different terms that just happen to be spelled alike (as in "The *square root* of 9 is 3" and "Look! This beet has a *square root!*"). And if disputes about the meanings of laws typically refer to semantic meanings, then it might seem that for our purposes in this chapter we should just forget about nonsemantic meanings.

Would that this were possible! The problem is that in practice, the semantic and nonsemantic usages often tend to blur into each other. That is because statements, or texts, can have evidentiary implications and causal consequences that are connected to their verbal quality but are not properly part of their semantic meaning. Indeed, nonsemantic meaning may result directly from a statement's verbal quality and yet be the antithesis of the statement's semantic meaning. Writers of detective stories sometimes take advantage of this possibility by having a suspect with no way of knowing that a murder has occurred blurt out something like, "I swear it wasn't me who killed Jones!" In one sense (a semantic sense), the statement means that the suspect *didn't* kill Jones, while in another sense (an evidentiary, nonsemantic sense) it may mean that he probably *did* kill Jones. So a detective might interpret the statement to mean that the speaker is guilty. Even so, it would be an error to say that the statement *in its semantic meaning* is a confession of guilt (in the way, for example, that we perhaps *could* say this if the speaker spoke similar words in a deliberately ironic tone of voice: "Of course I didn't kill Jones. Would a nice guy like me lift a finger against a sweet, harmless soul like him? I'm shocked that you could even suggest it.").

In this example we can, with a little care, sort out the statement's semantic from its nonsemantic meanings. But that task is not always easy, or even possible. Consider the observation: "So, the hiring partner said, 'I'll call you,' did she? You understand what that means, right? It means: 'Go away and leave me alone.'" Is this an observation about the semantic or nonsemantic meaning of the partner's "I'll call you"? It could be either. Perhaps the partner consciously intended (and assumed that you would understand) her statement to mean for you to go away; so that if you come back uninvited she might say, "Are you deaf? Didn't I say to go away and leave me alone?" Conversely, the hiring partner might have been trying to be polite; she might be mortified to know that anyone had taken her statement as evidence of her (actual) desire not to be bothered. Without more information, it is hard to tell.

Because these disparate usages of "mean" employ the same word and sometimes blur into each other, equivocation and slippage are constant dangers here. I expect that we will see such slippage from time to time: it may even be a leading cause of the notion that texts can have meanings apart from authors' intentions. That is because, in a sense (though not in the appropriate sense), they can.

## The Ontology of Semantic Meaning

Though nonsemantic meanings are real enough, however, and though they may rise up to complicate our inquiry, it remains true that in the interpretation of statutes, regulations, and constitutional provisions, lawyers and judges are typically concerned with semantic meanings. So our question asks how or from where that sort of semantic meaning arises. What sort of thing is it? I have already disclosed my answer to that question: legal meaning—or the semantic meaning of legal texts—must be equated with the semantic intentions of an author or authors of some sort. That is just what legal meaning is. But why?

### Practical Considerations

Some scholars argue for this conclusion on practical grounds that draw on our everyday practice of communication. We read the newspaper, or talk with friends or colleagues, or prepare letters for potential employers, or write scholarly articles or books for (we hope) the academic community. And when we are engaged in this process of communication, we regularly associate the meaning of a statement or text with the semantic intentions of a speaker or author. It only makes sense: if I am trying to communicate with you about, say, where to meet for lunch, I will naturally use your words as a means of figuring out what you are trying to communicate. There would be no point in imagining meanings other than the one you intend: to do so would only interfere with my purpose in "interpreting" (which is to succeed in agreeing on a meeting place).

Likewise, legal utterances and texts might be understood to be part of a process of communication—between principals and agents, or between rulers and subjects. And if that is what legal texts are, then once again it makes sense to identify their meanings with what their authors intended to say.[1] For this reason, as Thomas Merrill notes, "the judicial view" (which Merrill contrasts with the "academic view") traditionally "presupposes that interpretation means searching for and enforcing the specific intentions of the enacting body."[2]

This logic can overwhelm even academic presentations that try to flout it. For example, Gary Lawson is an eminent constitutional scholar and a proponent of the textualist view that the meaning of a law is "objective" and equivalent to what he calls "original public meaning," *not* to the "subjective" intentions of the law's enactors; and in support of that position he engages in an extended reflection on the theme that the Constitution is a "recipe" for government and hence should be interpreted in much the same way that we would interpret an eighteenth-century recipe for fried chicken.[3] Lawson advances a proposition "so obvious that it can be obscured only by an advanced degree: The presumptive meaning of a recipe is its original public meaning."[4] So in deciding what words like "lard," "salt," and "pepper" mean in the recipe, Lawson says, the presumption is that we should look to the "original public meaning"—to what "the words meant" at the time, not to the merely "private" or "subjective" intentions of the cook who wrote the recipe. But far from being obvious, Lawson's proposition seems positively perverse. After all, if we are reading the recipe in an effort to cook fried chicken and on the assumption that the recipe was written by someone who was a specialist in the art, then what we care about in reading the recipe is *what the cook intended.* Conversely, we care not at all about the recipe's original public meaning—except perhaps as an aid to figuring out what the cook actually meant.

Thus, suppose that the recipe says to sprinkle the chicken with "sugar" and that most people two centuries ago used the word "sugar" to refer to the same sweet, white, crystals that people refer to today when they use the word; but we also have good reason to believe that the particular cook who wrote the recipe had an idiosyncratic usage (or just slipped up in this case) and that by "sugar" he really intended what most people (then and now) would call "salt." What sense would it make to say, "Although as a 'private' and 'subjective' matter he probably *intended* 'salt,' the fact is that he *said* 'sugar.' That was the objective, *public* meaning. So sugar it is." Pity the poor diners who are victims of a chef with this textualist approach to reading recipes.

And indeed, Lawson himself concedes that "if there is good reason to think that a particular recipe was designed only for private rather than public consumption, then one must take account of *both* its original public meaning *and* its original private meaning to its intended audience." And, apparently sensing that this concession still doesn't go far enough (because if we know that the cook meant "salt" there is no apparent reason why we should try to negotiate between the cook's "subjective" meaning and the "original public meaning"—maybe mixing a little sugar with a little salt?), Lawson grudgingly acknowledges that "[i]n that case, the original private meaning might even be the standard one"—"though," he adds enigmatically, "that is an empirical matter for linguists to explore."[5] (I confess that I have no idea what Lawson—or is it Lawson's text?—means by this last qualification.) But these concessions and puzzling qualifications merely serve to distract from a point that is "so obvious that it can only be obscured," if not "by an advanced degree," then by rarified jurisprudential commitments: in reading a recipe, what we care about is what the author— the cook—intended to communicate. If the cook meant "salt," salt is the meaning we want to extract from the recipe. Conversely, we care about original public meaning only insofar as it helps us understand what the author of the recipe intended.[6]

So if he wants to establish an interpretive presumption for "public meaning" over "private" or "subjective meaning"—that is, over "authorial intentions" as the basis of meaning—it seems that Lawson has made exactly the wrong argument. What he needs to argue is that interpreting legal texts such as the Constitution is *not* like reading a recipe. More generally, opponents of the position that equates legal meaning with authors' intentions need to argue that legal interpretation is not like ordinary communication— where, as noted, we routinely interpret to ascertain authors' or speakers' intentions and have good practical reasons for doing so.

But that argument—though it is not the one that textualists like Lawson typically make—might well be plausible nonetheless. When you stop and think about it, after all, reading an ancient and authoritative legal document like the Constitution, written by a group of diversely minded people we have never met and under circumstances very different from our own, is not all that much like reading a chatty letter from your grandmother back home—or a recipe for fried chicken. It might well be that different interpretive assumptions should govern these different types of reading. In any case, the differences between ordinary communication and legal interpretation are why the merely practical reasons for equating "meaning" with "author's semantic intentions," though powerful, fall short of being conclusive.

### Ontological Considerations

The more conclusive reason for equating "meaning" with "authors' semantic intentions," I believe, is not practical but ontological in character. The basic point can be put simply: under the ontological conceptions that most of us entertain, and in a world in which most of us have discarded "animistic" notions, *persons* have the property or capability of being able to mean. *Objects* do not have this property. Meaning is not just "there," like the moon or the Grand Canyon. Instead, like government in Lincoln's famous description, meaning is *of* the people, *by* the people, *for* the people. (For present purposes we need not worry about other entities arguably possessing some of the same mental capacities as persons, such as whales or dolphins—or angels). By contrast, *objects* do not, strictly speaking, have the property of being able to "mean" in a semantic sense.

There are, to be sure, various senses in which we talk about objects as meaning things: we will notice some of these senses shortly. But on reflection, none of them authorizes us to view objects—including marks on a page—as being capable of forming and conveying semantic intentions. "Meaning," Patrick Brennan observes, "is something only persons make. . . . It is Subjects—not black marks—who mean."[7]

An intriguing thought experiment suggested by Paul Campos may serve to clarify the central point. Drawing on similar analyses by the literary theorists Walter Benn Michaels and Steven Knapp, Campos imagines that while walking in the desert near the border between the United States and Mexico, you come across marks in the sand forming the figures "R E A L," and you wonder what these marks mean. Your first step will be to guess whether the marks were made by an English-speaking or Spanish-speaking agent. If you think the marks were made by an English speaker, you probably will interpret them to mean something like "real" in the sense of "actual" or "existing." If you suppose instead that the marks were made by someone speaking Spanish, then you will understand them to mean something like the English term "royal." But if you think the marks were made by no one, and were instead simply the fortuitous effect of wind on the desert sand, then you will not suppose that the marks actually mean anything at all: they are merely a strange accident devoid of meaning.[8] The most you might do (and this will turn out to be a tremendously important possibility) is to imagine that *if* the marks had been made by an English speaker, they *would* mean . . . , and so forth. But even here, it is an author (albeit a hypothetical one), not the marks in themselves or as free-floating entities, that supplies meaning.

This elementary point is often obscured, Campos suggests, because we routinely do things with texts other than read them. For example, we may *misread* a text, inadvertently or even deliberately, ignoring or distorting the authorial intentions that produced it. Or we can *reauthor* texts. ("I don't care what Jefferson meant by 'all men are created equal.' *I'm* the one who's talking now." Or, "Forget the framers: the Constitution means what the Supreme Court says it means.")[9] Such practices of misreading or reauthoring are familiar, perhaps necessary, and they do indeed create distance between the original or historical author's intentions and something else that we might for various purposes choose to call the text's "meaning."[10] But these practices do not dispense with the need for *an* author as the source of meaning, Campos observes: they merely substitute a different author (myself, or the Supreme Court) for the historical one. It simply makes no sense to talk about the marks having a meaning except by reference to what someone meant by them. Indeed, Campos argues, *what the author was trying to say* and *what the text means* just are the same thing.

### Clarifications and Qualifications

This is a modest and commonsensical claim, I think, but it is also, paradoxically, a confusing one that can easily be taken amiss and can thus come to seem deeply implausible. In hopes of averting such misunderstanding, I offer a qualification and two clarifications before proceeding with the argument.

First, the qualification. It is surely true that objects (such as marks on a page) can be used *by persons* to convey meanings; and so in a shorthand expression we may refer to the "meaning" of an object (in the same way that we may say, as a shorthand expression, that the "purpose" of a bus is to transport people, or that the "purpose" of a hammer is to pound nails).

Taken too literally or simple-mindedly, such statements might seem to lapse into primitive animism—as in the assertion that "rocks fall because they crave the earth." But in fact we readily understand such statements to be shorthand expressions of more complex propositions, such as "People make and use hammers to pound nails."

In addition, as discussed above, objects can have nonsemantic meanings; they can be connected in evidentiary and causal ways to other facts or objects. In one or both of these senses (namely, the shorthand and nonsemantic senses), we *do* often talk about objects as meaning something. But neither usage implies that objects *in themselves* can "mean" in a semantic sense. In *that* sense, objects don't mean; *people* mean.

To be sure, in talking about what some text means, we may not make any explicit reference to any persons for whom it has that meaning, but our talk of necessity contains implicit personal references (on peril of collapsing into nonsense). Larry Solum suggests a helpful analogy in assertions about "price."[11] If you say that the price of a dozen tortillas is two dollars, you may not explicitly mention any persons for whom the tortillas have this price, and you may not even have any such persons consciously in mind: your conscious thoughts might be limited to just the tortillas and the price. Even so, you necessarily refer, at least implicitly, to such persons (buyers and sellers). Otherwise, your talk of "price" loses its sense. In this respect, "price" and "meaning" are similar: both are what we might call "person-relative" qualities. Deprived of that relation, they lose their sense. You cannot have pure, "objective," person-independent meanings any more than you can have person-independent prices—or person-independent spouses, or uncles.

To see the point, take the more obvious example and then try imagining someone who does not grasp it. "I'm an uncle," your neighbor tells you. "Wonderful," you reply. "And how many nieces and nephews do you have?" "None. You misunderstand: I'm not *that kind* of uncle—not just *somebody's* uncle, not just a *relative* uncle. I'm an uncle pure and simple, an uncle period, full stop, *tout court*. An 'objective' uncle, if you like." My suggestion is that if, in the ontological schemes that most of us hold, persons can "mean" and objects cannot (except in the shorthand and nonsemantic senses noted above), then talk of "objective" meaning (except, again, in the shorthand or nonsemantic senses) is as nonsensical as talk of "objective" unclehood.

Now for the clarification. What do I mean by saying that the connection of *meaning* to *persons* is an "ontological" connection? Is this claim meant to state some sort of logically necessary or *a priori* truth? Am I proposing this as a truth that will obtain in, as philosophers say, all "possible worlds"? Offered in these extreme forms, the claim connecting meaning with persons would be implausible, I think, because if we want to fantasize, we can *imagine*, for example, impersonal or inanimate entities somehow forming themselves into what look like words and sentences that in fact turn out to convey accurate information. Larry Solum points out to me (with an allusion to Campos's "marks in the sand" example) that we can imagine a world containing the following bizarre occurrences:

- On January 3, 2002, the following letters appeared in the sand: "Tomorrow, there will be an unusual hail storm in the Kearny Mesa area. Park your car in the garage." The reader parks his car in the garage that night, and avoids the damage inflicted on his neighbors' cars.
- On April 7, 2001, the following letters appeared in the sand: "Buy stock in Amalgamated Widgets and hang onto it for a year. Then sell." The reader doesn't follow the advice, but the stock triples during the one-year period, and then falls back to its original value within a few weeks.
- On October 8, 2002, the following letters appeared in the sand: "There is a really good deal on Charmin at Costco." The reader goes to Costco, and buys one of those enormous containers of Charmin at half the usual price.

I think Solum is right: we *can* imagine such a world—in fact, we just did—and that possibility suggests that the claim connecting meaning with persons is not an assertion of logical necessity or an *a priori* claim applicable to all possible worlds. In *Alice in Wonderland*, after all, or in Disney movies, there is nothing especially surprising about, say, a teapot bursting into song. Indeed, we need not even resort to fantasy: historians and anthropologists tell us of animist cultures in which rivers and rocks act with conscious intentions. But Solum goes on to observe of his hypothetical communications by inanimate objects that "[i]n the actual world, this will never happen"; and that of course is the point. In *our* world, or within the ontological inventories that most of us employ, *persons* have the capacity to form and convey semantic meanings. Impersonal objects (such as rocks and rivers and teapots—and marks on a page) do not have this capacity; at most they can serve to convey *persons'* meanings.

One further clarification is essential. The ontological point that I am making here suggests that textual meaning must be identified with the semantic intentions of *an author*—and that without an at least tacit reference to an author we would not have a meaningful text at all, but rather a set of meaningless marks or sounds—but it does not necessarily insist that the author be the *historical author,* or the "empirical author," as Umberto Eco says.[12] We can assign meaning in accordance with the intentions of some other author—ourselves, or some other contemporary or historical person, or some hypothetical author of our own devising. Consider again the words "I'll call you." We might understand that when Joe says these words he really means we can expect to hear from him, but when Elizabeth says them she means that the conversation is over; and we can imagine hypothetical speakers who might utter similar words to convey any number of other meanings.

Whether as a practical matter it is sensible or merely silly to look to hypothetical authors for meanings presents a separate question—one we will consider in Chapter 6. And a purist might insist that the "true" or "real" meaning of a text is what the "real" author—Eco's "empirical author"—intended. We can for the time being remain agnostic on those questions. My point for now is merely that statements about meaning that refer to hypothetical authors are not nonsensical. We *can* meaningfully say, in other words, that whatever the historical author may have intended by a particular text, if written by someone else—by some actual historical person, or perhaps by some fictional person of our own construction—the text *would mean* such-and-such.

In sum, the practice of reading texts to determine authors' semantic intentions is not only a familiar and useful one; it is a practice necessitated by the basic ontological proposition that "meanings"—semantic meanings, that is—are properties of persons, not of objects (except in the shorthand sense mentioned above). In this vein, Stanley Fish explains that "[t]here is only one style of interpretation—the intentional style—and . . . one is engaging in it even when one is not self-consciously paying 'attention to intention.'"[13]

This is a crucial and, I think, obvious point, but it is also routinely rejected in (among other places) legal literature. Critics of the conclusion quickly point to what they take to be alternative sources of meaning—sources that are not persons, or at least not authors. First, don't we routinely recognize that meaning is not so much a property of speakers or authors but rather something that inheres in the rules or conventions of *the language?* Second, even granting that meaning is a property of persons, why must the meaning-conferring person be the *author?* Why isn't it as plausible—indeed, more plausible—to suppose that the *reader* supplies the meaning?

## Meanings without Authors?

If these alternative sources can in fact provide meanings, then the claim equating meaning with authors' intentions would be mistaken. But I think a careful consideration of the leading alternatives in fact reinforces that claim.

### Do Linguistic Conventions Create "Meaning"?

A common source of resistance to the equation of semantic meaning with authorial intention lies in the idea that meaning comes not from speakers or authors but rather from language—or from "the laws of language," as Holmes put it,[14] or "linguistic conventions." A whole movement of "textualists" (Justice Scalia being the most prominent) is currently perhaps the most conspicuous group to advance this view.[15] The textualist or "rules of language" position is beguiling because it contains a large measure of truth. But that truth confounds rather than enhances understanding when it is taken as reversing the basic ontological proposition that persons, not objects, have the property of being able to mean.

Linguistic conventions are of course real enough, and without them it would be well-nigh impossible for communication to occur. The necessity of conventions becomes painfully apparent to us whenever we find ourselves in a country or culture where we do not share such conventions—that is, where we don't speak the language (as I am reminded on my occasional trips into Mexico). Nonetheless, linguistic conventions do not obviate authors or speakers as the underlying and indispensable source of meaning. On the contrary, conventions are simply the common patterns that speakers and listeners, authors and readers, use in communicating. Consequently, conventions can at most provide an account of (and the resources for conveying and ascertaining) *persons'* meanings; they cannot establish a meaning independent of these meanings.

Understood as establishing a source of linguistic meaning independent of speakers' or authors' meanings, the conventionalist account is like the schoolchild's notion of a dictionary: it is a sort of legislated linguistic code, enacted by some duly ordained language autocrat, that dictates what the meanings of words shall be whether we, the speakers, like it or not. The schoolchild may believe that particular words just have particular meanings, period—even if people rarely use the words in the "correct" ways and routinely use them in other, "incorrect" ways. ("Kids say 'cool' when they mean that something is really good. But 'cool' doesn't *really* mean that; it means 'a little bit cold.'") Lexicographers understand that this notion turns reality on its head. Dictionary meanings come from, and attempt to track, the usage of actual language users. Usage is primary; dictionaries are derivative.

Consequently, a Samuel Johnson or a Noah Webster does not achieve his position by campaigning to be appointed "language czar" and then, once in office, proceeding to legislate meanings for words. No one this side of Adam has enjoyed that prerogative[16] (and even then, with a human population of one, there could scarcely be any distinction between speaker's meaning and conventional meaning). Instead, the lexicographer studies the ways in which people actually use words, and then tries to give succinct and accurate reports of those usages. To be sure, a dictionary may help you understand what a writer or speaker was trying to communicate. And if you are writing or speaking and you deviate from dictionary meanings, you risk being misunderstood. But neither of these observations changes the fact that meanings ultimately come from persons—from speakers—not from dictionaries.

The same point applies to linguistic conventions, of which dictionaries are one kind of report. Indeed, how could it be otherwise? What sense would it make, after all, to say, "Although speakers in this culture *intend* this phrase to mean *X*, and although listeners *understand* speakers who use the phrase to mean *X*, nonetheless according to the 'conventions of the language' the sentence *actually means Y*." If persons understand that speakers use the phrase to convey a particular meaning, then it is nonsensical to suppose that there could be conventions that "really" give it a different meaning.

Indeed, this conclusion would hold even if there were an appointed language autocrat who purports to dictate the meaning of words. Suppose that a country has a Ministry of Language (as I am told some countries do) that issues rulings—backed, if you like, by stiff criminal sanctions—about what particular words shall and shall not mean.[17] Actual speakers in that linguistically regulated land will either conform to the Ministry's rulings or, risking punishment, they will not conform. Suppose that nonconformity becomes widespread. So conversations occur, letters are sent, and books are written in which speakers convey their intentions using words in ways that deviate from the Ministry's regulations. In this situation, it still seems more natural and plausible to say that what the conversations and letters and books mean is determined by the speakers' actual usage and their semantic intentions as reflected in that usage—not by the Ministry's regulations. And it would seem pointless and obtuse to insist that these expressions and communications "really" mean what the official regulations prescribe, even though neither speakers nor listeners understand them that way.

Conversely, suppose that speakers choose to conform to the regulations. In this case, meanings will correlate with official prescriptions. But even so, it is the usage and understanding of speakers and listeners that gives the words their meaning. The prescriptions will affect meaning only indirectly—by causing speakers to use (and listeners to understand that speakers use) words in particular ways.

### *"Speaker's Meaning" versus "Sentence Meaning"?*

How then has the notion that linguistic conventions obviate, or at least stand as an alternative to, speakers' or authors' meaning become so prevalent? Primarily, it seems, the notion arises because for some purposes it is helpful to distinguish between what we might call "normal" uses of words and deviant or idiosyncratic usages (such as, for example, the communicative glitches we acknowledge when we say "I misspoke" or "I didn't mean what I just said"). In the same way, we might say that "although Jones may have intended *X*, most people who use those words in that context would intend *Y*." In this way, philosophers sometimes distinguish between "speaker's meaning" and "sentence meaning" (or between "utterer's" and "utterance" meaning). And lawyers talk about the "objective" meaning of the terms of a contract. The point is not to imply that the words themselves just have a particular meaning, period (regardless of how speakers use the words), but rather to screen out hidden or idiosyncratic meanings—private meanings that might lead to misunderstanding and injustice. So-called objective meaning does this by tying the legally enforceable meaning to, as Holmes explained, "what those words would mean in the mouth of a normal speaker of English, using them in the circumstances in which they were used."[18] Modern textualists are likewise animated by a strong aversion to letting the meaning of law turn on "private, potentially idiosyncratic meanings"—meanings that might be "deviant" or characterized by "subjectivity and imprecision."[19]

But though this distinction may be serviceable for some purposes,[20] three points should be kept in mind. First, philosophers' references to "sentence meaning" or lawyers' talk of "objective meanings" should not be taken to show that words can have a context-free meaning independent of *any* author's semantic intentions. At most, such terms can focus our attention on the meanings intended by someone like Holmes's "normal speaker of English." So it would be a mistake to suppose that in thus recognizing something we call "sentence meaning" we have thereby freed meaning from its ultimate dependence on persons—and indeed on persons speaking in particular contexts in an effort to communicate particular meanings.

Indeed, Holmes's own description of "objective" meaning by reference to what the "normal speaker" would mean by words—"using them in the circumstances in which they were used"—calls attention to this point. In a similar vein, Gerald Graff explains:

> Speech act theorists like John Searle and H. P. Grice distinguish between "sentence meaning" and "utterance meaning" to distinguish between the kind of understanding we can have of a context-free sentence like "keep off the grass" and of the same sentence when actually used by somebody to commit a speech act, say, of warning. One might suppose that the expression's familiarity probably depends on our imagining a standard situation with which we associate words—a sign seen on a well-manicured lawn, say, or the cry of a gardener working on such a lawn while somebody is walking across it. "Keep off the grass" would *mean* something entirely different if we overheard the expression uttered by a narcotics-counselor, in appropriate circumstances, to a person known to us as a marijuana user. . . . [I]*nterpretation is concerned not with what words or sentences mean "in themselves" but with how speakers actualize the semantic potential of words and utterances in particular speech acts.*[21]

Second, even for the limited purpose of distinguishing normal from idiosyncratic or deviant language uses, we should be wary of distinctions between "speaker's meaning" and "sentence meaning" or "conventional meaning." When we say that a particular speaker's intended meaning departs from conventional meaning, we are very likely just employing a stunted conception of linguistic conventions. For example, it is sometimes said that "speaker's meaning" diverges from "conventional meaning" when a speaker uses words ironically. But this description distorts. Irony itself is typically used and understood by means of conventions; if it were not, we would almost never have any way of detecting or understanding it. The ironic speaker employs these conventions to convey her meaning, and (just as with nonironic speech) listeners use the same conventions to discern that meaning.

So, for example, there seems to be no warrant for concluding that an expression such as "Yeah, right" (meaning something like "No way!" or "Are you crazy?") is a case in which "speaker's meaning" differs from "sentence meaning"[22]—or that the sentence "That's just *great!*" uttered in a sardonic tone indicates praise under "the rules of the language," even though most speakers would intend and most listeners would understand the utterance to mean just the opposite. Only an obtuse view of linguistic conventions would support that description. To be sure, listeners sorely lacking in linguistic proficiency might fail to grasp the usual and intended—and *conventional*—meaning of such expressions. But why should inept or clumsy speakers and listeners get to determine the rules and conventions of the language?

It is also true that some conventions turn on inflection or tone of voice or gestures that are hard to represent in a printed transcript. This fact reflects a limitation in our system of writing, but it hardly supports a fundamental distinction between "speaker's meanings" and "sentence meanings" (with the misleading implication that there is some "conventional" or "sentence" meaning not dependent on speakers). To be sure, someone who reads a transcript of a conversation might interpret it differently than would someone who was actually present and thus directly observed tone of voice, facial expressions, gestures, and the like. In the same way, someone who because of a bad telephone connection could not make out every third word might interpret the conversation differently than would someone who could hear the speaker perfectly; and a reader whose tattered paperback is missing numerous pages might understand it differently than a reader who has the full text. But we do not therefore create distinctions contrasting "speaker's meaning" with "audible meaning," or "author's meaning" with "preserved meaning," as if these were *independent kinds of meanings*. We simply recognize that although there is one source of meaning (a speaker or author) and one kind of textual meaning (semantic), the communication and reception of that meaning is less than perfect in a variety of ways.

Finally, the limited purposes that may be validly served by distinctions between speaker's and sentence meanings, or between "intended" and "objective" meanings, have scant relevance in any case to the interpretation of legal enactments. Parties to private contracts may sometimes use language in tricky or deviant ways that courts need to guard against by focusing on what they may choose (at their and our peril) to call "objective" meanings: Holmes emphasized this justification for not indulging "the idiosyncracies of the writer."[23] But the drafters and enactors of statutes and constitutional provisions do not tend to be highly idiosyncratic in their use of language after the manner of, say, humorists or poets. On the contrary, legislative drafters incline to dullness—to a numbing standardization—in their expressions.[24] Nor do they typically set out to trick their audiences. To be sure, legislators may conceive of themselves as addressing a specialized audience—government officials, perhaps—and not the general public.[25] But whomever they conceive of themselves as addressing, it is in the legislators' interest to communicate their purposes as clearly as they themselves can formulate those purposes; otherwise, the interpreters are unlikely to further those purposes.

Linguistic conventions matter, in sum—indeed, they are indispensable—and they may in some contexts permit us to contrast what some particular speaker intended by an expression with what most speakers (or the "typical speaker") would intend by that expression. But linguistic conventions do not in any way negate the ontological point that *meaning* is a capacity of persons—of speakers or authors communicating with listeners or readers—not of objects in themselves.

### Readers' Meanings?

Alright, you say, meanings come from persons, or are "person-relative" qualities: even so, why must those persons be *authors* (or speakers)? A popular view, sometimes associated with "reader response" theory, suggests that meaning is in fact conferred by interpreters, or by *readers*. This is a deceptive suggestion, in part because (like the linguistic conventions objection) it contains an important element of truth.

In the first place, if we understand "meaning" by reference to our pervasive experience with communication, as we often do, then it would seem to follow that communication (and hence meaning) cannot occur without readers or hearers. Since the reader is in a sense the last link in the communicative chain (author → text → reader), and since meaning will be successfully communicated and realized only when that last link is in place, it is tempting to say that the reader supplies the meaning. In addition, we often observe that the meanings a reader or hearer takes away from a communication do not always match up well with what an author or speaker was trying to communicate. This disjunction may be especially glaring when a text is ancient, so that author and readers are separated by vast stretches of time, space, and culture. Moreover, in some cases a reader may not even have any clear notion of who the actual author was (as in the "message in a bottle" situation). So the author may have to be inferred or "reconstituted" by the reader.

All of these observations seem sound enough, and they identify important senses in which we might say that readers "give" meaning to texts. And in fact there is no harm in a "readers' meaning" theory so long as it is understood simply as an expression of the sorts of observations just listed. The mischief occurs when we move from the (admissible but dangerous, because slippery) proposition that "*readers* give meaning to texts" to the (incorrect and fallacious) proposition that "readers, *not authors*, give meanings to texts" or, perhaps, that "textual meaning is not dependent on authors." The slippage is barely perceptible, because the latter propositions may seem like just rephrasings of the first, or a clearer expression of what was necessarily implicit in the first. But in fact the second set of propositions goes well beyond the first. Moreover, these propositions mislead by aggressively omitting to notice the crucial fact (colorfully presented in Campos's "desert sand" thought experiment) that the activity of reading or interpreting—of responding to a text *as a reader*, rather than in some other way—is by its nature an effort to discern the meaning that an *author* has sought to convey through a text. Readers may give meanings to texts, that is, but they do so (at least when they are engaged in *reading*) by assuming and trying to discern the meanings that they suppose an author has expressed.

So, from the fact that in some modest but important senses readers give meanings to texts, it does not follow that readers rather than authors confer meaning, and therefore that meaning is somehow independent of some author's (inferred, or presumed, or projected) semantic intention. Any such conclusion would almost exactly parallel the claim that because baseball umpires call balls and strikes and outs and runs, it is really umpires, *not players*, who make outs, score runs, and win baseball games—and hence that it is plausible to say "the Yankees won the game" without thereby essentially and primarily describing what the players in pinstripes did in the game. One might as cogently argue that because accused persons are innocent until a jury finds them guilty, it is really the jury, not the accused, that "determines guilt," . . . and hence that "confers guilt," . . . and hence—why stop here?— that "perpetrates crime." The overzealous application of "reader response" theory is guilty of the same fallacy—of confounding *the agent who must authoritatively pronounce upon a thing* (the baserunner's touching the plate, the defendant's innocence or guilt, the text's meaning) with *the thing itself.*

And indeed, in the proper context everyone understands that the reader response idea cannot be taken in any very far-reaching sense. If it could, then every reading would be as valid as every other reading, and it would become illogical to suggest that any interpretation is incorrect. I might read your learned and deeply reflective essay on reader response theory to *mean* (and not just in a nonsemantic, evidentiary sense) that you are a goofball and a moron ("That's what it meant to me!"); and you would be helpless to defend yourself (although of course you could retaliate by reading my interpretation of your essay as asserting that *I* am a goofball and a moron).[26] Nor is it cogent to fend off such wanton interpretations by suggesting that they are insincere, or that I "don't really believe" your essay meant what I said it meant. Probably I *don't* really believe your essay meant (not semantically, at least) that you are subcompetent; but that is precisely because I know that this is not actually what you were trying to communicate. More generally, the notion that an interpretation could be insincere or dishonest makes little sense except on the presupposition that there is some meaning conveyed by the text that a reader might choose to acknowledge or, conversely, to ignore, falsify, or misrepresent.

Why then have legal thinkers sometimes supposed that the undeniable role of readers in interpretation somehow removes the need to connect meaning to an author? We might notice several possible sources of this confusion—several senses in which it is tempting to say that readers have supplied meanings not originating with an author. First, as noted, readers often misread or misinterpret texts; they purport to find meanings in a text that no author ever intended to convey. We *could* say in these cases that the meaning came from the reader rather than the author. But it would be more straightforward simply to say that the reader erred in ascertaining the text's meaning. Mistakes are mistakes. So the possibility of misinterpretation no more obviates authors than the fact that umpires and juries sometimes "get it wrong" means that we can have baseball without players or crime without criminals.

In addition, as also noted, we *can* read texts to discern the intentions not of the actual historical author, but rather of some other person, or of some hypothetical author of our own devising. In a sense, we might say that the reader chooses the author of the text. (This statement would need to be heavily qualified for any real-world situation involving reading, but for now we can let it pass.) But even if we suppose, implausibly, that the reader is completely free to choose or create an author that will make the text mean anything she wants it to mean, it still does not follow that *in reading the text* the reader confers the meaning without reference to an author. It would be as cogent for me to assert that because the library has books saying almost anything I can imagine on almost every subject, and because I am free to pick any book I choose, it follows that I, not the author, in fact give the book I am holding in my hand its content.

A further source of confusion is the possibility of using texts as sources of nonsemantic meanings that are perceived by someone who is a "reader" (though not by a reader acting *as reader*) and that do not correlate with the intentions of any author. But although the distinction is easy to smudge (because, as discussed, semantic and nonsemantic meanings often blur into each other), we also understand that, at least in principle, these nonsemantic meanings are foreign to *the meaning* of a text, or to the semantic meaning that we seek when we are engaged in interpretation. Suppose you ask for my interpretation of the meaning of *Anne of Green Gables* and I say, "Well, to me, it's a book about human violence and cruelty." Surprised, you ask why I think this, and I explain, "Because my family had a large, hard-bound copy, and my sister hit me over the head with it when I was a little kid." We understand that this response, though entirely genuine, does not figure in the meaning of the book. Even if I am *also* a reader of the book, this is not the sort of "reader response" that counts as the book's meaning.

The same conclusion applies even when the text's verbal quality is part of the causal chain that produces the nonsemantic meaning. Suppose I ask what you think of T. S. Eliot's poem "Little Gidding," and you say, "To me, it's an irresistibly erotic poem. Pornographic, actually." Taken aback, I point out that this reading is unusual and that most people have thought the poem is profoundly religious in nature, but you explain, "You see, I used to know this gorgeous, really petite girl whose last name was 'Gidding'—Paula Gidding she was—and we used to go to the movies and afterwards back to my place, and—well. . . ." In a sense it is the words—and your reading the words—that produces this response, but the response still does not give the meaning of the poem. Nor would it matter if you insisted, "That really is what the poem *means* to me." We could take your report as perfectly sincere and yet understand that you are not talking about the poem's meaning in an interpretive sense.

Finally, and perhaps most importantly for law, for various purposes of our own you or I may not care about what meaning the author intended to convey; we may care, rather, about what meaning a reader derived from a text—or about what the reader "*thought* the text meant," as we might say. Suppose my wife has e-mailed my daughter to meet me at a certain time and place for dinner. In this situation, I will want to know how my daughter (the reader) understood the instructions, not what my wife (the author) intended her to understand. I care about the "reader's response," not about the "author's intention." But—and this is the crucial point—my daughter could not even go about reading or responding to the directions at all, or assigning any meaning to them, unless she began by assuming that they were an expression of someone's intent to communicate something. Without that assumption, the instructions would simply be scribbling, or "spam"—meaningless marks. And the "meaning" of the directions, for her, will correlate with what she believes that intended communication to be.

So if I do not treat my wife's semantic intentions as dispositive, it is not because her instructions (the text) have some meaning independent of those intentions, but rather because I ultimately do not care what either the text or my wife meant: I am interested in meeting up with my daughter, and so care about what *she thought* the text meant. (We could, of course, complicate the story by adding that my daughter in the final analysis also does not care what the text means: she wants to meet up with me, and so may ask not what the text means, but rather what *I think* the text means—or perhaps what I think *she thinks* the text means. And knowing this, I may ask myself what she thinks I think she thinks. . . . But however many layers we add, we will still not have constructed any nonauthorial source for what the text means.)

So in the end, yes, we can say (if we want to seem insightful, or vaguely enigmatic) that *you*, the reader, confer meaning on the text. We can *say* this, and in a certain restricted sense we will be right. But (and this again is the crucial point) you confer meaning by attempting to discern or recognize the semantic intentions of an (inferred, or perhaps imagined) author.

## Reframing the Debate

The discussion thus far has suggested that semantic meaning always depends on and refers to the semantic intentions of an author—of *some sort* of author. Conventionalist and reader response accounts convey a good deal of truth and insight (and they can also perpetrate a good deal of sophisticated confusion), but they do not obviate the need for an author as the source of meaning.

This conclusion, however, is not an endorsement of "intentionalism" in the usual sense, or of constitutional originalism. That is because the discussion has also repeatedly recognized that the "author" to whom we look for textual meaning need not be the historical, flesh-and-blood person who put pen to paper or fingers to keyboard (or even the legislators or ratifiers who called out "Aye" when the vote was taken). The "author" might be a constructed or hypothetical figure, such as Holmes's "normal speaker of English," or perhaps the "Model Author" hypothesized by Umberto Eco.[27] We can—and we often do—interpret statements or texts by reference to the constructive intentions of some such artificial speaker or author.[28]

In short, authors are necessary for (semantic) meaning, but the authors can be constructed or hypothetical. Taken together, those conclusions suggest that the usual debates about legal interpretation—and the usual positions in those debates—might helpfully be reframed. The debates are not in reality about whether to equate textual meaning with authorial intentions, or about whether to get our meanings from authors or from some other source. Rather, they are about either or both of two somewhat different questions. First, *which author* should we look to in trying to discern the meaning of a legal text? And second, should a legal decision turn on what a text meant or means, or rather on other factors, such as what someone else—the public *then*, the public *now*, the Supreme Court?—*thought* the text meant (or thinks the text means)?[29]

What is often called "intentionalism" would make legal decisions turn on textual meaning and would equate legal meaning with the intentions of "the legislature," or perhaps "the legislators." (We will look briefly at the possible difference between legisla*tors* and legisla*tures* as authors in Chapter 6.) By contrast, the position often described as "textualism," as endorsed by self-proclaimed "originalists" such as Justice Scalia, can best be understood as claiming one or both of two things. First, the authoritative author whose semantic intentions are the source of meaning is someone like the "normal speaker of English."[30] Second, for legal purposes what controls is not the *actual* intentions of the author (whether real or hypothetical), but rather what competent speakers *at the time the text was enacted* would have understood this author to mean.[31] Though textualists may often embrace both claims (or conflate them), either seems capable of standing on its own—and of supply-

ing a coherent textualist position. So textualist assertions about meaning being "in the text" itself or in the "public understanding"—assertions that if
uncharitably considered might seem nonsensical, or else vestiges of primitive animism—can be taken as abbreviations for the position reflected by
one or both of these claims—a position that is neither nonsensical nor
animistic. (Whether the textualist position thus understood is attractive is
a question we can defer to the next chapter.)

Of course, if legislators are usually fairly conventional in their use of language, then one might expect that in practice intentionalism and textualism
would usually tend to converge: legislators, we would suppose, *are* "normal
speakers of English." But on rare occasions we might have evidence showing that legislators have used language in surprising or idiosyncratic ways,
perhaps by mistake.[32] So the debate between intentionalists and textualists
would be about whether, in these exceptional cases, legal meaning should
be determined by the semantic intentions of the actual legislators or, instead, of the hypothetical "normal speaker of English." Even if such cases
are rare, moreover, we could never be sure in advance whether a given
case falls into this category; so the difference between intentionalism and
textualism might also have important practical implications for whether, for
instance, it is helpful and proper for interpreters to consult legislative history—and for what purposes.

Still, the practical differences between intentionalism and textualism begin to seem rather tame. But, of course, these theories and their authorial
candidates—the actual legislators (or legislature) and the hypothetical "normal English speaker" (or would it be the "normal English-speaking legislator"?)—do not exhaust the possibilities. We can imagine all sorts of possible
authors for legal texts, ranging from the obtuse and the depraved to the
imaginative and noble, and situated in all sorts of times and places. This,
incidentally, is why once textual meaning is divorced from the semantic intentions of the historical author, or at least of some specified hypothetical
author, "deconstruction" or the demonstration of radical indeterminacy becomes child's play. You can *imagine* an author who might mean literally anything by a given utterance. You can even imagine, following a game that in
fact *is* literally a form of child's play, speakers using a language very much
like English except that "yes" means "no," "I will" means "I won't," and so
forth.

Some authors we might hypothesize would make texts "the best they can
be"—"best" according to a range of contestable criteria. Other hypothetical

authors might make texts "the worst they can be"; these more benighted authors might be useful for assigning meaning to texts we believe to derive from wicked or depraved sources.[33] Indeed, when engaged in polemics we routinely employ something like this "worst it can be" device in interpreting our opponents' texts. (I trust no one will adopt that technique with *this* text.)

Or, to mention just one not especially exotic possibility that some scholars find attractive: we might interpret legal texts as expressing the intentions of a hypothetical author who is a normal speaker of the language but who, unlike the hypothetical author implicit in Justice Scalia's textualism, is speaking *today* (or would it be yesterday?)—not in 1787 or 1868 or at the time the text was enacted. Alexander Aleinikoff in essence proposes such an author when he urges courts to "treat the statute *as if it had been enacted yesterday* and try to make sense of it in today's world."[34]

In sum, legal meaning depends on the (semantic) intentions of an author, but we have a broad array of choices about who that author will be. So it seems the real question is: "*Which* author?"

There is also a more worrisome question lurking in the background: "Will any of the authorial candidates be up to the job?" We take up these questions in the next chapter.

# CHAPTER 6

# *Author(s) Wanted*

In the previous chapter, we saw that the meaning of a legal text is equivalent to the semantic intentions of an author. Many theorists and jurists appear to deny this: consequently, debates about legal interpretation appear to pit "intentionalists" who equate the meaning of a statute with "legislative intentions" against "textualists" and other more exotic theorists who purport to separate meaning from authors' intentions. The preceding discussion has suggested, however, that this appearance is misleading. In fact, interpreting a text for its semantic meaning *always* involves a search for the semantic intentions of *some sort of author*. Even theories of interpretation that avoid explicitly featuring authors are still best understood as implicitly referring to some author—if not the "empirical author" (that is, the actual, historical person who wrote the text, such as a legislator or draftsperson), then a constructed or hypothetical author, such as Holmes's "normal speaker of English." So the real debate is not over *whether* to equate meaning with author's semantic intentions; it is over *which* author (or authors) to accept as "the author(s) of the law."

We can conceive of our inquiry, therefore, as a sort of job search. The position of "author(s) of the law" is open, and we are looking for an author or set of authors capable of filling that position. Not every author is equally serviceable for every authorial job: we would not employ a poet to write technical scientific reports, or a sports columnist to do obituaries. As with any job search, therefore, it is prudent to begin by reflecting on the nature of the position to be filled and previewing the leading applicants or candidates for the position. Having framed the search in this way, we can then get down to the hard business of considering which of the candidates, if any, might have the necessary qualifications.

## In Search of a (Qualified) Author

The position we are seeking to fill is, as noted, that of "author(s) of the law." That position is one with truly remarkable and audacious duties calling for a very special sort of author.

### The Job

So, what are the functions that an author of the law must perform? Though no simple job description is on file, we can notice some of the job's central responsibilities.

First, law provides "a framework for the citizen within which to live his life," as Lon Fuller put it,[1] and in doing so it allows citizens to *coordinate* their activities and decisions with others'. Second, as legal thinkers throughout the twentieth century emphasized, law *establishes policy* for society: it may attempt to mold and direct a society toward some happier or more prosperous or just condition. "The law of a community," Steven Burton suggests, "straightforwardly should be understood as the representation of a possible social world to be brought into empirical being by coordinated human action."[2] Third, law serves a *dispute resolution* function. "This doing of something about disputes," Karl Llewellyn observed, "this doing of it reasonably, is the business of law. . . . What . . . *officials do about disputes is, to my mind, the law itself.*"[3]

Among these tasks, "dispute resolution" may seem the most modest. The term conjures up images of petty landlord–tenant squabbles or the litigation of personal injury claims—messy matters that, while important to the people involved, seem mundane by contrast to law's social coordination and policy-setting functions. But in fact, dispute resolution is not just a dirty necessity; it is arguably the most majestic and even mysterious of law's roles. In the first place, the disputes can be momentous in their significance. Should George Bush or Al Gore be declared the winner in a close and disputed presidential election? Is a president impeachable for philandering with an intern and then prevaricating about his behavior under oath? Should giant computer or telecommunications companies be broken up, with all of the consequences (good and bad) that such a decision may have for consumers, employees, shareholders, and owners? Should a church that neglects to supervise abusive clergy be sanctioned with severe criminal or civil penalties?

All these controversies present disputes that, in our society, are resolved by appealing to the law.

Moreover, as we saw in Chapter 3, law attempts to resolve these disputes not in the pragmatic, down-to-earth way that, say, a mediator or a diplomat might use. In our legal system, that is, we typically do not simply take a hard look at the questions or disputes that arise and then work out a resolution or compromise that seems morally or pragmatically acceptable. Instead, we submit ourselves to "the rule of law," and thereby seek to answer such weighty questions in accordance with textual meanings—meanings that we say are authoritative or "binding." "It's really a shame we have to strike down this program (for, say, remedial education) that by consensus has done so much good and little if any harm," the Supreme Court says, with what almost sounds like genuine remorse, "but, alas, the law makes us do it."[4]

The law, in short, is entrusted with some truly daunting tasks. What qualifications would be needed for the author or authors who will give meaning to the law that tries to perform these tasks? Given the formidable nature of the job, it is hard to know where to begin. But we can briefly mention three qualifications that seem indicated, and then elaborate on these as our search progresses.

In the previous chapter we have already observed one qualification, which we can call "communicative capacity." More specifically, our author or authors must be capable of having and conveying a semantic intention. This is no light matter. The requirement may have seemed simple enough to satisfy when we were talking about ordinary communication: in the everyday ontology, persons have the capacity to "intend," and to have and convey semantic intentions. But when we come to large and diverse groups of persons—legislatures, for example—intention becomes more problematic.

Already implicit in this requirement (but for convenience we can break it out as a separate or corollary qualification) is what we might call a requirement of "intelligibility." It is no help that author can form a semantic intention, that is, if no one can figure out what that intention is. We all know of speakers or authors—particular poets or lyricists, perhaps, or philosophers or politicians, or even, alas, law professors—who utter words that sound as if they might be meaningful, or even profound or portentous, but that we simply cannot decipher. Such utterances may have their uses. They can sponsor gnostic movements, for example, in which an elite few who believe they have been initiated into a realm of esoteric meaning bask in the satisfaction of knowing that they stand apart from, and above, the rest of humanity. Not surprisingly, the academy is rich with such cryptic utterances and such movements. But because law is a practical and necessarily encompassing enterprise, its author or authors cannot afford to be profoundly or portentously inscrutable.

Finally, we can hardly rest content with just any old hack who is capable of communicating intelligibly: more is obviously required. For now, we might describe that more as "cogency." We want an author who will speak to our questions and needs, and who will do so thoughtfully and wisely. In setting social policy or in resolving an important dispute, in other words, we might defer to the advice of a person who has reflected seriously on a matter and who has sufficient wisdom to dispense meanings with enough political judgment and ethical content to elicit our respect. Conversely, we would not willingly defer to a game of chance, or a coin flip, or a configuration of stars—to phenomena that lack any capacity to think about the questions we might pose. Nor would we take authoritative guidance even from an undisputed sage who happened to be speaking to *someone else* about some question other than the one we need answered.

Probably there are other qualifications, but these are enough to get us started. We want an author with gifts of communicative capacity, intelligibility, and cogency. Are there any authorial candidates who meet these requirements?

## The Candidates

Let us have a quick preview of the leading candidates. We noted in Chapter 5 that once hypothetical or constructed authors are included, the pool of potential authors becomes almost limitless. We can organize and reduce the field, however, by lumping the candidates into two broad groups—we can call these "real" authors and "hypothetical" authors—and then by noticing what seem to be the leading candidates in each category.

REAL AUTHORS    In order to give meaning to law, we might choose a real author—one or more living, breathing human beings (or at least persons who at one time were living, breathing human beings). This is a large category, of course, potentially including several billion members. But we can narrow the field drastically by observing that only two subgroups seem to have any serious *prima facie* claim to the job; and one of these subgroups can be eliminated quite summarily. The first subgroup is that of *legislators* (which we can understand broadly to include enactors and drafters of all sorts—constitutional "framers" and "ratifiers," city council persons, and so forth). This group has an obvious claim: in our system legislators are elected, after all, precisely to enact law. So it is at least *prima facie* plausible to suppose that they should be the ones to give the meanings to the laws they enact. And of course one major position in the interpretation debates—often called "intentionalism"—advocates just this view.

A second, initially interesting group of candidates might include the *interpreters* of the law—meaning, primarily, judges. Indeed, a certain version of "reader response" theory would suggest that interpreters are of necessity the persons who give the law its meaning. The previous chapter criticized that view, but conceded that interpreters *could* act as the effective authors of the law, through a process that Paul Campos calls "reauthoring."[5]

Once we look past appearances, though, it seems that this group has no very plausible claim and no substantial supporting constituency. Proponents of judicial creativity, or "judicial activism," are plentiful enough, to be sure. But far from encouraging judges to reauthor law, these proponents nearly always insist that judges must be limited to interpreting the law—albeit in inventive or dynamic ways not dependent on the intentions of the historical enactors. Ronald Dworkin is exemplary in this respect. Dworkin is famous as an energetic proponent of an active judicial role in the manner of the Warren Court—and as a long-standing critic of "originalists" like Robert Bork. Indeed, Dworkin's conception of the judicial role often seems to border on the grandiose.[6] Dworkin also rejects a "speakers' meaning" theory of interpretation.[7] Nonetheless, Dworkin insists that judges must limit themselves to interpreting the law. Thus, in early writings Dworkin assailed the view (which he ascribed to H. L. A. Hart) that judges have the discretion to legislate when the meaning of positive law runs out;[8] and he has strongly criticized a "pragmatist" view that would encourage judges to use the materials of law—the precedents, statutes, and so forth—to make whatever decisions seem best according to their own notions of good policy.[9]

Other scholars or citizens, of course, hold pragmatism in higher esteem. And indeed Dworkin's disputes with Judge Richard Posner—probably the leading recent proponent of Legal Pragmatism—are well known. But Posner does not suggest that pragmatism should be carried out by instructing judges to reauthor legal texts adopted by legislatures. There are also a few scholars who would confer on judges an even more ample power than Dworkin allows to implement prescriptions derived directly from moral and political philosophy; but once again, this more exalted assignment contemplates *freeing* judges from the constraints of legal texts, not encouraging them to *reauthor* those texts.[10]

And indeed, it is hard to think of any good excuse for a system in which elected legislators and their aides draft, debate, mull over, scrutinize, and amend texts, after which these texts are then handed over to a wholly separate set of officials—such as judges—on the understanding that they will deliberately reauthor the texts to mean what they, the judges, would want the texts to mean. I say it is hard to imagine any excuse for such a system: it is not impossible. Suppose we are deeply distrustful of democracy, and sympathetic to a more aristocratic regime in which an educated elite (composed of, say, professors and judges) governs; but we find ourselves in a political community in which democratic commitments and assumptions are deeply entrenched. In this situation, we might favor a system in which elected officials enact texts—thus maintaining a facade of democracy calculated to appease the masses—but judges are then free to reauthor those texts to carry out their own intentions, thereby ensuring aristocratic governance. Critics of unpopular Supreme Court decisions or of judicial review in general often accuse our own regime of operating in pretty much this fashion,[11] and indeed it is arguable that the description fits. Still, I cannot think of anyone who *admits* to favoring such a position. And even if some people do tacitly favor it, its reauthoring dimension is still only a necessary evil, even for them; it is a desperate, dishonest expedient for disguising the fact of government by judiciary. On its own merits, reauthoring by judges has little or nothing to recommend it—either for those who love and trust judges or for those who don't.

Instead, the form of judicial activism that appears to enjoy substantial support insists that judges interpret the law, not reauthor it; but they should interpret in a creative fashion and not be confined to ascertaining the supposed intentions of the enactors. This position can be more accurately expressed by saying not that judges are elevated to being the authors of the law, but rather that they should construe the law in accordance with the intentions of some more idealized author other than the actual legislators. Thus, the position nominates for "author(s) of the law" *not* judges, but rather some more idealized author. (As we will see, this nomination is close to being explicit in Dworkin's writings.)

So it seems that among real authors, enactors are the only serious candidates. There are other possible real authors, of course. In theory, *I* might be chosen for the job. Or *you* might be. It could be anyone. We *could* treat the pertinent legal question, in other words, as something like "What would Woody Allen (or George Will, or Jesse 'The Body' Ventura, or whoever) mean if he uttered the words of the Fair Labor Standards Act, or the Robinson-Patman Act?" In one not so old case, a disputed issue regarding the meaning of the Federal Tort Claims Act was settled on the basis of a memorandum written by an obscure Justice Department attorney fifteen years before the law was actually enacted—even though, as Justice Stevens noted in dissent, "[t]here is no indication that any Congressman ever heard of the document or knew that it even existed."[12] But cases like this seem almost comical: their very wackiness serves to reinforce the point that other than legislators (or "enactors" generally), no real authors have any very plausible claim to be "author(s) of the law."

HYPOTHETICAL AUTHORS    If we turn to hypothetical or constructed authors, we have a wider range of potentially attractive choices. Indeed, we might seem to have the luxury—one we never have in actual job searches, or elections—of fashioning our ideal candidate.

But in fact, the candidates who get talked about the most seem to be characterized by one of two features: they are distinctive either for being extraordinarily ordinary or, conversely, for being exemplary. In other words, the leading candidates among hypothetical authors are, first, our old friend "the normal speaker of English," who is notable not for any special gift or insight but rather for being wholly free of linguistic idiosyncracies, and, second, the idealized lawmaker who is somewhat superior to—or perhaps vastly superior to—your average citizen or official. The first kind of candidate is obtained by *subtracting* from ordinary human beings. Thus, the "normal speaker" author is like real people except that he lacks our ability to use language in imaginative or creative or personalized ways: in that sense we might say he is a dull fellow, or even a bit less than human. The idealized author, by contrast, is constructed by *adding* some quality that ordinary people do not have, or by augmenting some quality beyond the normal level: the idealized author is more intelligent or virtuous or articulate than the typical citizen or official.

Theorists vary, of course, in how much wisdom or virtue they mix in to conjure this idealized author. In the 1950s, in their famous "Legal Process" materials, Henry Hart and Albert Sacks asked interpreters to imagine authors who are equal to, or at most just a little bit better than, the more respectable among the officials we actually see in government. We should construe statutes, Hart and Sacks thought, by assuming that "the legislature was made up of reasonable persons pursuing reasonable purposes reasonably."[13]

Ronald Dworkin is much more lavish in endowing his idealized author, reflecting his high aspirations for law and legal theory. A theory of law, Dworkin thinks, must account for "the moral authority of the law" by "provid[ing] a justification for the use of collective power against individual citizens or groups."[14] Moreover, Dworkin rejects the most familiar accounts of law's authority, such as the account that suggests that authority is based on some sort of actual or tacit consent of the citizens.[15] The alternative account he proposes is complicated: it involves imagining that we live in a "community of principle" in which collective legal decisions are not merely political compromises, but instead are consistently derived from "a single, coherent set of principles."[16] And this assumption in turn implies a unified author or legislator lurking behind the tangled mess that law appears to us to be. Thus, Dworkin's account "instructs judges to identify legal rights and duties, so far as possible, on the assumption that *they were all created by a single author*—the community personified—expressing a coherent conception of justice and fairness."[17]

Though Dworkin says little about this hypothetical "single author" of the law, his author is evidently possessed not only of the virtues of justice and fairness but also of the capacity to comprehend and render consistent the vast labyrinth of the law all at once. We can appreciate the magisterial scope of Dworkin's author by recalling the attributes of Hercules, Dworkin's hypothetical judge who is a sort of hermeneutical conversation partner for this ideal "single author." Hercules is a truly heroic figure who combines the philosophical aptitude of a Kant with the encylopedic knowledge of a Jacques Barzun and the integrity of a Thomas More. It would be wonderful to encounter such a paragon. Or perhaps not.

In any case, we have a range of authorial candidates to choose from—some real and some constructed, and ranging from the slightly less than human to the quasi divine. But do any of these candidates measure up? If we consider them in turn, we will see, I think, that although each has something to recommend it, each falls short in significant respects. Some of our authors may be suitable for law's more modest tasks. But when it comes to the more demanding functions, they all appear to suffer from one of more of three principal deficiencies. These deficiencies (which correspond inversely to the job qualifications we noted earlier) might be called the "problem of communicative incapacity," the "problem of inscrutability," and "the problem of misdirection."

## Real Authors and the Problem of Communicative Incapacity

We can start with the most promising and popular among the real author candidates—legislators (or, more broadly, "enactors"). As noted, this group has a strong point in its favor: it includes the people who were actually elected to make law. In a constitutional democracy, this is no mean recommendation.

Unfortunately, this candidacy promptly runs into a well-established (and essentially ontological) challenge asserting that the candidacy flunks the first and most basic requirement for the job—namely, the capacity to form and convey a semantic intention. *Legislative intention*, the familiar criticism argues, does not exist. In ordinary situations, a person communicates with one or more other persons. But with statutes there is no person to serve as speaker or author: legislatures are not persons. *Legislators* are persons, to be sure, but there is no recognized way of aggregating a host of different (and differently intending) legislators into a composite person capable of engaging in personal communication. Consequently, "legislative intention," as Max Radin declared in what may be the classic statement of the objection, is a "transparent and absurd fiction"—"an illegitimate transference to law of concepts proper enough in literature and theology."[18] Modern textualists such as Justice Scalia reiterate this criticism.[19]

Defenders of intentionalism try to answer the criticism, but their answers are only partially successful. We can consider two quite different strategies for defending legislative intentions. The bolder strategy responds to the criticism by asserting outright that a legislature *qua* legislature *can* form intentions that are not simply derivations from or aggregations of the intentions of individual legislators. The second, more modest strategy suggests that although only individual persons truly have intentions, these individual intentions can converge to form what we can properly call "collective intentions." I will suggest that the first strategy is implausible under prevailing ontologies. The second strategy is partially successful: it explains how legislative intentions can be said to exist in many contexts. Unfortunately, the "convergence" account is not helpful in supplying legal meanings responsive to the questions we care about and debate the most.

## Can Legislatures Intend?

The most direct answer to the challenge posed by critics like Radin and Scalia is to assert that groups—including legislatures—*can* have intentions separate from and not reducible to the intentions of the individual human beings who are members of those groups. I confess that I do not recall seeing this view advocated in legal literature[20] (though somewhere in the endless libraries of law review articles *someone* surely has taken this position). Ronald Dworkin may appear to suggest something akin to this view when he proposes that we think of "communities" as being committed to principles "in some way analogous to the way particular people can be committed to convictions or ideals or projects." But Dworkin concedes that this suggestion "will strike many people as bad metaphysics," and he hastens to clarify that what he is proposing is a sort of imaginative exercise in "personification" that treats a political community "*as if* [it] really were some special kind of entity distinct from the actual people who are its citizens."[21] The "as if" is crucial. "I do not suppose," Dworkin emphasizes, "that the ultimate mental component of the universe is some spooky, all-embracing mind that is more real than flesh-and-blood people, nor that we should treat the state or community as a real person with a distinct interest or point of view . . . of its own.[22] So Dworkin's "personification" exercise does not appear to endorse the possibility of what we might call "*real* group intentions."

I believe we can find a proponent, however, in a different and surprising quarter. In his effort to give an ontological account of social phenomena, John Searle contends that "collective intentionality" exists as "a primitive phenomenon," not reducible to or derivative of the intentions of individuals.[23] "No set of 'I Consciousnesses,' even supplemented with beliefs [about what other individuals intend], adds up to a 'We Consciousness,'"[24] Searle argues. Nonetheless, "We Consciousness" clearly exists. By this view, it would seem that a "legislature" might intend a particular meaning even though not all of the legislators—or a majority, or perhaps even one—had any such intent.

Searle's argument for this position is disarmingly direct. Many of our collective activities—Searle mentions playing football, performing in an orchestra, and prizefighting, but legislating might easily be added to the list—

depend on some sort of collective intention. And we do in fact engage in these activities. So it follows that collective intentions *must* exist. Moreover, although most people who have considered the matter have tried to derive collective intentions in some way from individual intentions, "all these efforts to reduce collective intentionality to individual intentionality fail." But if collective intentionality exists, and if it is not derived from individual intentions, then collective intentionality must exist as a primitive phenomenon.

Though the argument seems logical enough, it is nonetheless surprising, coming as it does close on the heels of Searle's contention that we noticed in Chapter 2—namely, that all phenomena must be explicable in terms of a scientific ontology dedicated to "a world made up entirely of physical particles in fields of force."[25] So how do these particles and force fields somehow add up to create collective intentionality as a "primitive phenomenon"? Searle notes that many thinkers have worried about this question, but he thinks their concern is needless.

> The argument is that because all intentionality exists in the heads of individual human beings, the form of that intentionality can make reference only to the individuals in whose heads it exists. So it has seemed that anybody who recognizes collective intentionality as a primitive form of mental life must be committed to the idea that there exists some Hegelian world spirit, a collective consciousness, or something equally implausible. . . . It has seemed, in short, that we have to choose between reductionism, on the one hand, or a super mind floating over individual minds, on the other.[26]

Searle asserts that this common way of framing the problem presents a false dilemma. But he does not actually explain where its error lies. The familiar anxiety that he notes but dismisses reflects a straightforward ontological proposition: so far as we understand, intentions exist in, or are a property of, minds. *Persons* have minds; therefore, persons have the capacity to intend. *Groups*, by contrast, do not have collective or group minds—or at least they are not treated as having minds in our usual ontologies, which at least in this respect Searle does not wish to challenge. So it is not apparent how groups can intend. Searle simply declares that collective intentionality exists, but he gives no account of how it exists, or of how it is real, or of how his quite limited inventory consisting of particles and forces could satisfy an ontological audit into the nature of collective intentions.

On reflection, this curious performance is perhaps not so surprising after all. Given the limited scientific ontology that Searle declares to be exhaustive and nonoptional, explaining collective intentionality is only one—and neither the first nor the foremost—in a whole host of seemingly insurmountable metaphysical challenges. It is hard enough—some would say impossible—to explain *individual* consciousness or intentionality in those reductive terms. As Searle elsewhere observes, "[w]e are at present very far from having an adequate theory of the neurophysiology of consciousness."[27] (Some theorists, such as Thomas Nagel, suggest that we will never have such a theory—that it is impossible in principle.)[28] Searle and similarly minded thinkers are thus forced to say that although science does not *yet* have anything like a full account of the affair—of consciousness, or belief, or mind—we can be confident that in principle such an account exists. We can be confident of this because . . . well, we *know* that mind and consciousness exist—as Searle has argued elsewhere, we have direct, first-person knowledge of these things[29]—and we also know (don't we?) that the scientific ontology of particles and forces is the complete and correct one. So it follows that there *must be*, in principle, a scientific account of mind (even if we do not yet have any inkling what such an account would look like). Right?

So not to worry. And having become accustomed to such casually spectacular leaps of faith (which would make even an Evel Knievel cringe), such a theorist will hardly find it embarrassing to say that something like collective intentionality exists—even if he has no intelligible account of it.[30]

For our purposes, by contrast, this situation supports a judgment not of falsity, exactly—we *do* seem to believe that collective intentionality exists in some sense, as Searle says—but of "nonsense" in the technical sense in which we have used the term in earlier chapters. So we should consider a less brash account of collective intentions that seeks to avoid that judgment.

### The Convergence Account of Collective Intentions

In an article defending what they call "expressivist" jurisprudence, Elizabeth Anderson and Richard Pildes address head on the problem of assigning semantic intentions—or, more generally, "states of mind"—to a collective agent. Anderson and Pildes thoughtfully defend the notion that a collective intention or mental state can exist, and can be more than an illusion or metaphor or fiction, as the familiar objection contends.

They begin by noting that in everyday conversation "we speak without puzzlement about social groups or collective actors having beliefs, emotions, attitudes, goals, and even characters." For example, "[p]eople say that the big tobacco companies knew they were lying when they denied that cigarettes are addictive; that Russia is angered at NATO's expansion plans; that rival gangs hate each other; that the Congressional Budget Office is trustworthy and nonpartisan."[31] The observation is surely correct, and it can easily be extended: people also *say* that "the government" decided to do such-and-such, or that "the legislature intended" this or that. But this observation is of little help. Such talk might be metaphorical. Or it might be nonsense. After all, critics of legislative intention like Max Radin and Justice Scalia have never denied that people commonly *talk* in these ways; such talk is precisely the target of their criticism, which suggests that this talk is careless, misconceived, or at best metaphorical.

But Anderson and Pildes go on to defend this common usage, explaining with some rigor the conditions in which it seems sensible and accurate (and not merely a loose, metaphorical "personification") to talk of collective mental states. They give a formal statement of these conditions: "A group, $G$, has a mental state $M$ if and only if the members of $G$ are jointly committed to expressing $M$ as a body."[32] Anderson and Pildes illustrate this possibility with examples of people self-consciously and by mutual understanding hiking *together* (as opposed to hiking unilaterally in close proximity to each other), cooking together, and shoveling snow together pursuant to a common agreement.[33] They explain that

> [w]hen groups share beliefs, they are often the product of successful conversational exchange. Suppose, while waiting for the bus, two people discuss whether the clouds in the sky threaten rain. One says, "Those clouds look like they are getting dark, so we'll be getting rain." The other replies, "No, they just look dark because the sun is setting." The first says, "Oh," nodding in agreement. This conversation establishes, through joint acknowledgment of the claim that the clouds do not indicate rain, a belief held by the conversation group.[34]

Having established the possibility of a collective mental state, Anderson and Pildes go on to argue that groups "can also share principles of actions, social norms, or conventions."[35] These groups might include "legislatures, political associations, or social groups."[36]

This analysis helpfully clarifies the idea of a collective mental state, which might include an intention such as a semantic intention or an intention to convey a particular meaning. Anderson and Pildes's analysis shows, I think, that legal meaning determined in accordance with legislative intention is in principle *possible*. The strong objection that would assert that such notions are *a priori* nonsensical, or that collective intentions or meanings are necessarily an illusion, is thus mistaken.

This is at least a valuable conceptual insight, I think; but the critic after the manner of Max Radin or Justice Scalia might well respond that as a practical matter this insight is largely beside the point. Granted that it is possible *in principle* for members of a legislature to reach a deep shared understanding in the way that two neighbors might: still, *how likely* is it that such a meeting of multiple minds will in fact occur? The more sensible construction of the familiar objection to legislative intent, perhaps, would interpret that objection as claiming not that legislative intention is impossible *a priori* or in the abstract—in theory, legislators *could* all agree on a single shared meaning for a law—but rather that in reality the convergence necessary for such an intention rarely occurs. And indeed, although Anderson and Pildes purport to extend their point about collective mental states to legislatures, social groups, and even "the democratic state," a close reading suggests that in fact they simply leave the analysis behind when considering these larger and more amorphous groups.

Thus, Anderson and Pildes make little effort to show that a legislature could *in fact* satisfy the conditions that they have so carefully specified—the conditions, that is, of their "members [being] jointly committed to expressing [a particular meaning] as a body"—or that these groups could engage in the "successful conversational exchange" attributed to partners in hiking, cooking, and shoveling snow. Instead, they promptly retreat to a different (and all too familiar) position—that we often treat laws *as if* they reflected some such collective intention. For example, they observe that "Congress has adopted various mechanisms, institutional structures, and conventions through which it understands itself to be manifesting its purposes"; consequently, members of Congress "are *deemed* to have accepted these mechanisms or structures by virtue of accepting their seats."[37]

Taken as an empirical proposition, this claim is contestable at best. In reality the "mechanisms" and "conventions" for ascribing meaning to enactments are far from being uniformly understood or accepted: on the contrary, they are hotly debated.[38] So any "deeming" that occurs will be a flimsy and artificial affair. Anderson and Pildes do not list the specific conventions, seemingly for good reason: any ostensible convention—for example, the erratically honored "conventions" that an ambiguous law means what its sponsor said it means, or what the committee report said it means—would be controversial, not settled or uniformly accepted.[39]

For present purposes, though, the more important point is that even if the "mechanisms" and "conventions" were settled, the resulting "constructive" mutual understandings and intentions (based on what members of Congress would be "deemed to have accepted") would still not be the *actual* mental states or intentions that Anderson and Pildes earlier seemed to be arguing for. Rather, they would be precisely the sort of fictional construction that critics like Radin have all along said they are. Thus, Anderson and Pildes's rigorous "if and only if" quickly lapses into the more licentious "as if."

But perhaps this retreat is premature. To be sure, critics of intentionalism have a heyday ridiculing the idea of convergence when the issue concerns the *motives* that led legislators to support a particular law. Justice Scalia's dissent in *Edwards v. Aguillard* provides a colorful instance. "Discerning the subjective motivation of those enacting the statute is, to be honest, almost always an impossible task," Scalia argues.

> The number of possible motivations, to begin with, is not binary, or indeed even finite. In the present case [of Louisiana's "balanced treatment" education act], for example, a particular legislator need not have voted for the Act either because he wanted to foster religion or because he wanted to improve education. He may have thought the bill would provide jobs for his district, or may have wanted to make amends with a faction of his party he had alienated on another vote, or he may have been a close friend of the bill's sponsor, or he may have been repaying a favor he owed the majority leader, or he may have hoped the Governor would appreciate his vote and make a fundraising appearance for him, or he may have been pressured to vote for a bill he disliked by a wealthy contributor or by a flood of constituent mail, or he may have been seeking favorable publicity, or he may have been reluctant to hurt the feelings of a loyal staff member who worked on the bill, or he may have been settling an old score with a legislator who opposed the bill, or he may have been mad at his wife who opposed the bill, or he may have been intoxicated and utterly unmotivated when the vote was called, or he may have accidentally voted "yes" instead of "no," or, of course, he may have had (and very likely did have) a combination of some of the above and many other motivations. To look for the sole purpose of even a single legislator is probably to look for something that does not exist.[40]

Scalia's criticism focuses on legislators' motives, but similar mockery is readily forthcoming if we ask about the purposes legislators attribute to a law: different legislators may have acted with a host of different objectives, hopes, and expectations.

It is crucial to recall, however, that the meaning of a law—or of any text, including a text written by a single author—is given not by the author's motives or purposes, but rather by his *semantic intentions*. The question is not what the author hoped to achieve, or why, but rather what the author *intended to communicate*. This seems a more tractable question, and one much more likely to support the requisite convergence among disparate legislators or enactors—a convergence, that is, of semantic intentions.

Suppose a bill introduced in Congress proposes to exempt the airline industry from age discrimination prohibitions by allowing compulsory retirement of pilots at the age of fifty-five. Legislators will disagree about whether this is a good or bad proposal. And even those legislators who decide to support the bill may do so for any or all of the types of varied motives described by Scalia. For similar reasons it might be difficult or impossible to find convergence on any *general purpose* for the law: some who voted "Aye" view it as safety legislation, while others may see it as an employment measure designed to open up jobs to younger pilots, and still others may see it as a small step toward a more general repeal of antidiscrimination legislation that they disfavor in principle. Despite these differences, it is plausible to suppose that the various legislators' semantic intentions have converged, at least to a significant extent: they understand that the law allows compulsory retirement of pilots who are fifty-six but not of pilots who are fifty-four, and so forth. On these matters, it is arguable that Anderson and Pildes's conditions for establishing a collective intent are satisfied.

So, does this reminder that meaning lies in semantic intentions—not in motives or general purposes—show that an intentionalist approach nominating actual legislators for the role of "authors of the law" is viable after all? The answer, it seems, is "It depends." The convergence account shows, I think, that the notion of "legislative intention" is not inherently nonsensical, as critics sometimes argue. Legislative intention is ontologically possible *in principle,* and it should often be possible in practice as well. Indeed, the notion seems largely unproblematic so long as we are thinking about textual provisions such as "the age of fifty-five": legislators might well converge in their semantic intentions expressed in such phrases.

But if we move to more abstruse language—"contracts in restraint of trade," or "due process of law," or "equal protection of the laws"—the likelihood of meaningful semantic convergence quickly vanishes. It is more plausible to suppose, with measures like these, that legislators had quite different semantic intentions or understandings—or perhaps, in some cases, none at all; they might have had no clear notion what the provision they enacted was supposed to mean. Historical research into, say, the origins of the Fourteenth Amendment can sometimes provoke this suspicion. So if the question is posed, "What did the enactors mean by these words?" the best answer may well be "They didn't."

Note that the difference here is not between statutory and constitutional provisions, but rather between those expressions that are precise enough, realistically, to support a convergence of semantic intentions and those that are not. Many statutes have a great deal of broad or abstract language; conversely, the Constitution has many relatively precise provisions (such as the provision that every state gets to elect two senators—not one, not three, but *two*). The difference is obviously one of degree. But the point—hardly a shocking one—is simply that for some statutory or constitutional language it seems plausible to suppose a convergence of relatively definite semantic intentions, and for other statutory or constitutional provisions this supposition is *not* plausible.

Both halves of the point are important. The first is crucial because it explains how, for a host of everyday legal matters that no one would think to litigate, the "legislative intention" account of legal meaning works tolerably well. Cars should drive on the right-hand side of the road; tax returns should be filed by April 15; and so on. Frederick Schauer lists a host of "easy" constitutional cases where the rules seem perfectly clear.[41] For these matters, which compose a large part of law's coordination function, legal meaning presents no deep mysteries. "Legislative intention" seems a perfectly serviceable notion, and fancy Derridean challenges seem the work of slightly deranged academics with too much time on their hands. A scholar wonders, perhaps, whether the constitutional provision specifying that the President must be at least thirty-five just *might* mean that the President can be a teenager but cannot have acne. (As Dave Barry says, I am not making this up.)[42] And of course we *can* imagine a world in which the provision would mean this (just as we can imagine a world in which the provision would mean anything at all.) But the practical lawyer will see no need to engage with this sort of objection. "The law doesn't mean that in *this world*," she will observe—or perhaps, less diplomatically, "Get a life!"[43]

But of course the controversial and difficult legal questions that result in legal disputes tend to arise precisely in those cases where no such semantic convergence has occurred, and where there is consequently no intent of the legislature that can be said to exist in any ontologically plausible sense. Such cases may represent only a small fraction of the matters that arise under the law. Indeed, the answers to many legal questions may seem so clear that the questions do not perceptibly arise at all.[44] But the instances of indeterminacy constitute a large percentage of the cases that legal scholars devote their attention to (and also of the cases that reach the Supreme Court).

We can still talk about legislative intent in these cases if we like. But there is no actual legislature, or collection of legislators, possessed of the communicative capacity needed to resolve the case. So if we nonetheless appeal to legislative intention, it seems we must be invoking a fiction, or a stand-in for something (or someone) else.

But for what (or whom)? For these "hard cases," it seems we need to look for a new, different author.

So crank up the job search again.

## Hypothetical Authors: Can a Fictional Figure Do the Job?

The new author we are looking for will likely be hypothetical. Who else is there? And on first reflection, hypothetical authors offer wonderful possibilities: we can fashion them, it seems, to be whatever we want or need. So we can easily endow a hypothetical author with the capacity to form and convey a semantic intention: the perplexities that have afflicted the concept of "legislative intention" are thus waved away with a stroke of the jurist's or law professor's wand (or with a click of the mouse). In addition, we might decide to avoid other difficulties with real legislators that we have not so far considered but that are obvious enough. Real legislators are all too often thoughtless, or foolish, or corrupt. In constructing a hypothetical author we can easily replace these qualities with virtue, wisdom, and integrity.

Initially, therefore, the possibility of interpreting law according to the intentions of a hypothetical author seems almost a panacea. It seems almost too good to be true. And it is. On further reflection, this strategy provokes an obvious and rudely uninspired complaint: What good is a *hypothetical* author for a *real* job? To be sure, we can imagine an exquisitely qualified author—just as we can imagine a perfect presidential candidate, or a perfect dean, or an ideal marriage partner. And there is no harm, perhaps, in occasional innocent day-dreaming. But when someone starts to treat these phantoms as if they could do real work or meet real needs . . . well, we know what to do with such people, don't we? Remember *A Beautiful Mind* (the movie version)? So why should a sustained lapse into "as if" fantasy, which might ordinarily call for therapy or even commitment to an institution, be regarded as worthy of the highest jurisprudential respect when it occurs in law?

This is not a purely rhetorical question; and indeed I think there is even a partial answer, though it is one that supports only a relatively modest role for law. First recall that hypothetical authors fall into two main categories. One sort is obtained by *subtraction* from the qualities of ordinary people and is a slightly lesser-than-life figure. The other is created by *addition* to ordinary human qualities and is morally or cognitively superior to—perhaps, as in Dworkin's theorizing, vastly superior to—ordinary mortals. These different types of authors raise different types of concerns.

### The Virtues—and Limitations—of (Sub-)Normalcy

Consider first the slightly less-than-human figure—the "normal speaker of English"—who is uncannily like the people we live and work with every day except a bit more boring. She has, we might say, no personality: at least in her legal incarnation, she never jokes, or speaks ironically, or indulges in imaginative or creative or idiosyncratic uses of language. How does this person measure up against the job requirements we noted at the outset—the requirements of communicative capacity, intelligibility, and cogency?

By hypothesis the normal English speaker meets the first two requirements: indeed, the ability to communicate intelligibly is her very essence, and the reason and measure of her creation. But she is not likely to be of much help when disputes over textual meaning arise. Suppose, to revert to the standard example of the "no vehicles in the park" ordinance, that one lawyer says, "Skateboards *are* 'vehicles'" while another insists, "No they're *not*." If we ask what the normal speaker of English would mean, these antagonistic claims will merely reassert themselves. ("She'd say they *are* 'vehicles.'" "Oh no she wouldn't.")

In fairness to this speaker, we should acknowledge that she was not called into existence to answer *that* sort of question. Rather, she was concocted for a different purpose—to avoid the injustices that might flow from deferring to "the idiosyncrasies of the writer," as Holmes put it.[45] The normal speaker, in other words, was created for the sort of situation in which most of us would use words in a particular way—so we agree on what the *usual meaning* of text would be—but we also have reason to suspect that the contracting parties or the actual legislators may have used words in a more idiosyncratic or perhaps more devious way.

To embellish on an example from Robert Bork,[46] suppose a historian were to discover a letter from George Washington to Martha, written from Philadelphia while George was presiding over the constitutional convention, and explaining that the delegates were writing the Constitution in a code that could only be deciphered with the help of a translating key that would be buried in Roger Sherman's back yard. It is not hard to list excellent reasons why this secret or private intention should not be taken as establishing the authoritative legal meaning of the Constitution. And the normal speaker serves to prevent any such surprising construction. We can say to the framers: "Whatever meanings *you* may have intended, the normal speaker would not use these words to convey any such meanings; and consequently the normal *reader* would not get any such meaning from the text. Normal usage controls—not your private intentions."

So the normal speaker serves to avoid this (rather far-fetched) danger. In reality, of course, the normal author's semantic intentions will usually coincide with those of actual legislators, who after all do not typically write law in secret codes. So in their practical consequences, what are called "intentionalism" and "textualism" (which is best understood as refering to the semantic intentions of the "normal speaker" author as understood by normal speakers of the time)[47] will usually tend to converge: that is no doubt why originalists have been able to slide so easily from the former view to the latter one.[48] Understood in this way, textualism is little more than a modification of intentionalism adapted to satisfy "rule of law" values such as publicity, intelligibility, predictability, and consistency.

The "normal speaker" author is thus well suited to supply meanings for all of those rules in which, as we say, it matters less what the rule is, exactly, than that there be a clear rule. It does not matter much which side of the road drivers use—the right side or the left—but it matters tremendously that there be a clear rule on the subject. The normal speaker gives us that rule— or at least prevents it from being subverted by private or secretive legislative intentions. In sum, this excessively ordinary and even less-than-human hypothetical author may serve some of law's more modest (though still tremendously important) functions—in particular the coordination function.

Conversely, the normal speaker has no apparent qualification to perform law's more ambitious functions. There is little to recommend her, for in-stance, as an agency for establishing social policy. Nor is the normal speaker of English an auspicious candidate to turn to in the case of hard or high-level disputes—for example, if we are considering the proper grounds for im-peaching the President, or declaring the winner in a disputed presidential election, or determining the civil or criminal liability of a church in a sexual abuse case. The very fact that the law is hotly disputed in such cases suggests that what the normal speaker has to say on these questions is not enough to resolve the differences in interpretation. And at that point, asking "What would the normal speaker mean by this provision?" (or, more deceptively, "What does this text *really* mean?") seems obtuse. The normal speaker, if we could find her and ask her, would evidently say something like "I'm not sure. I never really thought about that." And even if we could wheedle an answer out of her, there is no apparent reason why we should care what she thinks on this sort of contested issue.

For these more challenging functions, it seems, our practice of resolving disputes or setting policy on the basis of what "the law requires" makes sense only on the supposition of an author with more impressive qualities of mind than the normal speaker possesses—or perhaps than we ourselves possess. We need for these purposes not just any old normal speaker, but rather an exemplary author for the law. We need a paragon, or at least a sage; or at the very least we need a few "reasonable persons pursuing rea-sonable purposes reasonably."

### The Idealized Author and the Problem of Inscrutability

Given the need for an idealized author, it is perhaps not surprising that legal theorists have offered us such a figure. Indeed, as noted, they have proposed an assortment of exemplary authors. But these more idealized authors pro-voke the objection noted earlier: "It would be wonderful if we had such an author for the law: but *we don't*. And a merely fictional author isn't much help."

This objection covers two related but independent criticisms. The first can be presented in the form of a dilemma. The idealized author, especially when significantly enhanced as in Dworkin's account, is by hypothesis wiser and more articulate than we are. But how then are we supposed to know what this author would have meant by a legal text? One possible answer is simply, "We can't." But there is another response, along these lines: "*Of course* we can know that this author would intend. After all, we created him. So he will intend whatever we say he intends." But this response, by reducing the fictional author's intentions to those that we project onto him, forfeits the advantage of wisdom superior to our own. Indeed, making decisions by "interpreting" a text according to the intentions of a hypothetical author who says whatever we tell him to say seems a bizarre charade: it is a lot like the child's exercise of constructing an imaginary friend who must be consulted before any decision can be made. ("Do I want to go to the zoo? Well, *I* think it sounds fun, but I have to ask Jane. Jane, do we want to go to the zoo?. . . . Jane says 'yes.'")

So the dilemma is this: it appears that either we can conjure an author whose sagacity transcends our own but which for that very reason is also beyond our ken, and thus is not intelligible to us (so what would be the point?); or else we can construct an author who is intelligible but no wiser than we are (so what would be the advantage?). The more worthy of deference our hypothetical author is, the less accessible he becomes (and vice versa). Either way, he is of little help either in resolving hotly disputed questions or in fashioning policy for our society.

Indeed, a similar objection applies to an author whom we believe to be real but absent. "What would Mother say?" Or WWJD: "What would Jesus do?" Such questions may be useful in provoking us to think about a problem seriously or in a different light, or in motivating us to act in accordance with our better natures, as we say. But in the end they cannot convey any wisdom we do not already have. I may assume that Jesus would always do "the right thing," or that Mother would always say to do the right thing, but by hypothesis I do not know what "the right thing" is in a particular situation: that is why I am asking the question. So I simply don't know what Jesus would do or what Mother would say to do. In the same way, if we imagine an author for the law whose wisdom exceeds our own, or whose semantic intentions are superior to ours, then by hypothesis we cannot know what this author would have meant by a particular expression or text. We can only project our own intentions onto that author.

## The Ideal Author and the Problem of Misdirection

Suppose, though, that we somehow find a way around this objection: we create an ideal author, wiser than ourselves, but we also find a way to ascertain this author's thoughts (perhaps through the sort of philosophical inquiry advocated by Dworkin). Now a new objection arises: if we could actually gain access to the wisdom of some such superior being, then it would seem that we ought to pose our questions to her or him *directly*—our questions about social policy or social justice or about how to resolve a difficult dispute—rather than asking the altogether different question of what this idealized author *would mean* by legal texts that have come to us through a different process and from less exemplary historical authors. Indeed, *that* question seems to misdirect our inquiry along an irrelevant tangent.

Thus, we can imagine how the hermeneutical dialogue might unfold:

*Us:* We have a case, O sagacious Author, under the provision of the Sherman Act that prohibits all contracts "in restraint of trade." What do (or did?, or would?) you mean by these words, O Author?

*Ideal Author: I* don't, and didn't, and wouldn't mean *anything* by them. I never wrote those words at all.

*Us:* We know you didn't actually write them. They were written by some nineteenth-century congressmen who weren't too swift when it came to economics. But what would you have meant if you *had* written them.

*Author: I wouldn't* have written them. To me, the whole provision seems very clumsily designed. Why don't you people just forget that silly law—ignore it, or repeal it, or whatever—and start over?

*Us:* Well, it's pretty widely acknowledged that the provision wasn't carefully thought out. You definitely have a point there. But a statute like this is hard to amend. And it's *the law*—meaning that as long as it stays on the books, we're bound by it. So this is what we're stuck with for now. And so we still need to know: What would you have meant, O ideal Author, if you had written these words?

*Author:* What kind of inane question is this? If you want my counsel on whether Microsoft or AT&T should be broken up, I'll be pleased to tell you. Or, for a nominal fee, I can give you some good advice about antitrust policy in general. In fact, I have a really nifty theory about monopolies, based on the latest research in microeconomics. But what I can't fathom is why you keep asking *what I would have meant by words I never wrote*—and never would write. The question makes no sense.

In short, construing law according to the understanding or intentions of a hypothetical author, even one possessed of extraordinary wisdom and whose understanding we can somehow tap into, seems simply to be a misdirected kind of inquiry. The question has no cogency: it does not solicit the guidance of any act of mind directed to the real controversies or questions of policy we are seeking to address.[49]

### A Dose of Cynicism?

The argument given here may strike the more hardened reader as entirely too ingenuous. Was I born yesterday? Isn't it clear what is really happening? According to the cynical view, the ideal author to whom some interpreters ostensibly appeal (if not explicitly, then by talking about a law's general "purpose" or implicit "principle," or about a "living Constitution") is in reality just a sort of mannequin for the interpreter himself or herself. "Interpreting" judges, or "interpreting" scholars, are using the words that have come down to us in the Constitution or in statutes to advance their own visions of what is just and good: they simply bend the words to fit their own political or philosophical agenda. The interpreter "puts a meaning into the text as a juggler puts coins . . . into a dummy's hair," as Roscoe Pound commented, "to be pulled forth presently with an air of discovery."[50] Certainly the creative interpretations that Ronald Dworkin has offered over the years for various statutes and constitutional provisions do nothing to dispel the suspicion that they are merely artful presentations of Dworkin's own political or philosophical commitments.[51]

The cynic might go on to suggest that the question we constantly ask—What does this law mean?—is not misdirected, exactly; its real direction and import—that is, its tacit appeal to the judgment of the interpreter himself—has merely been disguised. And our practice of resolving difficult questions by purporting to "interpret" statutes or constitutional provisions is not nearly as crazy or mindless as the preceding discussion may have suggested. The practice is just more complicated—more sophisticated and, yes, a bit more disingenuous—than we have been supposing.

But in fact we have not ignored this possibility. On the contrary, we have already considered it in connection with the proposal that judges or other interpreters should "reauthor" law. And as we saw, this is a position that has few if any open supporters—and little to recommend it. The best that can be said for such a reauthoring practice is that sometimes deception—"noble lies," if you like—might be useful in the service of valuable ends.

Whether that observation is plausible is something we need not worry about for our purposes, because even if this sort of deception is practicable or morally desirable, it is not in itself a jurisprudence. The deceptive presentation is still necessarily parasitic on some other, more primary process of *interpretation*, or at least of *decisionmaking*—some more primary process that the deception serves to conceal. So we might concede, for purposes of argument anyway, that the cynical view is descriptively accurate, and even (though this is more of a stretch) normatively attractive. With respect to the most central normative questions of law and jurisprudence—How *should* controversial disputes for which there is no predetermined answer be resolved? How *should* social policy be established?—the cynical view offers no answer.

### A Failed Search?

Our search has considered what appear to be the leading candidates for "author(s) of the law" but has produced no authors that seem suitable for a very demanding job. Some of the candidates appear qualified to perform some of law's more modest functions. Thus, either the actual legislators (converging as the legislature) or the "normal English speaker" seem capable of providing the meanings needed for law's basic coordination function. Insofar as what we want, in other words, is simply rules that are basically sensible and that are clear enough to guide the ordinary practical business of life, either of these authors seems adequate to the job. Indeed, these authors turn out in practice to be almost interchangeable, though the hypothetical normal speaker has perhaps a slight edge because she is by definition indisposed to harbor any sort of private or idiosyncratic meanings.

If we were content to limit law to these basic coordination functions (which could of course include punishing people for violating norms deemed important enough to be supported with criminal sanctions), these authors would seem to meet our needs. Not surprisingly, therefore, these *are* the authors to whom we often resort.

The problem, though, is that we are not content with a law that sets and enforces coordinating rules. If we were, then whenever a question arises for which no reasonably determinate rule exists, we would have a simple answer: "Sorry. No law on that one." At that point the issue could be dismissed, or turned over to the legislature (or perhaps delegated to the courts, deliberately commissioned to act as a legislature), or relegated to whatever default position or institution we might choose to defer to. A great deal of the law would no doubt still exist, and courts would still have a mass of business (in resolving *factual* disputes, for example); but the litigation of *legal* issues would be greatly reduced.

Most of the constitutional disputes that capture our attention, for example, would be transformed—expelled from the domain of legal issues. Did Bill Clinton's misconduct satisfy constitutional requirements for impeachment? Can a macho military educational institution dedicated to what is euphemistically called the "adversative" method admit only men? Is there a right to abortion? Or to the assistance of a physician in ending one's life? These questions would seemingly all have received the same answer: "No law on that one." Supreme Court justices would have a lot more time for reading or golf. Constitutional law casebooks, which in their current form can cause crippling injury if you are unfortunate enough to drop one on your foot, would be reduced to virtual pamphlets.

In fact, we *are* comfortable with approximately this sort of approach in many contexts. In families, in universities, in law firms, in associations of various types, we are often presented with matters about which we say, simply, "There isn't any rule covering that." So we either leave the matter to the individuals involved to work out, or else we self-consciously create a new rule for the situation.

But we have not been content with this sort of modesty in our law. Important questions such as those listed above arise, and it becomes clear that the only answers furnished by any genuine convergence of semantic intentions of enactors or by the normal speaker of English speaking through the statutory or constitutional text would be something like "We didn't think about it" or "I don't know." We nonetheless insist that interpreters proceed to tell us "what the law means"—or "what the law is"—on the subject. (This, by the way, is why analogies commonly made by legal scholars to other rule-governed activities—baseball and chess seem especially popular—are of limited relevance: we make no equivalent demands of those activities.)

For these more demanding functions, it seems, we need some author or authors beyond the usual candidates. But where might such an author be found? Or, if no such author is available, what should we conclude about the nature of the activity in which as lawyers, scholars, or even citizens we are all involved?

## The Classical Account Revisited

Would the classical account of law, briefly presented in Chapter 3, be more successful in addressing these problems? We are by now far removed, of course, from times in which such an account could be presented openly and discussed respectfully. For many of us, the classical account is a distant memory; for others it is not even that. So perhaps all we can confidently say is that the classical account, if it were admissible and believable, *might* be of some help.

As discussed in Chapter 3, the understanding of law broadly shared in different forms by thinkers from Aquinas to Fortescue to Coke to Blackstone posited a sort of dual authorship for law. Law's ultimate author was God, whose providential plan for the cosmos constituted what Aquinas described as an "eternal law," and all law—human and divine—derived its legal character from that law. But what we would call "positive law" comes into being only as it is promulgated by human legislators. Moreover, very little of the detailed content of positive law can be "read off" of the eternal law; the content is given, rather, by the decisions of human legislators. So those mundane authors supply the substance of the law that serves, for example, the function of coordination. But the law is also connected to a higher or deeper source of meaning through its underlying, divine authorship. So the partnership between law's dual authors just might provide both the clarity given by normal speakers—clarity needed for law's coordination function—and the deeper wisdom provided by a greater-than-human author that might justify deference to law in resolving our most important and difficult issues.

There are many assumptions here, of course—that a transcendent author exists, that this author has actually promulgated an eternal law, that human beings can have at least qualified access to this transcendent code, and that the pronouncements of this superhuman author can actually be integrated with those of the human, all-too-human legislators who make positive law. Are these assumptions believable today? For many, the answer is straightforward: No. "As long as law was felt as something ordained of god," Karl Llewellyn observed, "or even as something inherently right in the order of nature, the judge was to be regarded as a mouthpiece, not as a creator; and a mouthpiece of the general, who but made clear an application to the particular." But this classical view of law, we now understand, was nothing but "superstition."[52] Or at least, thus spake Llewellyn.

It is understandable that modern thinkers would reject this view of law. It does not square with modern metaphysical assumptions that dominate the academy; and it probably does not square very comfortably with the way most religious believers view the world either. Still, there is an uncanny resemblance between the classical account and the jurisprudence of, say, Ronald Dworkin. In Dworkin's account, as noted, law is likewise conceived to be the product of a "single author" whose legal outpourings form a single "coherent set of principles." Those principles are just and fair, justifying the use of force in their implementation. So it seems that the classical account, though long discarded, echoes still in modern jurisprudential thought.

The difference, of course, is that in the classical account the law's transcendent author was taken to be real, while in the modern account that author is understood to be a fiction—"as if." And that observation brings us back to the familiar question: What is the good of a superhuman author who is merely fictional?

Suppose your baseball team is struggling, largely because of pitching problems. The team's owner proposes that what you need is someone who can throw 100 mph fastballs with pinpoint accuracy; and when you observe that unfortunately no such pitcher is available in the free agent market this year, the owner responds, "I know that. I'm not stupid. But we can play 'as if' we had such a pitcher." The proposal would be laughable. So why do analogous proposals produce not howls of laughter but rather furrowed brows and pensive strokings of chins when offered by, say, an Oxford professor of jurisprudence?

In short, we face a dilemma. The authorial candidates who are actually available seem grossly underqualified to perform the weightiest functions we ask law to perform. We can fantasize an author who *would* be qualified to perform these functions but, alas, that kind of author does not seem to be available. This is (or at least it is one way of describing) law's quandary.

# PART IV

# Mind the Gap

For us, in our time and place, law persists in an ontological gap. The gap can be described in different ways. Part 2 suggested that our discourse and practices—our law-talk and what we do with that talk—routinely and pervasively presuppose commitments to (and often explicitly invoke) something like "the law" of the classical account. Confronted with these apparent commitments, however, we profess not to believe in any such thing. We are compelled to that profession, almost, because "the law" —the "brooding omnipresence in the sky" of Holmes's derision—does not square with either the everyday ontology or the scientific ontology that people in academic settings regard as axiomatic, at least for professional purposes. So our talk and practice make sense, if at all, only on assumptions that we feel compelled, or at least obligated, to disavow.

Part 3 described the gap in different terms. The practice of law pervasively involves soliciting "meanings" from legal texts, and those meanings presuppose authors—not necessarily the flesh-and-blood authors who actually wrote the texts, but at least hypothetical or constructed authors. Moreover, not just any authors will be qualified to fulfill the lofty functions we assign to law; for those functions we need authors who can satisfy requirements of communicative capacity, intelligibility, and cogency. But no such authors appear to be available—not, at least, for law's more pretentious functions.

The classical account, which supposed a sort of working partnership between a divine author and human legislators, *might* have been able to meet the requirements—from our vantage point it is hard to say—but once again, that account has been widely rejected by modern legal thinkers as mere "superstition," as Karl Llewellyn said. So it seems we have been reduced, as in Ronald Dworkin's jurisprudence, to *pretending* that we have an "as if" author possessing the requisite qualifications while denying any actual belief

155

in the substantial existence of such an author. Once again, the ontological assumptions that we presuppose in our daily talk and practice do not square with the ontological assumptions that we are willing to affirm.

This disjunction—between what we presuppose and what we profess to believe (or *not* to believe) is reflected in the quirky combination of skeptical sophistication and apparent naivete that lawyers and legal scholars so often exhibit regarding the ontological status of "the law." As noted, if the issue is raised in a context calling for critical self-consciousness, lawyers and especially legal scholars will scoff at the notion that "the law"—an entity exhibiting some of the qualities of a "brooding omnipresence"—somehow exists. But then the conversation changes ("Did the Fifth Circuit get the law right in *Smith v. Jones?*" or "Does section five of the Fourteenth Amendment authorize Congress to expand constitutional rights?") and these same worldly wise skeptics will immediately launch into earnest arguments that make no apparent sense except on the presupposition that "the law" *does* exist. Or the lawyers will mock "legal formalism" and recite that "we are all realists now," but they go on writing briefs or opinions or articles that sound for all the world like the work of formalists; and then if a critic raises antiformalist objections, they will yawn and say, "We all understand that. Please don't be patronizing."

So what are we to make of this peculiar situation? That is the question addressed in this part of the book.

# CHAPTER 7

# Law in a Quandary

On the eve of the twentieth century, as we have seen, Oliver Wendell Holmes was sure that law was on the verge of a new era. Reform—radical reform—was inevitable: it was inconceivable that law-talk could continue in the archaic modes that it had adopted in an earlier time ruled by a wholly different worldview. Since Holmes, veritable legions of legal thinkers have echoed this assessment. And, thus far, they have been wrong. More than a century later, lawyers and judges and even legal scholars talk largely in the same vocabulary and tacitly operate on the same jurisprudential assumptions that they have been using for decades and even centuries. "The traditional conception of law is as orthodox today," Holmes's most faithful jurisprudential heir laments, "as it was a century ago."[1]

How have we come to this pass? And how should we understand the peculiar persistence of conventional law-talk, and of the ontological gap in law that has appeared over and over in these pages? This chapter considers four different (though not mutually exclusive) interpretations of our predicament. Any or all of them may contain a measure of truth; taken together, those measures of truth might add up to a satisfactory account of our situation.

Or perhaps not.

## The "Survival" Interpretation

Perhaps the most obvious and common explanation of the persistence of conventional law-talk suggests that lawyerly discourse as we continue to practice it is a holdover, or a "survival," from an earlier era when that discourse made sense in terms of prevailing assumptions about reality. So lawyers are like erstwhile religionists who, though they have lost their primitive faith, still instinctively cross themselves, or utter traditional prayers, or engage in other forms of religion that made sense under beliefs they formerly held. Just as these neophyte nonbelievers persist in certain religious practices out of *habit*, conventional law-talk continues on the strength of *tradition*.

Thus, in his "Path" essay, Holmes attributed much of what he found nonsensical in law to a lingering—and lamentable—traditionalism. A little later, Felix Cohen described the "Restatement" project as "the last long-drawn-out gasp of a dying tradition."[2] In a similar vein, though from a very different religious and jurisprudential perspective, Harold Berman proposes a similar "survival" interpretation. "Western legal science is a secular theology," Berman explains, "which often makes no sense because its theological presuppositions are no longer accepted."[3]

For all of its initial plausibility, however, this explanation of our situation gradually depletes its credibility as the decades pass and conventional legal discourse retains its vigor. For Holmes, the classical worldview in which conventional law-talk had its home was a fresh memory: prominent professors at Harvard, where he had studied and later taught, had self-consciously defended that position in one version or another.[4] So the demise of the classical worldview was recent—or still in progress—and it was hardly surprising that a legal discourse grounded in that framework would persist for a period.

A century later, though, this explanation seems more suspect. If conventional law-talk is a holdover, it is surely a tenacious one. Indeed, far from withering away, legal discourse has in recent decades not only maintained itself but expanded its jurisdiction, as more and more areas of life have been subjected to the governance of the law: developments under the Warren Court (such as the expanded application of "due process") can be offered here as "Exhibit A."[5]

Thomas Kuhn has famously observed, to be sure, that even a struggling or decrepit "paradigm" will be maintained until a new and better paradigm emerges.[6] But this observation cannot account for the persistence and even expansion of a legal discourse grounded in an older, rejected worldview, because in fact other paradigms *are* available. For example, there is the "policy" paradigm proposed by Holmes and developed with increasing sophistication by countless legal thinkers ever since. To put the point differently: we *can* readily imagine other, more obviously sensible ways to resolve disputes and to make important decisions. Legal thinkers from Holmes to the Legal Realists to (leaping forward in time) Bruce Ackerman and Richard Posner *have* imagined and elaborated other decisionmaking approaches that square better with prevailing assumptions about the world, and about what rationality would mean in our sort of world. Moreover, in other fields and disciplines and in many areas of life, we routinely employ other methods— nonlegalistic forms of practical reason, such as straightforward cost–benefit analysis—for making decisions. These methods are so familiar and attractive, in fact, that law's peculiar methodology and discourse often seem, as Cass Sunstein says, "weird or exotic."[7]

Nonetheless, this weird or exotic discourse persists—and is used to resolve many of the most important issues both of our personal lives and, even more so, of our public life. *Perhaps* its persistence reflects a clinging to tradition. But the dogged resilience of that tradition suggests that there is something more at work here—something that infuses continuing vitality into the tradition.

## The "Bad Faith" or Idolatry Interpretation

So what might that something more be? One possibility, presented by different thinkers in different ways, is that law has come to serve as a resource for satisfying our personal and collective needs for meaning and spirituality. Religion, it is often observed, is not merely a set of dry propositions about the world: it is a response to a human need for transcendent meanings. If religion is rejected, this need nonetheless persists, and it will strive to find satisfaction elsewhere. "There is in all men a demand for the superlative," Holmes wrote, and that demand is so inexorable that "the poor devil who has no other way of reaching it attains it by getting drunk."[8] Dostoevsky had earlier made the same point in explicitly religious terms: "Man cannot exist without bowing before something. . . . Let him reject God, and he will bow before an idol."[9]

No doubt the intensity of this "demand for the superlative" varies from person to person. And of course, the substitute for religion need not be law. It might be almost anything. A. N. Wilson's engaging history of nineteenth-century atheism is among other things a story about how converts to the brave new atheistic worldview projected their religious needs and passions onto other objects, of varying plausibility and dignity. Sometimes the projections could be almost comical—or pathetic. For example, reflecting on John Stuart Mill's extravagant claims asserting the surpassing intellectual and aesthetic virtues of his (comparatively ordinary) wife Harriet Taylor—"I venture to express the opinion," a friend remarked regarding Mill's claims, "that no such combination [of virtues] has ever been realized in the whole history of the human race"—Wilson suggests that Mill's delusions reflected a kind of "Harriet-worship." And he comments that "[a]s [Mill's] encomiums of Harriet Taylor remind us, the human race can easily deprive itself of Christianity, but finds it rather more difficult to lose its capacity for worship."[10]

Mill himself did not regard his devotion in this way, of course. But he explicitly contemplated, as many others have done, that literature and art might serve as a suitable substitute for religion.[11]

So there are many religions and, for those not drawn to religion itself, many religion-substitutes. Among the more eligible objects of veneration, however, *law* surely appears near the top of the list. Its power, its majesty, its imperial scope, its deep roots in tradition, and its well-honed ceremonialism all fit it for the role.

Law's attractiveness as a religion-substitute becomes even stronger when it is considered in its social and political context. For centuries, and at least until the adoption of the U.S. Constitution, it had been almost universally assumed by "[e]very responsible thinker, every ecclesiastic, every ruler or statesman who gave the matter any attention," that "religious solidarity in the one recognized church was essential to social and political stability."[12] For thinkers like Émile Durkheim, this assumption represented a sort of universal sociological truth. John Noonan explains that, for Durkheim, "religion unites the collectivity and gives society its 'unity and personality.' So defined, religion becomes essential to every society. . . . The relation of religion and society is reciprocal: the collectivity creates religion, religion creates the collectivity. Society itself is a religious phenomenon."[13]

Under the U.S. Constitution with its disestablishment provisions, of course, this identification of political society with religion is problematic, and Noonan goes on to discuss some of the complicated and devious ways that what he calls "Durkheim's dilemma" has worked itself out in American history. An important part of that development, however, has been the substitution of law—or the "rule of law," or the Constitution—for traditional religion as a unifying force and an object of common loyalty. Thus, Morton Horwitz observes that "[i]f you look at the relationship between law and religion in American society, you will see the tremendous connection between the two and the ways in which law came in the late nineteenth century to replace religion as one of the dominant forms of certainty and legitimacy in social life."[14] Numerous constitutional scholars have noticed the ways in which law—constitutional law in particular—has operated in a way analogous to religion, or has performed the functions elsewhere served by religion.[15]

If law is conscripted to perform the *functions* of religion, however, we should hardly be surprised if law comes to be endowed with some of the *attributes* of religion—including some of its references to more transcendent realities or sources of meaning. Scholars like Robert Bellah have studied how law makes up part of a "civil religion" in American society.[16] And in a more jurisprudential vein, Pierre Schlag describes modern law as "the continuation of God by other means."[17]

Schlag explores parallels between the classic philosophical arguments for the existence of God and the defenses of the enterprise of law made by modern thinkers ranging from formalists such as Joseph Beale to contemporary mainstream, pragmatist, and postmodern scholars like Owen Fiss, Margaret Jane Radin, Frank Michelman, and Jack Balkin.[18] These legal thinkers do not explicitly or consciously embrace the theological framework that they inadvertently imitate; nonetheless, Schlag argues, their ways of thinking and arguing show that they are engaged in a "residually theological discourse."[19] Much of the discussion in the preceding chapters lends support to Schlag's assessment.

Indeed, to an attentive outsider, Schlag's diagnosis may seem evident even on the face of the way lawyers talk. Several years ago I participated in an academic conference in which most of the participants were lawyers; but one presenter was an accomplished historian. Midway through the conference he indicated to me that in all his years in the academy he had never before worked much with lawyers or law professors, and he found the lawyerly discourse extremely curious. "All of the talk about *doctrines*, all of the invoking and distinguishing of authorities," he commented. "Where else except in theology departments do people talk like this?"

Of course, any endowment of law with transcendent qualities will clash with prevailing modern assumptions. Law is not *really* a proper object of worship, we think. Law is made by and for human beings: it is not a superhuman source of wisdom. From a religious perspective, therefore, treating law as if it had such qualities is a form of idolatry.[20] A more secular perspective—one grounded more in Sartre than in Scripture—points to a similar judgment, couched in a different vocabulary: the secular view sees the religious use of law as a manifestation of "bad faith." Thus, Schlag suggests that the modern practice of law is pervasively in bad faith. In a similar spirit, Roberto Unger famously described the pre–Critical Legal Studies professoriat—and the characterization would seem at least as applicable to the post–CLS profession—as "a priesthood that had lost their faith and kept their jobs."[21]

More recently, Duncan Kennedy has offered an extensive diagnosis of modern legal culture that pervasively depends on ascriptions of bad faith (though Kennedy emphasizes political rather than spiritual needs as the source of this bad faith). The puzzle Kennedy seeks to explain is much like the ontological gap discussed above; it is "the simultaneously critical and 'believing' character of American legal consciousness, its paradoxical combination of skepticism and faith."[22] This puzzling condition, Kennedy thinks, reflects bad faith, which arises from the conflict between our commitment to "rule of law"—a commitment that requires law to transcend mere interests and partisan ideologies—and our knowledge that in fact law does not and cannot actually be what we need it to be. Judges resolve this conflict by presenting decisions as deductive, and by half-believing that law in fact has this character, even though at another level they know this is not so. They do not engage in "conscious, deliberate, strategic misrepresentation," and probably *could not* do so, because law "would then have the instability of any conspiracy that involves many thousands of people and has to constantly renew itself by recruiting new Grand Inquisitors."[23] Instead, the denial of the ideological character of legal decisions is "half-conscious, or conscious and unconscious at the same time."[24]

Drawing on the work of Freud and Sartre, Kennedy suggests that "there is some part of the psyche that registers the possibility of the unpleasant truth and then mobilizes to keep from knowing it."[25] Consequently, "[t]he ideological element [in law] is a kind of secret, like a family secret—the incestuous relationship between grandfather and mother—that affects all the generations as something that is both known and denied."[26]

Kennedy's diagnosis of modern legal culture is a nuanced one. He acknowledges that denial and bad faith work differently in different judges.[27] And he does not depict law as simply and purely an exercise in bad faith. Legal texts *do* effectively and legitimately constrain in a nonideological way to a limited extent. Hence, critical claims that exaggerate the indeterminacy and ideological quality of law are implausible, and may themselves reflect bad faith on the part of radical critics who "have commitments to the presence of ideology in adjudication that it would be hard to give up."[28] Nor is the bad faith representation of law as nonideological a conspiracy by which one class—judges and lawyers—cynically deceive and oppress other classes. On the contrary, the bad faith engulfs us all—perhaps for our benefit: "Judges keep the secret, even from themselves, in part because participants in legal culture and in the general political culture want them to. Everyone wants it to be true that it is not only possible but common for judges to judge nonideologically. But everyone is aware of the critique, and everyone knows that the naive theory of the rule of law is a fairy tale."[29]

In short, we manage to maintain faith (albeit "bad faith") in the law because we think "the rule of law is . . . a beneficent illusion." To be sure, the illusion confers a dangerous authority on judges. But who knows?—if the illusion were shattered, then perhaps "judges would tyrannize us worse than they do already."[30] Consequently, the legal academy and the legal culture have cause to ignore or censure anyone who would threaten the illusion by telling the truth about the law.[31]

In this respect, Kennedy may have a surprising ally in Justice Scalia. In a recent interpretation, Daniel Farber and Suzanna Sherry suggest that although Scalia usually advocates a rigorously formalist view of law, "there is some evidence that he views [this account of law] . . . as a sort of noble myth to which judges ought to give their allegiance even if it is not wholly true." Farber and Sherry quote a provocative statement in which Scalia observes: "That is why, by the way, I never thought Oliver Wendell Holmes and the legal realists did us a favor by pointing out that all these legal fictions were fictions: Those judges wise enough to be trusted with the secret already knew it."[32]

Although in some respects this seems a plausible interpretation of our situation, the "bad faith" or "noble myth" account fails to register the full complexities of the internal dissonance in contemporary legal culture. It may be true, as Kennedy suggests, that judges routinely present their decisions as the product of deductive, formalist reasoning. But Kennedy seems insufficiently attentive to another important feature of legal culture— namely, that judges and lawyers today typically do *not* avow a belief in the sort of law—"the law"—that, as we saw in Chapter 3, their practices seem to presuppose. In this respect, legal culture departs from the familiar pattern of bad faith.

In ordinary bad faith, in other words, a person professes (to others, and perhaps to himself as well) *to believe* in something that at some level he does not really believe. His hypocrisy or self-deception serves his interests, because without a (false, or at least inauthentic) profession of belief he would have to relinquish something he values. In contemporary legal culture, on the contrary, practitioners profess *not to believe* in something—"the law," or the law's metaphysical presuppositions—that their discourse and practice would suggest they in fact *do* at some level believe in. And since their practice—or, more generally, the "rule of law" itself—is something that they evidently value, their dissonant professions of unbelief in the presuppositions of law are not self-serving in any straightforward sense.

To put the point differently, if lawyers were practicing bad faith in the typical sense, then one would expect them to protect their practice by *avowing* the assumptions presupposed in the practice, not by *disavowing* those assumptions. Disillusioned ministers or pastors, it is said, sometimes do this; they pretend, for selfish or perhaps even altruistic reasons, to believe in the literal reality of God or the soul or the resurrection even though in fact they regard these doctrines as myths at best. Unger's comparison of law professors to a "priesthood that had lost their faith but kept their jobs" draws on this sort of reference. But on closer examination, it seems that lawyers and law professors do just the opposite of the bad faith pastor: they persist in the practice while *denying* its ontological presuppositions. They avow belief *in the practice*, that is, but not in *the metaphysical premises that seem necessary to support the practice*. Or, to shift to the religious vocabulary, if contemporary law is a species of idolatry, it is a peculiar and confusing sort of idolatry in which the devotees regularly *deny* that the idol has the transcendent qualities it would need to justify the uses they make of it.

This perplexing condition invites us to consider a different and almost opposite possibility: Could it be that at some level legal practitioners *do* sincerely believe in "the law" (as Tess argued in Chapter 3), and that if they are guilty of bad faith, their misrepresentation or self-deception occurs *not* when they engage in the practice and discourse of law but rather when they consciously or explicitly disavow its metaphysical commitments? In short, although lawyers and judges might be in bad faith when they engage in the *practice* of law, their overall behavior seems more consistent with the hypothesis that the self-deception occurs when they engage in explicit *theorizing* about law—and when in the course of such theorizing they deny the metaphysical commitments that they in fact hold.[33]

## Ad Hoc Platonism

So we need to consider the possibility that lawyers and legal scholars do in fact believe in something more metaphysically robust and exotic—something to which we could fairly attach the label "the law" in something akin to its classical sense. But what might that metaphysical something be?

Platonism—or if not Platonism in its full majesty, at least something that I will call "ad hoc Platonism"—offers one possibility. The term needs explanation. The philosophical orientation called "Platonism" has cropped up again and again through the centuries, but in different guises: the position advocated by classical neo-Platonists like Plotinus may look to us very different (and much more mystical) than Plato's own theories, and the more modern (and much less mystical) incarnations of Platonism look different still. These variations work to frustrate any general account of Platonism—even by those who (unlike myself) would otherwise be qualified to give one. Fortunately, no such account is needed here. For present purposes, what I have in mind is a particular kind of "move" that thinkers sometimes make in an effort to escape ontological difficulties of the kind we have been considering.

The move works in this way: suppose you are trying to give an account of something—let us just call it *X*—that you are sure is real, and that you also ardently *hope* is real because you and your friends actually depend on it for various purposes (like the delusional brother-in-law who thinks he is a chicken in Woody Allen's "But we need the eggs" joke). But you find that *X* cannot easily be accounted for in terms of the kinds of items that appear on your ontological inventory. So you appear to be trapped in what I have been calling an "ontological gap." What to do? How to climb out? Of course, you could just admit that your understanding is confused or incomplete: you are confident that *X* exists but you can't explain exactly how. But if you are averse to admitting confusion, you might try to avoid this embarrassment by simply declaring that *X* is a thing-in-itself, so to speak, or a "primitive phenomenon"—by adding *X* to the ontological inventory in its own right. Now, if someone asks you to explain in what sense *X* is real or what sort of thing it is, you have a ready response: "It's *X*. Not reducible. Just plain *X*."

Plato himself *might* have been resorting to this move—it is hardly for me to say—by hypothesizing a realm of nonmaterial "Forms" that are somehow more real than the things we see, feel, and handle in our everyday world. Suppose we cannot give a good account of courage, say, or temperance. Our difficulties might leave us in perplexity, or aporia, as in the most Socratic dialogues. But if we find this condition intolerable, we might try to escape it by simply asserting that courage and temperance themselves exist in their own right—as abstract items or Forms, perhaps—and that earthly actions or characters get their quality of courage or temperance through some sort of re-

semblance to or "participation" in the Form that is the real essence of courage or temperance.

Whether this is in fact the nature of Plato's own position is a question that
is absolutely beyond my competence and also, fortunately, not necessary to
the present discussion. But I am confident that the Platonist move is not
something I just dreamed up. We have already seen a stark instance of it,
I think, in the previous chapter. "Collective intentionality" is surely real,
John Searle argued, and we need to believe it is real in order to make sense
of activities such as playing football or performing in an orchestra. But collective intentionality cannot be accounted for by aggregating individual intentions: therefore, it must exist as a "primitive phenomenon." Searle did
not overtly describe this argument as Platonist. But Charles Larmore happily
embraces the label as he makes a similar move in the realm of moral theory.
The ontology of scientific naturalism cannot adequately account for morality, Larmore argues, so we must expand our ontologies to include "moral
facts."[34] "Basically, Plato was right."[35]

To describe this move as a form of ad hoc Platonism is to imply that there
is something vaguely unseemly or opportunistic about it; and that implication is intended. But it might also be unfair. If we are certain something is
real but cannot otherwise account for it, simply adding it in its own right to
our ontological inventories may seem the only sensible thing to do. Still, the
Platonist move can leave us with the feeling that there is something fishy
going on. The "solutions" derived in this way have the feel of being purely
verbal. And the entities that are posited to relieve our metaphysical distress
have a sort of jerry-rigged or "tacked on" quality; that is because they do not
seem to "fit" the overall character of our inventory. Thus, I have already
noticed the oddity of an argument like Searle's that, after insisting that the
ultimate building blocks of everything that exists are particles and force
fields, goes on to postulate collective intentionality as a primitive phenomenon: an ontology listing particles, force fields, and collective intentionality
looks like a Periodic Table containing squares for hydrogen, helium, carbon,
scrambled eggs, and Mozart's "Jupiter" symphony.

These objections may reflect the awkwardness of resorting to Platonism in
a world that finds any such ethereal entities hard to take seriously. In this
environment, we may be tempted to resort to Platonism opportunistically,
on the sly, and in a tacit, half-hearted, almost apologetic way. Like metaphysical dieters, we want, it seems, *not* to have our (ontological) cake and
eat it too. So contemporary Platonists (or closet Platonists) may disavow re-

liance on religious notions such as God, or a purposeful cosmos, or an imma-
terial soul—indeed, its ability to grant its adherents immunity against association with actual religion may well be a principal attraction of Platonism
today—and they are also eager to disclaim belief in anything "spooky" or
"queer," like the mysterious "nonnatural" moral properties posited early in
the twentieth century by the philosopher G. E. Moore.[36] Their inclination is
to declare the deficiencies of ordinary naturalism—that is, of the scientific
ontology discussed in Chapter 2—while clinging as closely to that worldview
as they possibly can.

Thus, some contemporary theorists—who though perhaps not Platonists
exactly nevertheless exhibit Platonist tendencies, or at least yearnings—may
assert that moral qualities are "objective," not merely subjective or relative
or emotive, but then hasten to assure us that they themselves are of course
not so naive as to suppose that these qualities are part of "the fabric of the
universe."[37] Other self-proclaimed moral realists may suggest that moral
qualities like goodness or justice, while not exactly identical to natural properties like pleasure in a crude utilitarian sense, are also not a separate or
nonnatural order of existence either. Rather these qualities "supervene
upon" the natural order: they are the same as natural facts—except, of
course, insofar as they are different.[38] Such analyses seem calculated more
to show what morality *is not*—it is not something in the dreaded categories of either the religious or the nonnatural—than to explain what sort
of thing it actually *is*. So the inquirer who is mainly interested in that more
affirmative question—What *is* morality?—will emerge from these impressively intricate analyses as clueless as she was going in. Commenting on this
version of moral realism, which he describes as the "new cognitive naturalism," Larmore argues that it "does not account for the specifically *normative*
character of moral beliefs." In short, Larmore argues, this version of natural
realism does not account for our sense that moral realities are qualitatively
different than natural facts. "Nor is it at all clear," he adds, "what such an account would look like."[39]

The criticism seems apt, but it seems almost equally apt for Larmore's own
more avowedly Platonist position that, though disclaiming naturalism and
asserting that moral facts are "real and non-natural," also insists that moral
facts are *not* "an additional feature of the world" but rather "facts containing
*reasons*."[40] Larmore's description seems akin to Michael Moore's account of a
"moral property" as one that "has 'has-to-be-doneness' built into it."[41]

What can we say about these claims? I cannot speak for others, of course, but for myself I can only say that although I can read these words, that is all they are: "just words." Facts often provide us with reasons, to be sure. The fact that you are hungry gives you a reason to eat. The fact that it is snowing outside gives you a reason to put on your boots before going out. Depending on who you are and what you are trying to do, just about any fact might give you a reason for doing or thinking something. But I confess that I cannot picture what a special "fact *containing* a reason" would be. Nor can I grasp what it would mean for a "property" to have "'has-to-be-doneness' built into it." I don't know about you, but for me, these expressions seem nonsensical. They bring to mind William Barrett's observation: "For a concept to have meaning, we must be able to represent it, directly or indirectly, through some concrete intuition or intuitions. More simply and perhaps crudely: we have to be able to make some kind of mental picture of the concept. Otherwise our thinking becomes empty, and the words we use merely empty verbalisms."[42]

Thus far, my examples of ad hoc Platonism have come mostly from work in moral theory, where thinkers like Larmore have explicitly invoked Platonism in an effort to account for the nature of morality. It is harder to think of *explicit* invocations of Platonism in modern jurisprudential writings. But the possibility is plain enough (and has been proposed to me in informal conversations as the solution to the quandary described in earlier chapters). Asked to explain what a "right" or a "legal duty" or an "immunity" is, in other words, someone could decline to give the standard reductionist explanations (dissolving these legal entities into predictions of what judges will do, for example, or mere features of lawyerly discourse) and instead assert that rights and duties and immunities—and, more sweepingly, "the law" itself—somehow exist as entities in themselves, independent of our recognition of them in our practice and discourse.

And indeed, Platonism is arguably exploited routinely, albeit without attribution, by lawyers and scholars. Though few lawyers or scholars make a point of claiming to be Platonists, the label *is* sometimes attached to the positions and views of others—usually but not always in derision. Richard Posner suggests that Langdellian formalism was "a form of Platonism; just as Plato had regarded particular chairs as manifestations of or approximations to the concept of a chair, Langdell regarded particular decisions on contract law as manifestations of or approximations to the legal concept of contract."[43] Brian Bix describes Michael Moore's natural law theory as "Platonist."[44] David Luban argues that the Warren Court and especially Justice Douglas adopted a "Platonic way of viewing legal rights."[45] Luban offers this interpretation enthusiastically because he thinks the Platonist "theory of legal rights" is "true";[46] he thereby suggests the possibility of a more thorough-going Platonic account of law. Patrick Brennan notices that legal thought today operates "[u]nder the sway of an unanalyzed Platonism."[47] And indeed, going back to Chapter 3, we might say that our hypothetical visitor Tess was in essence arguing that legal discourse is Platonist to the core: we routinely talk of "the law" as something that exists independent of our particular practices and references to it.

But as we also saw, modern legal thinkers have steadfastly resisted this characterization, at least when it is bluntly presented; indeed, they have mocked the notion that "the law" is "real" as any sort of independent entity—a "brooding omnipresence." Richard Posner notes that "the modern secular intellectual finds Plato's, and the successor Christian [worldview], . . . unbelievable."[48] The second half of Posner's claim is contestable[49]—unless, that is, the qualifier "secular" is meant to make the claim tautologically true. But the conspicuous dearth of legal thinkers rushing to wrap themselves in the mantle of Plato, or to proclaim that "'the law'—the 'brooding omnipresence'—*is* real!," suggests that at least the first half of Posner's claim is correct. So if contemporary lawyers and legal scholars hold to a Platonist view of law, we (or most of us) do so unconsciously.

That description—of a legal culture composed of unconscious Platonists—strains credulity. But there is a deeper deficiency with the Platonist account of our situation. The problem is not so much that we do not believe in Platonism, but that today Platonism is not something that we can meaningfully either believe or disbelieve. For lawyers and legal scholars, that is (I cannot speak for philosophers—or for mathematicians, for whom Platonism is said to have powerful appeal), Platonism simply does not offer the sort of fleshed-out, intelligible ontological inventory that we could meaningfully either accept or reject.

The point can be clarified by comparing the two positions that the statement I just quoted from Judge Posner linked together for common dismissal: Platonism and Christianity. Leaving aside the question of its truth, we can nonetheless appreciate that Christianity continues to offer a view of the world that is ontologically rich[50] (or, if you prefer, ontologically promiscuous). At least in some of its versions, Christianity affirms the reality of a personal (indeed three-person) God, of seraphim and cherubim, of fallen angels or devils, of souls that survive death, of an afterlife, and so forth. Some of this imagery may be metaphorical, of course, but Christian thinkers through the centuries have also provided thoughtful accounts of why metaphor is needed and of how it relates to realities that transcend mundane, literalistic description. The Christian picture thus contains an elaborate content about which one can say, meaningfully: "I believe in that" or "I *don't* believe in any of that." Platonism may once have offered similarly fleshed-out possibilities—for example in its classical versions that, as Arthur Lovejoy explained, owed at least as much to the *Timaeus* (with its creative "demiurge") as to the *Republic* (with its more ethereal Forms and its "Idea of the Good").[51] But Platonism as it loosely presents itself today—or at least as it casually drops in from time to time in legal conversations—seems a flickering ghost of its former robust self. So you might *say* that you favor or oppose Platonism. But what is it, really, that you would be coming down for or against?

Suppose a law professor today were to affirm, for example, "I believe 'the law' *is* real" (or that rights or legal duties are real); and when asked for an explanation of that reality ("'Real' in what sense? *How* are they real?"), he answers, "In a Platonist sense. I'm a Platonist." What would this answer even mean? The affirmation does not illuminate—does not add anything to the assertion that the law is real. It supplies no "mental picture," as Barrett puts it, but instead seems to be mere "verbalism." Just words. Consequently, a Platonist interpretation of our quandary seems not so much wrong as empty; it is not so much an interpretation at all as a description of our perplexed situation in different, perhaps more dignified, but mostly more obfuscating terms.

## The Neoclassical Interpretation

If we are not exactly Platonists, however, or if it adds little to say that we are Platonists, we might be tacit neoclassicists. We might be believers, that is, in something like the classical account of law in its more substantial form, with its reliance on the sort of ontological inventory associated with religion. A few so-called natural law thinkers—though not, it seems, the most prominent current proponents of what they choose to call "natural law"[52]—appear to advocate the classical position in something like its standard form. For present purposes, though, we can profitably consider the less conventional and often cryptic version of neoclassicism contained in the work of one of the most provocative but elusive legal thinkers of our time—Joseph Vining.

Vining's most searching investigation of this counterintuitive possibility occurs in his book *From Newton's Sleep*. The book offers no linear analysis leading to any definite and confident conclusion, but rather a series of reflections ranging from near aphorisms to short essays. The argument—and despite its self-consciously meandering method[53] the book contains an overall argument—advances slowly, haltingly, with many changes of direction and detours and returns; and in the end the argument leaves a good deal open or uncertain. But some recurring central themes can be identified.

## How Do We Know What We Believe?

On one level, Vining's purpose is to discover what lawyers believe—what we believe about the law, and what we believe more generally in order to believe the things we believe about the law. But this task is both complicated and perilous because Vining does not assume that our beliefs are transparent or immediately accessible (even to ourselves) through casual inspection or introspection. "We hardly know ourselves," he confesses.[54] Consequently, what I *think* I believe is evidence—but *only* evidence—of what I *really* believe. The ways I use language (beyond what I explicitly assert), and the ways in which I act and plan and live are also evidence of what I believe.[55] So discovering what I believe entails a careful reflection on what I think, say, and do in order to reveal the underlying beliefs that I truly hold.

In this respect, Vining's project is very much like that described by Michael Polanyi:

> I believe that the function of philosophic reflection consists in bringing to light, and affirming as my own, the beliefs implied in such of my thoughts and practices as I believe to be valid; that I must aim at discovering what I truly believe in and at formulating the convictions which I find myself holding; that I must conquer my self-doubts, so as to retain a firm hold on this programme of self-identification.[56]

By this view, the investigation of what lawyers (or human beings generally) believe involves a close examination not only of what people *say* they believe, but also of what they tacitly concede in the ways they talk and of the presuppositions that seem to underlie their actions. And what we do in and with *law* comprises a vital part of this examination. "[I]t is too often overlooked," Vining maintains, "that law is evidence of view and belief far stronger than academic statement and introspection can provide."[57] These various kinds of introspective and linguistic and behavioral evidence may often contradict each other—Vining frequently identifies statements or actions, for example, in which lawyers or scientists or philosophers tacitly deny what they explicitly assert, and vice versa[58]—so that the determination of belief is no easy task that we can know to be complete at any particular time.

### Searching for Authority

Acknowledging these daunting obstacles, Vining proceeds to consider the beliefs that manifest themselves in law. He observes that the activity of a lawyer involves the careful reading of texts—of statutes, cases, contracts, regulations. Moreover, lawyers read texts with a particular purpose in mind; they aim to encounter "authority"—something that deserves our attention and respect and hence that can guide our decisions. But it makes no sense to read carefully—much less to read a text seeking authority—unless one supposes that the text is the expression of some *person;* without a person speaking to us there would be no meaning in the words at all, much less a meaning that we would respect and struggle to understand.[59]

Thus, if we were to come upon what initially appears to be a text but then discover that in fact it is the product of random, mindless processes—of waves on the beach, or of a manual containing form letters, or of a computer programmed to string words together in grammatically and syntactically proper sequences—we would not engage in close reading to determine the text's meaning. Indeed, we would be embarrassed to be caught in such an activity, feeling "the blush of foolishness that comes with an awareness no one is speaking."[60] Much less would we regard the mindless marks as worthy of deference or respect.

The lawyer's search for authority, therefore, betrays a constant presupposition of *mind* behind and expressing itself in the texts lawyers study.[61] Law is, in effect, a restless "search for voices."[62]

Insofar as he insists that bare words have no meanings and that interpretation must look to what an *author* was trying to say, it might almost seem that Vining is arguing for the familiar "intentionalist" versions of constitutional or statutory construction. But Vining suggests that our practices cannot be accounted for by supposing that we are merely looking for the intentions of the historical, flesh-and-blood authors of a particular statute or constitutional provision. (Much less would a merely fictional author serve to justify our practices.) After all, not just any author would be worthy of deference. In order to merit our respect, and hence to justify our interpretive practices, the author would need to speak *to us*, and to us *now*—would need in some sense to be actually *present*.[63] The author would also need to address us not in a game of manipulation, but in "good faith."[64] And the author would need to display qualities of caring, and of mindfulness, to warrant our continued attention and respect.[65] Rarely if ever would the enactors of some dated statute or ancient constitution have these qualities.

Nonetheless, we continue to interpret the materials of law in ways that presuppose some such mind speaking to us through the assorted texts that lawyers study and invoke. So we must be seeking an author beyond the particular enactors.[66] "Lawyers are caught by legislation and their reading of it," Vining argues. "Either they must believe what they do with legislation is often foolish and deceptive; or they do believe and confess a belief in *an informing spirit* in the legislated words that is *beyond individual legislators*."[67]

## The Transcendent Author

We thereby reveal a tacit commitment to the reality of something—or, better, *someone*[68]—who communicates to us through the texts that lawyers study, but who transcends the flesh-and-blood authors of those texts. Just who or what that someone is remains obscure, an object of Vining's continual musings. He describes the ultimate author as "spirit," and as the "transcendent."[69] At times he hints at a sort of pantheism, in which through the practices of the law we come to know a universal mind, and at the same time we come to know our own true selves, and these somehow turn out to be the same thing. So "the question of what the law 'is' is not so very different from the question of what we 'are.'"[70] In this spirit, Vining wonders whether "our whole life outer and inner exists forever as a memory in a greater mind,"[71] and he asks: "What is that original mind if not a mind something like our own, and what are it and our own but points to a larger mind."[72]

But from these hints, and given Vining's own description of writing as "distillations of vacillations," one could hardly conclude that Vining is proselytizing for pantheism. Ultimately, the object of the faith that Vining finds in the practices of law lends itself more to poetic suggestion than to creedal formulation. Fittingly, therefore, the book ends with a poem, which itself ends not with a period but with a dash. The poem, called "Present Meaning," concludes:

> What we say—
>   Always behind us,
>   You, me,
> In the silence,
>   The present silence,
> Existing beyond words,
>   Always beyond words,
> In the clear silence,
>   The moving stillness—[73]

In any case, it is that someone—that "spirit," or that "transcendent," or "moving stillness," necessarily personal—that we actually seek in the practices of law. And what that someone speaks to us is what we call "the law." So the texts we study are not themselves "the law," Vining repeatedly asserts, but rather "evidence" of the law[74]—here Vining sounds very much like Story and Blackstone—which is to say that they are evidence of the mind we seek to understand and respect.

Vining insists that his approach is not incompatible with, and indeed is thoroughly grounded in, reason. "Reason in its largest sense, respect for evidence that includes all experience," he asserts, "is the very ground of faith."[75] We may want to banish "transcendence" and the "mysterium tremendum," but in doing so we are "not true to experience."[76] "The world is full of oddnesses and incongruities, and this is not the least of them, this departure from the empirical taken by so many whose chief pride is their empiricism."[77] Moreover, in starting with faith, he is only doing what lawyers always do—and must do: "the lawyer . . . approaches the words with a faith to be tested in her work with them."[78]

## Faith or Nonsense?

Vining's is an intriguing assessment of our situation. But it is safe to say, I think, that this assessment will not be widely embraced within the legal academy and culture anytime soon: it is too foreign to prevailing ontological assumptions. Vining acknowledges as much. Approached in this way, he concedes, law becomes "an object of amazement to the modern and postmodern mentality."[79] And he points out that, reflectively studied, law and its presuppositions will be "subversive" of twentieth-century thought—of the materialism evident in so much work in the sciences and social sciences, but also of "what goes by the name postmodernism in literary and philosophic studies."[80] He concedes as well that we *say*—that we *think*—we believe in no such mysterious or transcendent authority as his account posits. But he explains that our behavior shows that we *do* harbor some such belief.

> But if, the way we and the world and the universe are, we cannot do without authority, without saying you ought, you must, we will produce suffering and take responsibility for it, I ought, I must suffer if I do not—and if authority is impossible should this something more not exist—then we have some evidence that what we must believe, is. What we must believe, must be, not because it exists if we believe it exists, but because we exist and have been given the means, by our work, to continue existing.[81]

And if this sort of reflection involves a "leap of faith," so be it. "Without faith," he observes, "we know nothing beyond ourselves."[82]

For those averse to such leaps, what are the alternatives? We might try to eliminate dissonance by rejecting law as we know and practice it—by treating law (with its archaic talk of rights and duties and principles) as something to be "overcome," as Posner suggests. But as we have seen, this prescription has been offered in vain by countless thinkers, going back at least to Holmes, for over a century. By now that prescription ought to seem at least as quixotic as anything Vining proposes.

So what are the viable options? Should we just resign ourselves to slogging along in the bad faith described by Schlag and Kennedy? Should we opportunistically declare ourselves to be special purpose Platonists (whatever that might mean in our current situation) and pretend thereby to have filled our ontological gaps?

In our current predicament, living in the gap, what should we do? What *can* we do?

# Epilogue:
## Confusion and Confession

We have seen how law in our time persists in an ontological gap, and as a result, much of what we say about law—or what we say in the vocabulary of law—does not make sense. Much of our law-talk is, as so many have said or suspected already, "just words." Should we be worried about this situation? Is our predicament intolerable?

We might first observe that law is hardly alone in this embarrassment. Another worrisome gap—one that we have noticed but not dwelt on—exists as a consequence of the discrepancy between the ontology of everyday experience and the ontology of science. This discrepancy is particularly troublesome with respect to the ontological category of "persons." As we saw in Chapter 2, in everyday experience we treat persons as a discrete part of reality; and hence we take at face value, so to speak, personal qualities such as mind, belief, intention, and choice. References to such qualities are ubiquitous in our daily conversations, and in our legal discourse as well. Yet they all seem problematic from the ontological perspective of science, which is determined to reduce such entities to, as John Searle put it, particles and force fields. But few of us are prepared either to surrender persons and their distinctive properties to science or to sacrifice science for the sake of persons. The result is an ontological gap that looms over a good deal of the humanities and social sciences.

More generally, we might say that the modern era has been dominated by two converse movements. There is a movement in politics, law, and ethics that has attempted to give ever greater elaboration and practical realization to the idea that human beings have intrinsic value—that they are endowed with human dignity and entitled to equal concern and respect. We may associate this movement with terms like "Enlightenment," "humanism," "liberalism," and "progressivism." Then there is a reductionist and physicalistic movement in our underlying ontologies—we associate this movement with science—that quietly operates to make claims about human value and dignity look like sentimental nonsense.[1] Perhaps surprisingly (or perhaps not), the same people are often truculent proponents of both movements. As a consequence, our modern lives have for some time now been carried on in a sort of gaping ontological gap. In this respect, I am far from being the first to sense that "nonsense," or at least "bad faith," seems to be the prevalent condition of our time.

So law is not alone in its embarrassment. But this observation may not provide much consolation: my own observation, at least (contrary, perhaps, to the adage that "misery loves company"), is that a person who is suffering gets scant comfort from being told that other people are suffering too. And we may wonder how long things can go on this way—that is, in this condition of pervasive nonsense.

I confess that I have no idea what the answer to that question might be. But it may be at least mildly reassuring to recognize that our situation is not unprecedented—that cities and even civilizations seem to have survived and even prospered for extended periods in a condition of nonsense. It would be too much to suppose that *all* times and places are equally engulfed in ontological gaps. On the contrary, it seems (to simplify shamelessly) that our species is prone to wander from the path of metaphysical good sense in contrary directions. We may cultivate lush ontologies (filled with divinities and magical beings, perhaps) that can be invoked to account for almost everything, but precisely for that reason cannot really explain almost anything (why *this* and not *that?*). Or we can overcompensate by adopting ascetic ontologies that provide greater rigor in limited domains, such as physics and chemistry, but leave us unable to account satisfactorily for much of what we do and believe and care about. Some cultures—the popular culture of the medieval and early modern Europe, perhaps—seem to have chosen, or at least fallen into, the first of these alternatives. Other cultures (such as ours—or at least our academic culture) have embraced the latter alternative. And even so, they have not promptly fallen into chaos or paralysis. On the contrary, they have lived quite happily, for a time at least, "in the gap."

In Chapter 1, I suggested that Socrates lived in such a culture. Or at least, he thought he did. And he seems to have taken it as a sort of life mission— one he pursued with evangelical fervor—to wander around Athens interrogating people in order to expose the ontological gaps in their lives and to convict them of nonsense. Politicians, poets, philosophers, craftsmen: none of them, he thought, could really explain even their own fields of activity. The city was filled with "an abundance of men who believe they have some knowledge but know little or nothing."[2] They were all—or at least the self-confident and articulate ones were—"playing with words but revealing nothing."[3] And yet there was no denying that some of these people *were* possessed of certain virtues (even if they could not explain what virtue is), and some were very good at what they did. Ignorance and a propensity to nonsense, it seems, were not necessarily paralyzing. So the conclusion, Socrates said, was that "human wisdom is worth little or nothing," and that those who were virtuous and wise were acting with "a wisdom more than human; else I cannot explain it."[4]

Take, for instance, Socrates's brief encounter with Ion, a rhapsode, who was the Tiger Woods of his time in the much admired field of reciting and expounding on Homer in large competitions. Socrates begins the conversation by suggesting that Ion's skill must result from some sort of profound knowledge of the subject, and Ion, naturally, is happy to agree; but a few Socratic questions are enough to expose the gross error in this hypothesis. So Ion modestly acknowledges that, as Socrates says, his success is evidently not the result of any "knowledge or mastery."[5] But then how *does* Ion manage to do what he does? Some readers may view Ion as a sort of buffoon, but to me he exudes a fetching, child-like curiosity when he asks, "Then how in the world do you explain what I do, Socrates?"[6] Because the empirically verifiable fact is that when Ion recites, the spectators cry, and become terrified, and are "filled with amazement."[7]

In response, Socrates hypothesizes that Ion's skill is a product not of human wisdom but rather of a kind of divine inspiration originating with the Muse and channeled through Homer to interpreters like Ion, and through them to the audience. We may suspect that Socrates was less than serious in offering this explanation. But in that case, Ion's question would remain unanswered: "Then how in the world do you explain what I do, Socrates?"

In any case, Socrates's mission showed that although perplexity may be embarrassing—we would prefer, naturally, to think that we understand and control our world—it need not be debilitating. To be sure, the Athenians in general did not appreciate Socrates's enterprise. He seemed to them unconstructive and subversive, and in the end they put a stop to his pestering. But Socrates himself insisted to the end that in spreading perplexity—in convicting and convincing people of confusion—he was only seeking to benefit his fellow citizens. Among other blessings, the humility that could result from perplexity might render them more receptive to other sources and re-sources—to the influences (whatever we may think they were) that he de-scribed as "inspiration" and as a "wisdom more than human," or to the kind of inner "voice" that he himself heard and took to be a "divine or spiritual sign."[8]

Perplexity is not a resting place, to be sure, and it is uncomfortable (as some of us can attest) to have to be constantly choosing between speaking nonsense or just standing in silence. So we will surely continue, as Socrates did, to seek to enhance our understandings, or to fill in our ontological gaps. But in the meantime—and we look to be in the meantime for quite a while—and on the Socratic premise that "it is the most blameworthy igno-rance to believe that one knows what one does not know,"[9] we would per-haps be wise to confess our confusion and to acknowledge that there are richer realities and greater powers in the universe than our meager modern philosophies have dreamed of.

# *Notes*

## I. Law and Metaphysics?

1. Oliver Wendell Holmes, "The Path of the Law," 10 *Harv. L. Rev.* 457, 468 (1897).
2. Richard A. Posner, "The Path Away from the Law," 110 *Harv. L. Rev.* 1039, 1043 (1997).
3. Mary Ann Glendon, *A Nation under Lawyers* 190 (1994).
4. Norman F. Cantor, *Imagining the Law: Common Law and the Foundations of the American Legal System* 192 (1997).
5. Posner, "The Path Away from the Law," at 1040.
6. Richard A. Posner, *Overcoming Law* 20 (1995).
7. See generally Charles M. Yablon, "Law and Metaphysics," 96 *Yale L.J.* 613, 614–624 (1987).
8. Morris Cohen and Felix Cohen, *Readings in Jurisprudence and Legal Philosophy* 665 (1st ed. 1951).
9. Brian Bix, *Jurisprudence: Theory and Context* 6 (2d ed. 1999).
10. Michael S. Moore, "Legal Reality: A Naturalist Approach to Legal Ontology," 21 *Law & Phil.* 619, 704 (2002) (emphasis added).
11. Ibid. at 657.
12. Charles Larmore, *The Morals of Modernity* 116 (1996).
13. I take these examples from the table of contents to *Contemporary Readings in the Foundations of Metaphysics* (Stephen Laurence and Cynthia MacDonald eds., 1998).
14. William P. Alston, "Ontological Commitments," in ibid. at 46.
15. D. C. Williams, "The Elements of Being," reprinted in *Metaphysics: The Big Questions* 40, 43 (Peter Van Inwagen and Dean W. Zimmerman eds., 1998).

## 1. Just Words?

1. Deborah L. Rhode, "Legal Scholarship," 115 *Harv. L. Rev.* 1327, 1327, 1336, 1339 (2002).
2. Ibid. at n.64.

3. Ibid. at 1331.

4. Ibid. at 1337–1339.

5. Daniel A. Farber, "Missing the 'Play of Intelligence,'" 36 *Wm. & Mary L. Rev.* 147, 147, 157 (1994).

6. T. Alexander Aleinikoff, "Constitutional Law in the Age of Balancing," 96 *Yale L.J.* 943, 983 (1987) (emphasis added).

7. Michael Stokes Paulsen, "Captain James T. Kirk and the Enterprise of Constitutional Interpretation: Some Modest Proposals from the Twenty-third Century," 59 *Albany L. Rev.* 671, 674, 677 (1995).

8. Karl Llewellyn, "A Realistic Jurisprudence—The Next Step," 30 *Colum. L. Rev.* 431, 449, 443 (1930) (emphasis added).

9. Herman Oliphant, "A Return to Stare Decisis," 14 *A.B.A.J.* 71, 107 (1928) (emphasis added).

10. Roscoe Pound, "Mechanical Jurisprudence," 8 *Colum. L. Rev.* 605, 621 (1908).

11. W. V. O. Quine, "On What There Is," reprinted in *Contemporary Readings in the Foundations of Metaphysics* 32, 36 (Stephen Laurence and Cynthia Macdonald eds., 1998).

12. Ibid. at 42.

13. Ibid. at 37.

14. Ibid.

15. Oliver Wendell Holmes, "The Theory of Legal Interpretation," 12 *Harv. L. Rev.* 417, 420 (1899).

16. See, for example, Brian Leiter, "The Law School Observer," 5 *Green Bag* 101 (Autumn 2001).

17. Francis Bacon, "The New Organon," in *The Complete Essays of Francis Bacon* 179, 202 (1963) (emphasis added).

18. For a brief description of the movement, see A. J. Ayer, *Philosophy in the Twentieth Century* 114, 122–129 (1982).

19. 35 *Colum. L. Rev.* 809 (1935).

20. Jeremy Waldron, "'Transcendental Nonsense' and System in the Law," 100 *Colum. L. Rev.* 16, 53 (2000).

21. See Hilary Putnam, *Reason, Truth, and History* 105–106 (1981).

22. John R. Searle, *The Rediscovery of the Mind* 25 (1992).

23. Quine, "On What There Is," at 33.

24. See Terry Penner, "Socrates and the Early Dialogues," in *The Cambridge Companion to Plato* 121, 125 (Richard Kraut ed., 1992) ("The Socratic dialogues tend to be aporetic and without positive results").

25. See *Charmides* (temperance); *Euthyphro* (piety); *Meno* (virtue); *Laches* (courage); *Lysis* (friendship); *Protagoras* (virtue); *Republic,* Bk. I (justice). Unless otherwise indicated, citations to Plato's dialogues refer to the versions contained in *The Collected Dialogues of Plato* (Edith Hamilton and Huntington Cairns eds., 1961).

26. *Protagoras* 320d–328d.

27. See Gregory Vlastos, *Socrates: Ironist and Moral Philosopher* 57–58 (1991).

28. See, for example, *Republic* 340d–341c (Thrasymachus suggests that Socrates is a "pettifogger" who uses "shyster's tricks").

29. See Penner, "Socrates and the Early Dialogues," at 126. See also *Theaetetus* 202b–202d, 206c–207c. Although *Theaetetus* is regarded as one of Plato's later works, it is like the earlier, more Socratic dialogues in its aporetic quality.
30. Penner, "Socrates and the Early Dialogues," at 141, 168.
31. Ibid. at 168.
32. Cf. T. H. Irwin, "Plato: the Intellectual Background," in *Cambridge Companion*, at 51, 69 ("Socrates' efforts to define the virtues assume that objectively correct answers can be found, and that they must correspond to some objective realities independent of our beliefs and inquiries.").
33. Vlastos, *Socrates*, at 58–60.
34. Cf. *Republic* 498d.
35. *Gorgias* 489e.
36. *Greater Hippias* 298b (Paul Woodruff tr.)
37. Thomas Nagel, *The View from Nowhere* 4 (1986).

## 2. Ontological Dynasties

1. John R. Searle, *The Social Construction of Reality* 3–4 (1995).
2. Gilbert Ryle, *The Concept of Mind* 11 (1949).
3. Searle, *The Social Construction of Reality*, at 6.
4. Ibid.
5. Richard A. Posner, *The Problems of Jurisprudence* 167 (1990).
6. Gilbert Ryle, *Dilemmas* 71 (1960).
7. Daniel Dennett, *Brainstorms* 61 (1978).
8. Huston Smith, "The Ambiguity of Matter," in *CrossCurrents* 49, 55 (1998).
9. The theme is thoughtfully developed in E. L. Mascall, *The Christian Universe* (1966).
10. Michael S. Moore, "Legal Reality: A Naturalist Approach to Legal Ontology," 21 *Law & Phil.* 619, 661 (2002). Moore explains that the more familiar "Ockham's razor is for finer-grained work."
11. Ryle, *Dilemmas*, at 80.
12. For a perceptive overview, see Owen Chadwick, *The Secularization of the European Mind in the Nineteenth Century* 161–88 (1975).
13. Perhaps the most common instance of this tactic in modern times is the sort of reconciliation announced by scientists like Stephen Jay Gould. See his "Nonoverlapping Magisteria," *Natural History* (March 1997). Gould argues that science and religion do not and cannot conflict—they represent "nonoverlapping magisteria"—because they address wholly different concerns or "domains": science is concerned with "the empirical constitution of the universe"—or with the "factual"—while religion addresses moral questions, or "the search for proper ethical values and the spiritual meaning of our lives." Speaking "[a]s a man of good will, and in the interest of reconciliation," Gould urges the contending parties to accept this beneficent division of jurisdiction. In this spirit, he goes on to say that although he personally does not believe in "souls" and suspects that talk of this sort is a "device for maintaining a belief in

human superiority within an evolutionary world offering no privileged position
to any creature," he is nonetheless willing to "honor the *metaphorical* value of
such a concept [of 'souls'] both for grounding moral discussion and for expressing what we most value about human potentiality." In the same vein, Gould
confidently declares that, as a matter of scientific fact, "nature was not constructed as our eventual abode, didn't know we were coming (we are, after all,
interlopers of the latest geological microsecond), and doesn't give a damn about
us (speaking metaphorically)." But he also perceives that "such a position
frightens many people," and so graciously allows these more timorous souls
(speaking metaphorically, of course) to believe that there is "some intrinsic
meaning" in the universe—although it is not at all clear, once the empirical
framework that Gould insists on is accepted, how this notion of "intrinsic meaning" could be true or what it could even mean (as Gould himself well understands). In short, while proclaiming a "respectful, even loving concordat,"
Gould is quite plainly doing nothing more than declaring victory and dictating
terms—albeit in benign (or perhaps patronizing) tones.

14. Thomas Nagel, *Mortal Questions* 196 (1979). See generally ibid. at 196–213.

15. Luigi Giussani, *The Religious Sense* 42 (John Zucchi tr., 1997).

16. Plato, *The Laws* 889c–892c.

17. See John R. Searle, *The Rediscovery of the Mind* 90–91 (1992).

18. Norman Malcolm provides additional testimony. "[T]he fact [is] that science is a
    vastly greater force in our culture," Malcolm observes. By contrast, "religious
    belief is commonly regarded as unreasonable and is viewed with condescension
    or even contempt. It is said that religion is a refuge for those who, because of
    weakness of intellect or character, are unable to confront the stern realities of
    the world." Norman Malcolm, "The Groundlessness of Belief," in *Faith* 193,
    203, 197 (Terence Penelhum ed., 1989). Malcolm further explains: "[B]y and
    large religion is to university people an alien form of life. They do not participate
    in it and do not understand what it is all about." Ibid. at 203.

19. Charles Larmore, *The Morals of Modernity* 89 (1996).

20. See Jose Casanova, *Public Religions in the Modern World* 17 (1994).

21. See generally Thomas S. Kuhn, *The Structure of Scientific Revolutions* (3d ed. 1996).
    See also Harry Collins and Trevor Pinch, *The Golem: What Everyone Should Know
    about Science* (1993).

22. See generally Philip Jenkins, *The Next Christendom* (2002); *The Desecularization of
    the World: Resurgent Religion and World Politics* (Peter L. Berger ed., 1999).

23. Douglas Laycock, "Continuity and Change in the Threat to Religious Liberty:
    The Reformation Era and the Late Twentieth Century," 80 *Minn. L. Rev.* 1047,
    1078–1079 (1996). In a more recent conversation, Lindgren told me that the
    data Laycock referred to concern religious affiliation or identification, which
    may not correspond to actual belief: someone who was "raised Catholic" or
    Presbyterian or whatever might still self-identify as Catholic or Presbyterian
    even though he or she no longer shares the beliefs of that religion. Lindgren said
    he does not have actual belief data for law professors specifically. However, the

best data for persons with graduate degrees show remarkably high levels of religious belief, he said—far higher than secularization predictions would anticipate.

24. See, for example, Steven M. Barr, *Modern Physics and Ancient Faith* (2003); John H. Polkinghorne, *Belief in God in an Age of Science* (1998).

25. Laycock, "Continuity and Change in the Threat to Religious Liberty," at 1079.

## 3. Does "the Law" Exist?

1. Gilbert Ryle, *The Concept of Mind* 16 (1949).

2. Ibid. at 16–17.

3. Oliver Wendell Holmes, "The Path of the Law," 10 *Harv. L. Rev.* 457, 457 (1897).

4. Karl Llewellyn, *The Bramble Bush* 77 (1930).

5. 1 William Blackstone, *Commentaries on the Laws of England* 70 (1979) (first published 1765) (emphasis added). See also Matthew Hale, *The History of the Common Law of England* 67 (2d ed. 1716) (asserting that judicial decisions "are less than a Law, yet they are greater Evidence thereof, than the Opinion of any private Persons").

6. 41 U.S. 1, 37 (1842) (emphasis added).

7. Black & White Taxicab Co. v. Brown & Yellow Taxicab Co., 276 U.S. 518, 532–534 (1928) (Holmes, J., dissenting).

8. For an overview of different interpretations of what Justice Story meant by the statement in *Swift*, see Paul M. Bator et al., *Hart and Wechsler's The Federal Courts and the Federal System* 779–780 (3d ed. 1988).

9. Aquinas defined law as "an ordinance of reason for the common good, *made by him who has the care of the community and promulgated.*" *Summa Theologica* I–II, Q. 90, art. 4 (emphasis added), reprinted in *The Political Ideas of St. Thomas Aquinas* 9 (Dino Binongiari ed., 1953).

10. Q. 93, art. 1, ibid. at 30 (declaring that "the eternal law is nothing else than the type of divine wisdom, as directing all actions and movements"). See also Q. 93, art. 5, ibid. at 37–38 (explaining that all things both rational and irrational are governed by the eternal law).

11. Q. 93, art. 3, ibid. at 34.

12. Q. 95, art. 2, ibid. at 58. The "natural law" or law of nature is that part of the eternal law that is accessible to human reason without the aid of divine revelation.

13. Ibid.

14. Sir John Fortescue, *On the Laws and Governance of England* 17–18, 53, 82 (Shelley Lockwood ed., 1997) (first published *ca.* 1471).

15. Ibid. at 7.

16. Ibid. at 13.

17. Quoted in Jonathan Rose, "Doctrinal Development: Legal History, Law, and Legal Theory," 22 *Oxford J. Legal Studies* 323, 334 (2002).

18. See Blackstone, *Commentaries on the Laws of England* 38–43.

19. Ibid. at 41.
20. Stuart Banner, "When Christianity Was Part of the Common Law," 16 *Law & Hist. Rev.* 27, 29 (1998).
21. Ibid. at 43.
22. Ibid. at 61, 50. See also Stephen M. Feldman, *American Legal Thought from Premodernism to Postmodernism: An Intellectual Voyage* 159 (2000) (discussing Joseph Story's view that a natural law closely associated with Christianity undergirds all law).
23. Banner, "When Christianity Was Part of the Common Law," at 60.
24. But there are exceptions. Joseph Beale, for example, figures in the legends of American law schools as one of the arch-formalists of the early twentieth century. Learned Hand described Beale's outlook in this way: "Beale was a spiritual son of St. Thomas Aquinas. Himself deeply religious, he believed that, were we only true to ourselves, law would emerge as the will of God. There were principles of justice eternally true, from which if we were obedient and astute, we could deduce all, or at least most, of the specific rules of conduct necessary for our guidance." "Three Letters from Alumni," *Harvard Law School Bulletin* 8 (Jan. 1949). I of course cannot vouch for the accuracy of Hand's description.
25. Southern Pacific Co. v. Jensen, 244 U.S. 205, 222 (1917) (Holmes, J., dissenting).
26. Black & White Taxicab Co. v. Brown & Yellow Taxicab Co., 276 U.S. 518, 532–534 (1928) (Holmes, J., dissenting).
27. Erie Railroad Co. v. Tompkins, 304 U.S. 64, 79 (1938).
28. Llewellyn, *The Bramble Bush*, at 41.
29. Holmes, "The Path of the Law," at 457–461.
30. See, for example, Richard A. Posner, *The Problems of Jurisprudence* 221–239 (1990).
31. Cf. Connie S. Rosati, "Some Puzzles about the Objectivity of Law," 23 Law & Phil. 273, 316 (2004) ("Actual judges are . . . trying to discover the legal facts rather than discern their own judgments or reactions").
32. Karl Llewellyn, "A Realistic Jurisprudence—The Next Step," 30 *Colum. L. Rev.* 431, 456 (1930).
33. See, for example, Dennis Patterson, *Law and Truth* (1996).
34. Hart described law as a system of primary and secondary rules that exist in the sense that they are accepted by legal officials. See H. L. A. Hart, *The Concept of Law* 77–114 (1961). Hart sometimes presented this view of law as a kind of "descriptive sociology." Ibid. at v. MacCormick describes law as a complex "institutional fact." See, for example, Neil MacCormick, "On 'Open Texture' in Law," in *Controversies about Law's Ontology* 72, 78–79 (Paul Amselek and Neil MacCormick eds., 1991). See generally Neil MacCormick and Ota Weinberger, *An Institutional Theory of Law* (1986).
35. Felix Cohen, "Transcendental Nonsense and the Functional Approach," 35 *Colum. L. Rev.* 809, 830 (1935).
36. In an earlier period, common lawyers talked as if "custom" constituted the law,

but the same difficulty was apparent: there was in fact no established custom on most of the intricate issues considered by common law courts. See Brian Simpson, "The Common Law and Legal Theory," in *Legal Theory and Common Law* 8, 18–21 (William Twining ed., 1986).

37. Benjamin Sells, *The Soul of the Law* 24 (1994).
38. Ibid. at 29.
39. Ibid. at 27 (emphasis in original).
40. Black & White Taxicab Co. v. Brown & Yellow Taxicab Co., 276 U.S. 518, 533 (1928) (Holmes, J., dissenting).
41. Several of the following arguments and others in a similar vein are made, though in quite different and more analytical form, in Rosati, "Some Puzzles about the Objectivity of Law."
42. Llewellyn, *The Bramble Bush*, at 49.
43. Cass R. Sunstein, *Legal Reasoning and Political Conflict* 14 (1996).
44. Gerald Postema explains that "[a]lready in the seventeenth century, at the time of the self-conscious articulation of classical common law theory by Coke, Hale, and others, the doctrine [of precedent] was under severe attack." Gerald J. Postema, "Some Roots of Our Notion of Precedent," in *Precedent in Law* 9 (Laurence Goldstein ed., 1987).
45. Jonathan Swift, *Gulliver's Travels,* in *Gulliver's Travels and Other Writings* 203 (Ricardo Quintana ed., 1958) (first published 1726).
46. Robert Gordon, "The Path of the Lawyer," 110 *Harv. L. Rev.* 1013, 1013 (1997).
47. George C. Christie, *Jurisprudence: Text and Readings on the Philosophy of Law* 919– 960 (1973).
48. Ibid. at 921, 958, 921.
49. George C. Christie and Patrick H. Martin, *Jurisprudence: Text and Reading on the Philosophy of Law* (2d ed. 1995).
50. Antonin Scalia, *A Matter of Interpretation: Federal Courts and the Law* 8 (1997).
51. Brian Simpson, "The Common Law and Legal Theory," in *Legal Theory and Common Law* 8, 17 (W. Twining ed., 1986).
52. 347 U.S. 483 (1954).
53. See *Swift v. Tyson*, 41 U.S. 1, 37 (1842).
54. Llewellyn, *The Bramble Bush,* at 48.
55. Karl Llewellyn, *The Common Law Tradition* 77–91 (1960).
56. See, for example, Lon L. Fuller, *Anatomy of the Law* 112 (1968).
57. Ibid. at 45.
58. Ibid. at 92 (emphasis added). In a similar vein, but with more of the "poetic license" that Fuller eschewed, the historian and law professor Norman Cantor observes that the common law is sometimes described as if it were "a kind of fixed heavenly firmament, its procedures and principles shining down like beautiful and remote stars, infinitely set apart from the anxieties, confusions, and passions of particular human lives." Norman F. Cantor, *Imagining the Law: Common Law and the Foundations of the American Legal System* 377 (1997).

59. Fuller, *Anatomy of the Law,* at 93.

60. Rosati, "Some Puzzles about the Objectivity of Law," at 307–308.

61. Fuller, *Anatomy of the Law,* at 98 (emphasis added). Fuller noted that this characterization would typically be dismissed today as a "childish fiction," and he accepted the characterization while pointing out that the fiction was often a useful one. Ibid.

62. Guido Calabresi, *A Common Law Guide for the Age of Statutes* 5 (1982).

63. Lon Fuller discussed ten crucial differences that he believed separated statute law from common law. Fuller, *Anatomy of the Law,* at 89–112.

64. Aquinas, *Summa Theologica* I–II, Q. 90, art. 4 (emphasis added).

65. See Fuller, *Anatomy of the Law,* at 92 (emphasis added).

66. In statutory cases, of course, new interpretations are applied to events occurring before the interpretation was announced but usually not to events that occurred before the statute was enacted.

67. For discussion and collected materials on this practice, see William N. Eskridge Jr. and Philip P. Frickey, *Cases and Materials on Legislation: Statutes and the Creation of Public Policy* 441–457 (2d ed. 1995).

68. Llewellyn, *The Bramble Bush,* at 87.

69. Of course, this view of the matter still leaves open the question of whether it is fair to apply law to persons who could not have been expected to know its content.

70. For example, the argument is sometimes made that retroactive application is needed to give parties incentive to litigate in favor of beneficial legal change. See Larry Alexander and Emily Sherwin, *The Rule of Rules* 152 (2001). From an economic perspective, scholars have advocated retroactive application of common law rules on the assumption that actors will anticipate (presumptively beneficial or efficiency-enhancing) legal changes and will act accordingly. See, for example, Louis Kaplow, "An Economic Analysis of Legal Transitions," 99 *Harv. L. Rev.* 509, 598–602 (1986).

71. See, for example, Roger Traynor, "Quo Vadis, Prospective Overruling: A Question of Judicial Responsibility," 28 *Hastings L.J.* 533 (1977).

72. See, for example, Chevron Oil Co. v. Huson, 404 U.S. 97, 106–107 (1971); Linkletter v. Walker, 381 U.S. 618 (1965).

73. Jim Beam Distilling Co. v. Georgia, 501 U.S. 529, 535–536 (1991) (emphasis added). Two years later, in Harper v. Virginia Department of Taxation, 509 U.S. 86, 97 (1993), a majority of the justices reconfirmed this rule of retroactivity.

74. 501 U.S. at 549 (quoting Marbury v. Madison, 1 Cranch 137, 177 (1803)) (emphasis added).

75. Ibid. For an argument that Scalia's jurisprudential claims generally may be based on a self-conscious commitment to maintaining "noble myths" about law that he himself does not actually believe, see Daniel A. Farber and Suzanna Sherry, *Desperately Seeking Certainty: The Misguided Quest for Constitutional Foundations* 38–44 (2002).

76. Simpson, "The Common Law and Legal Theory," at 10 (emphasis added).

## 4. The Jurisprudence of Modernity

1. Karl Llewellyn, *The Bramble Bush* 4 (1930).
2. Richard A. Posner, *The Problems of Jurisprudence* 225 (1990) ("The law is not a thing [judges] discover; it is the name of their activity. They do not act in accordance with something called "law"—they just act as best they can. . . . The important thing is that law is something that licensed persons, mainly judges, lawyers, and legislators, *do*") (emphasis added, footnote omitted).
3. Deborah L. Rhode, "Legal Scholarship," 115 *Harv. L. Rev.* 1327, 1342 (2002) (quoting and agreeing with Robert Gordon).
4. Michael Moore, "Legal Reality: A Naturalist Approach to Legal Ontology," 21 *Law & Phil.* 619, 652 (2002).
5. Thomas Nagel, *Mortal Questions* 194 (1979).
6. Dennis Patterson, *Law and Truth* 181–182 (1996) (emphasis added).
7. Ibid. at 135.
8. See, for example, Philip Bobbitt, *Constitutional Fate* (1982).
9. Patterson, *Law and Truth*, at 136 n. 39 (second emphasis added).
10. Ibid. at 142.
11. Norman Malcolm, "The Groundlessness of Belief," in *Faith* 193, 203 (Terence Penelhum ed., 1989). See ibid. ("I do not comprehend this notion of belief in *the existence* of God which is thought to be distinct from belief *in* God.").
12. John Hick, "Seeing-as and Religious Experience," in *Faith*, at 183, 184.
13. For a similar analysis, see Moore, "Legal Reality," at 640–644.
14. Cover went on to suggest that this violent dimension of law is one that "the growing literature that argues for the centrality of interpretive practices in law blithely ignores." Robert Cover, "Violence and the Word," in *Narrative, Violence, and the Law: The Essays of Robert Cover* 203, 203–224 (Martha Minow et al. eds., 1992).
15. Arthur Leff, "Law and," 87 *Yale L.J.* 989, 1005 (1978).
16. A classic instance of this kind of claim is Richard Posner's seminal article offering an economic explanation of traditional common law negligence doctrines. Richard A. Posner, "A Theory of Negligence," 1 *J. Legal Stud.* 29 (1972).
17. Posner's more recent work seems more in this vein, viewing law as something to be "overcome." See Richard A. Posner, *Overcoming Law* (1995).
18. An example familiar to all first-year law students involves the central tort concept of "negligence": judicial talk of "reasonable care" and the "reasonable person" is often understood to be a figurative way of importing the more economic cost–benefit calculations of the so-called Learned Hand test.
19. Richard A. Posner, *Economic Analysis of Law* 21 (3d ed. 1986).
20. George Fletcher, "Fairness and Utility in Tort Theory," 85 *Harv. L. Rev.* 537, 546 (1972).
21. See, for example, Karl Llewellyn, "A Realistic Jurisprudence—The Next Step," 30 *Colum. L. Rev.* 431, 447–448 (1930) (distinguishing between "real rules" and "paper rules").

22. Grant Gilmore, *The Ages of American Law* 13 (1977).
23. Jed Rubenfeld, "The Anti-Antidiscrimination Agenda," 111 *Yale L.J.* 1141, 1177–1178 (2002).
24. See Oliver Wendell Holmes, "The Path of the Law," 10 *Harv. L. Rev.* 457, 466 (1897) ("[T]he logical method and form flatter that longing for certainty and for repose which is in every human mind. But certainty generally is illusion, and repose is not the destiny of man.").
25. Ibid. at 468.
26. Ibid. at 466–468.
27. See generally Robert Samuel Summers, *Instrumentalism and American Legal Theory* (1982).
28. See, for example, Roscoe Pound, "Mechanical Jurisprudence," 8 *Colum. L. Rev.* 605 (1908); Roscoe Pound, "The Scope and Purpose of Sociological Jurisprudence," 24 *Harv. L. Rev.* 591 (1910).
29. See, for example, Herman Oliphant, "A Return to Stare Decisis," 14 A.B.A. J. 71, 159–162 (1928); Felix Cohen, "Transcendental Nonsense and the Functional Approach," 35 *Colum. L. Rev.* 809, 829–849 (1935). See generally William Twining, *Karl Llewellyn and the Realist Movement* 60–67 (1973).
30. For an overview of the movement, see Anthony T. Kronman, *The Lost Lawyer* 201–209 (1993).
31. See, for example, "Symposium: Empirical Legal Realism: A New Social Scientific Assessment of Law and Human Behavior," 97 *Nw. U. L. Rev.* 1075 (2003); "Symposium: Preferences and Rational Choice: New Perspectives and Legal Implications," 151 *U. Pa. L. Rev.* 707 (2003); Jeremy A. Blumenthal, "Law and Social Science in the Twenty-first Century," 12 *S. Cal. Interdisc. L.J.* 1 (2002); Cass R. Sunstein, "Behavioral Analysis of Law," *U. Chi. L. Rev.* 1175, 1195 (1998); Edward L. Rubin, "Law and the Methodology of Law," 1997 *Wis. L. Rev.* 521, 541–555.
32. See Edward Rubin, "Legal Scholarship," in *A Companion to Philosophy of Law and Legal Theory* 562, 565 (Dennis Patterson ed., 1996).
33. Brian Z. Tamanaha, *Realistic Socio-Legal Theory* 241–242 (1997).
34. For a discussion of the failure to address any of the complex questions of "interest balancing" in constitutional law on either a conceptual or an empirical level, see T. Alexander Aleinikoff, "Constitutional Law in an Age of Balancing," 96 *Yale L.J.* 943 (1987).
35. See, for example, Indiana Harbor Belt Railroad Co. v. American Cyanamid Co., 916 F.2d 1174 (7th Cir. 1990).
36. Cf. Louis Michael Seidman, *Our Unsettled Constitution* 7 (2001) (arguing that citizens "are not fooled" by judges' claims that they are neutrally applying the law).
37. Holmes, "The Path of the Law," at 466–468. Cf..Posner, *Economic Analysis of Law*, at 21 (asserting that "legal doctrines rest on inarticulate gropings toward efficiency" and that "[a]lthough few judicial opinions contain explicit references to economic concepts, often the true grounds of legal decisions are concealed rather than illuminated by the characteristic rhetoric of opinions").

38. Bruce A. Ackerman, *Reconstructing American Law* 46–104 (1983).

39. See, for example, Posner, *Overcoming Law*, at 17.

40. Compare Richard A. Posner, "The Problematics of Moral and Legal Theory," 111 *Harv. L. Rev.* 1637 (1998), with Responses (by Ronald Dworkin, Charles Fried, Anthony T. Kronman, John T. Noonan Jr., and Martha C. Nussbaum), 111 *Harv. L. Rev.* 1718–1795 (1998). The condemnation of Posner's more pragmatic and policy-oriented position was often caustic. See, for example, Martha C. Nussbaum, "Still Worthy of Praise," 111 *Harv. L. Rev.* 1776, 1782 (1998) (asserting that "the reader who knows something about academic philosophy will be surprised at every point by the sheer casualness and inaccuracy of Posner's treatment"); ibid. at 1788 ("Posner's theoretical statement of his position is, to say the least, underdeveloped."). Charles Fried describes Posner's essay as "diatribe," full of "the ad hominen ridicule of opponents" and of argument that is "gross and unnuanced." Charles Fried, "Philosophy Matters," 111 *Harv. L. Rev.* 1739, 1739–1740 (1998).

41. Ronald Dworkin, *Taking Rights Seriously* 106–107 (1977).

42. See especially Ronald Dworkin, *Law's Empire* (1986).

43. Ibid. at 407. For Dworkin's own willingness to advise the judicial "princes," see, for example, Ronald Dworkin, *Sovereign Virtue* (2000); Ronald Dworkin, *Freedom's Law: the Moral Reading of the Constitution* (1996); Ronald Dworkin, *Life's Dominion* (1994); Dworkin, *Law's Empire;* Ronald Dworkin, *A Matter of Principle* (1985); Dworkin, *Taking Rights Seriously.* Dworkin and several philosophical comrades also famously—though futilely—submitted a "Philosophers' Brief" in the assisted suicide cases heard by the U.S. Supreme Court several years ago.

44. Cf. Dan Hunter, "Reason is Too Large: Analogy and Precedent in Law," 50 *Emory L.J.* 1197, 1243 (2001) (noting "the total absence of empirical evidence" supporting Dworkin's description of judicial decisionmaking).

45. Dworkin, *Freedom's Law*, at 37.

46. Ibid.

47. See Joseph C. Hutcheson, "The Judgment Intuitive: The Function of the 'Hunch' in Judicial Decision," 14 *Cornell L.Q.* 274 (1929).

48. Larry Alexander and Emily Sherwin demonstrate that the logic of Dworkin's approach necessarily prefers legal principles that achieve only a minimal or threshhold level of "fit." Larry Alexander and Emily Sherwin, *The Rule of Rules* 171–172 (2001).

49. The point is developed effectively and at length in Michael McConnell, "The Importance of Humility in Judging: A Comment on Ronald Dworkin's 'Moral Reading' of the Constitution," 65 *Fordham L. Rev.* 1269 (1997).

50. Dworkin, *Freedom's Law*, at 37.

51. See, for example, Dworkin, *Law's Empire*, at 271–275.

52. It would not be unfair to place part of the responsibility for this state of affairs on Holmes himself. As Louise Weinberg has pointed out, in his decades on the bench Holmes did virtually nothing to implement the jurisprudential changes he advocated, and toward which he promised "to press . . . with all my heart."

Holmes, "The Path of the Law," at 474. Measured against his own prescribed path, Weinberg concludes, Holmes's rhetorically memorable but jurisprudentially conventional opinions amounted to a "colossal waste." Louise Weinberg, "Holmes' Failure," 96 *Mich. L. Rev.* 691, 700, 707 (1997). Holmes's reticence or incapacity to carry out his own project might prompt doubts about the cogency of his prescriptions.

53. See Mary Ann Glendon, *A Nation under Lawyers* 184 (1994).

54. Holmes, "The Path of the Law," at 467–477.

55. Larry Alexander, "The Banality of Legal Reasoning," 73 *Notre Dame L. Rev.* 517, 519 (1998).

56. Norman F. Cantor, *Imagining the Law: Common Law and the Foundations of the American Legal System* 359 (1997): "Efforts made at Yale and Columbia University Law Schools in the 1930s and 1940s to integrate legal study with the leading edges of the social and behavioral sciences had a modest and mostly ephemeral impact. Except for market economics, social and behavioral science has remarkably little impact on American law schools today."

57. Ibid. at 376.

58. Richard A. Posner, "Against Constitutional Theory," 73 *N.Y.U. L. Rev.* 1, 10 (1998).

59. Deborah Rhode, "Professional Education and Professional Values," *The Newsletter* No. 98–2, April 1998, at pp. 1, 3.

60. Holmes, "The Path of the Law," at 467.

61. David Rosenberg, "The Path Not Taken," 110 *Harv. L. Rev.* 1044, 1045 (1997).

62. Ibid. at 1044.

63. For example, noting that the Supreme Court has sometimes addressed issues of jury behavior that have been extensively studied by social scientists, J. Alexander Tanford concludes that "[a]n examination of the written opinions in these cases reveals that the Justices ignored, misused, distorted and misinterpreted psychological literature about trials to justify decisions at odds with empirical data." J. Alexander Tanford, "The Limits of a Scientific Jurisprudence: The Supreme Court and Psychology," 66 *Ind. L.J.* 137, 145 (1990).

64. Rhode, "Legal Scholarship," at 1337, 1339, 1342.

65. Brian Leiter, "Is There an 'American' Jurisprudence?" 17 *Oxford J. Leg. Stud.* 367, 379 (1997).

66. Richard A. Posner, "The Path Away from the Law," 110 *Harv. L. Rev.* 1039, 1043 (1997) (asserting that Holmes's "article is a prophecy, and it is coming true").

67. See Cantor, *Imagining the Law,* at 192 ("A London barrister of 1540, quick-frozen and revived in New York today, would only need a year's brush-up course at NYU School of Law to begin civil practice as a partner in a midtown or Wall Street corporate-law firm."); id. at 73 ("Glanville wouldn't be surprised at what he would find if he were to sit in on a class on property in a law school today. It is still his common law.").

68. Cohen, "Transcendental Nonsense and the Functional Approach," at 833.

69. Jeremy Waldron, "'Transcendental Nonsense' and System in Law," 100 *Colum. L. Rev.* 16, 17 (2000).

70. Grant Gilmore, "Legal Realism: Its Cause and Cure," 70 *Yale L.J.* 1037, 1048 (1961).

71. See, for example, Daniel A. Farber, "The Inevitability of Practical Reason: Statutes, Formalism, and the Rule of Law," 45 *Vand. L. Rev.* 533 (1992); David E. Van Zandt, "An Alternative Theory of Practical Reason in Judicial Decisions," 65 *Tul. L. Rev.* 775 (1991); Steven J. Burton, "Law as Practical Reason," 62 *S. Cal. L. Rev.* 747 (1991). For a skeptical response to these invocations of "practical reason," see Larry Alexander, "Practical Reason and Statutory Interpretation," 12 *Law & Phil.* 319 (1993).

72. See Karl Llewellyn, *The Common Law Tradition* 121, 183–184, 206, 268, 447 (1960).

73. For a more scholarly albeit highly readable presentation of this view, see Paul F. Campos, *Jurismania: The Madness of American Law* (1998).

74. Cf. Sanford Levinson, *Constitutional Faith* 191–192 (1988) (arguing that constitutional law is best viewed as a "uniquely American form of political rhetoric" and observing that "[t]here is nothing that is unsayable in the language of the Constitution").

75. Cf. Gerard V. Bradley, "Overcoming Posner," 94 *Mich. L. Rev.* 1898, 1905 n. 15 (1996) (review essay) ("'Practical reason' is *reasoning . . . about what to do*.").

76. For an exposition of the origins of these distinctions in Aristotle's philosophy, see Joseph Dunne, *Back to the Rough Ground: Practical Judgment and the Lure of Technique* 237–244 (1993).

77. Cass R. Sunstein, *Legal Reasoning and Political Conflict* 14 (1996).

78. Emily Sherwin, "A Defense of Analogical Reasoning in Law," 66 *U. Chi. L. Rev.* 1179, 1186 (1999). See also Van Zandt, "An Alternative Theory," at 795–796 ("Although [judges] occasionally cite scientific studies, the most important source [of information] for judges is the pool of past decisions, precedent. . . . Precedents are derivative information").

79. Cf. Alexander and Sherwin, *The Rule of Rules*, at 146 ("The most persuasive reason for honoring incorrect precedents is to protect those who have relied on official decisions and to encourage such reliance in the future.").

80. Robin West, *Progressive Constitutionalism* 196 (1994).

81. See Posner, *Overcoming Law*, at 520.

82. A. W. Brian Simpson, *Leading Cases in the Common Law* 10–11 (1995).

83. Llewellyn, *The Bramble Bush*, at 36.

84. John Noonan, *Persons and Masks of the Law* ch. 4 (1976).

85. Simpson, *Leading Cases in the Common Law*, at 11.

86. See Richard S. Murphy and Erin A. O'Hara, "Mistake of Criminal Law: A Study of Coalitions and Costly Information," 5 *Sup. Ct. Econ. Rev.* 217, 218 (1997) ("'Ignorance of the law is no excuse' is so widespread a maxim that it is one of the few things many people do know about the law.").

87. Alexander, "The Banality of Legal Reasoning," at 527.

## III. The Metaphysics of Legal Meaning

1. See Peter L. Strauss, "The Common Law and Statutes," 70 *U. Colo. L. Rev.* 225, 227–229 (1999). For a succinct review of the ebbs and flows of these positions in the last century, see John Manning, "Legal Realism and the Canons' Revival," 5 *Green Bag* 283 (2002).
2. Umberto Eco, *Interpretation and Overinterpretation* 84 (Stefan Collini ed., 1992).

## 5. How Does Law Mean?

1. For a helpful discussion of this point, see Larry Alexander and Emily Sherwin, *The Rule of Rules* 98–100 (2001).
2. Thomas W. Merrill, "The Common Law Powers of the Federal Courts," 52 *U. Chi. L. Rev.* 1, 5 (1985).
3. Gary Lawson, "On Reading Recipes . . . and Constitutions," 85 *Geo. L.J.* 1823 (1997).
4. Ibid. at 1826.
5. Ibid. at 1826–1827.
6. For a succinct and pointed presentation of these and similar objections, see Larry Alexander and Saikrishna Prakash, "'Is That English You're Speaking?' Why Intention-Free Interpretation Is an Impossibility," 41 U. *San Diego L. Rev.* (2004).
7. Patrick McKinley Brennan, "Realizing the Rule of Law in the Human Subject," 43 *B.C. L. Rev.* 227, 312, 316 (2002).
8. Paul F. Campos, "Against Constitutional Theory," in Paul F. Campos et al., *Against the Law* 116, 118–119 (1996).
9. Cf. Cooper v. Aaron, 358 U.S. 1, 18–19 (1958).
10. Campos, "Against Constitutional Theory," at 128–131.
11. My references to Larry Solum in this chapter refer to some very helpful written comments he provided on an earlier draft.
12. Umberto Eco, *Interpretation and Overinterpretation* 84 (Stefan Collini ed., 1992).
13. Stanley Fish, "Play of Surfaces: Theory and the Law," in *Legal Hermeneutics* 297, 299 (Gregory Leyh ed., 1992).
14. Oliver Wendell Holmes, "The Theory of Legal Interpretation," 12 *Harv. L. Rev.* 417, 417 (1899).
15. For a helpful and approving overview of this movement, see Vesan Kesavan and Michael Stokes Paulsen, "The Interpretive Force of the Constitution's Secret Drafting History," 91 *Geo. L.J.* 1113 (2003).
16. The story, elaborated on for different ends and with different degrees of reverence by later writers such as Milton and Mark Twain, comes from Genesis 2:19–20.
17. If the establishment of the Ministry of Language is understood as a repudiation of the practice of determining meanings by reference to speakers' meanings expressed and understood with the use of linguistic conventions, then interesting problems arise. How will anyone make sense of the statutes or regulations creat-

ing and charging the Ministry? How will the ministers deliberate together about what semantic rules to adopt? And how will the public be expected to understand the rules when they are issued?

18. Holmes, "The Theory of Legal Interpretation," at 417–418.

19. Kesavan and Paulsen, "The Interpretive Force of the Constitution's Secret Drafting History," at 1132, 1138.

20. David Brink points out to me that a few theorists may use the "speaker's meaning"/"sentence meaning" distinction for a different purpose—not to establish a "conventional meaning" that is distinct from what the speaker intended, but rather to introduce the idea that the full meaning of a term or sentence is in part determined by the "true nature" of the thing or things referred to in the sentence. If I say "I found gold!," for example, my semantic intentions determine that it is gold, not silver or copper, that I am referring to, but the full meaning of "gold" may be determined by what gold really is, not by my (potentially mistaken) notions about gold. For an argument favoring this position, see Michael Moore, "Justifying the Natural Law Theory of Constitutional Interpretation," 69 *Fordham L. Rev.* 2087 (2001). By this view, as I understand it, speaker's meaning is still essential insofar as it determines the reference of the terms used, but "the way the world is" fills out the full meaning. This view raises complex and interesting questions—some of which can be important in practice to legal interpretation—but so far as I can see, the "authorial meaning" thesis advanced in this chapter does not necessarily commit one either to accept or reject this "natural law" version of meaning.

21. Gerald Graff, "'Keep Off the Grass,' 'Drop Dead,' and Other Indeterminacies: A Response to Sanford Levinson," in *Interpreting Law and Literature* 175, 177 (Sanford Levinson and Steven Mailloux eds., 1988) (emphasis added).

22. Both Larry Solum and David Brink point out to me—correctly, I think—that ironic meanings are typically dependent on, and play off of, "standard" or "literal" meanings. The ironic "Yeah, right" gets its effect from the fact that listeners understand that the speaker is making an assertion that if taken nonironically would be false, and he also intends that we understand this complex semantic intention. My point is simply that it is conventions that permit us to understand and negotiate this complex linguistic transaction: hence, it is a mistake to contrast "speaker's meaning" with "sentence" or "conventional" or "utterance" meaning.

23. Holmes, "The Theory of Legal Interpretation," at 417, 419.

24. To be sure, legislators may need to use language in technical or specialized senses that differ from speech patterns in nonlegal settings. But the legal linguistic conventions relied on by legal interpreters naturally take account of that sort of specialized usage (once again reflecting the fact that conventions operate as a way of expressing and discerning authorial intent, not as a source of meaning *independent of* such intent).

25. See Meir Dan-Cohen, "Decision Rules and Conduct Rules: On Acoustic Separation in Criminal Law," 97 *Harv. L. Rev.* 625 (1984).

26. You could, of course, argue that my response to your essay is idiosyncratic or unusual, but that claim, even if persuasive, would not show that my response is incorrect or that I have misinterpreted your essay.

27. Eco, *Interpretation and Overinterpretation*, at 69.

28. Indeed, a theorist touched by Kant might argue that we can never really have direct access to the *real* author—to the "author *an sich*," so to speak—but only to our representations of that author; so we will always and of necessity be looking to a sort of constructed or hypothetical author. It would not be profitable, I think, to pursue this refinement—or obfuscation—here.

29. In addition, we have not considered the question of whether legal decisionmaking should depend wholly on the meanings assigned to enactments or precedents. In written comments on an earlier draft, David Brink points out that "meaning is not the only constraint on interpretation." I would put what I think is an essentially similar point a bit differently: although interpretation is by its nature an inquiry into "meaning," it need not be the only component of legal decisionmaking. See generally Steven D. Smith, "Why Should Courts Obey the Law?" 77 *Geo. L.J.* 113 (1988). In addition, it may sometimes be helpful to distinguish between "interpreting" a text—that is, figuring out what it means—and "applying" that meaning to a specific set of facts. For a discussion emphasizing this distinction, see Michael J. Perry, *The Constitution in the Courts* 70–76 (1994).

30. See Holmes, "The Theory of Legal Interpretation." See also Kesavan and Paulsen, "The Interpretive Force of the Constitution's Secret Drafting History," at 1133 (quoting Robert Bork) (legal meaning should be derived from "an average, informed speaker and reader of that language at the time of . . . enactment"). Cf. ibid. at 1162 ("It does not matter what any actual Ratifiers thought . . . but rather what the hypothetical, reasonably well-informed Ratifier would have thought with all of the relevant information in hand.").

31. See ibid. at 1118 (arguing that constitutional interpretation should attempt to discern "the meaning the words and phrases . . . would have had, in context, to ordinary readers, speakers, and writers of the English language, reading a document of this type, at the time adopted," and should not attempt "to determine either the Framers' or the Ratifiers' *subjective intention*").

32. See, for example, In re Sinclair, 870 F.2d 1340 (7th Cir. 1989) (acknowledging that "textual meaning" was contrary to "legislative intention"). For an insightful analysis of the case and the problem it presents, see Paul F. Campos, "The Chaotic Pseudotext," 94 *Mich. L. Rev.* 2178 (1996).

33. See Pierre Schlag, "The Brilliant, the Curious, and the Wrong," 39 *Stan. L. Rev.* 917, 918 n. 2 (1987).

34. T. Alexander Aleinikoff, "Updating Statutory Interpretation," 87 *Mich. L. Rev.* 20, 49 (1988) (emphasis in original).

## 6. Author(s) Wanted

1. Lon Fuller, "Human Interaction and the Law," in *The Principles of Social Order* 234 (K. Winston ed., 1981).

2. Steven Burton, "Law as Practical Reason," 62 *S. Cal. L. Rev.* 747, 784 (1989).

3. Karl Llewellyn, *The Bramble Bush* 12 (3d ed. 1960).

4. The allusion is to Aguilar v. Felton, 473 U.S. 402, 415 (1985) (Powell, J., concurring), in which the Supreme Court concluded that "precedents of this Court require us to invalidate these two educational programs that concededly have 'done so much good and little, if any, detectable harm.'"

5. Paul F. Campos, "Against Constitutional Theory," in Paul F. Campos et al., *Against the Law* 116, 118–119, 128–131 (1996).

6. See, for example, Ronald Dworkin, *Law's Empire* 407 (1986) (describing judges as the "princes" of Law's Empire).

7. See, for example, ibid. at 313–337.

8. Ronald Dworkin, *Taking Rights Seriously* 14–45 (1977).

9. Dworkin, *Law's Empire,* at 147–164.

10. See, for example, Edward B. Foley, "Interpretation and Philosophy: Dworkin's Constitution," 14 *Const. Comm.* 151 (1997) (review essay).

11. See, for example, *The End of Democracy? The Judicial Usurpation of Politics* (Mitchell S. Muncy ed., 1997).

12. Kosak v. United States, 465 U.S. 848 (1984).

13. Henry M. Hart Jr. and Albert M. Sacks, *The Legal Process* 1374–1380 (William Eskridge Jr. and Philip Frickey eds., 1994).

14. Dworkin, *Law's Empire,* at 190, 109.

15. Ibid. at 192–196.

16. Ibid. at 211, 166.

17. Ibid. at 225 (emphasis added).

18. Max Radin, "Statutory Interpretation," 43 *Harv. L. Rev.* 863, 870–871 (1930). For a more recent and careful statement of the objection, see Matthew Adler, "Expressive Theories of Law," 148 *U. Pa. L. Rev.* 1363, 1389–1393 (2000).

19. See, for example, Antonin Scalia, *A Matter of Interpretation* 32–33 (1997).

20. For a possible exception, see Joseph Vining, *The Authoritative and the Authoritarian* 110–125 (1986). My own tentative view, however, is that the exception is only apparent. See note 34 below.

21. Dworkin, *Law's Empire* 167, 168 (1986) (emphasis added).

22. Ibid. at 168.

23. John Searle, *The Social Construction of Reality* 23–26 (1995).

24. Ibid. at 24.

25. Ibid. at 7.

26. Ibid. at 25.

27. John Searle, *The Rediscovery of the Mind* 91 (1992).

28. Nagel makes the argument in, among other places, his essay "What Is It Like to Be a Bat?" in Thomas Nagel, *Mortal Questions* 165–180 (1979).

29. See generally Searle, *The Rediscovery of the Mind.*

30. Searle has elsewhere suggested that "it is a very deep mistake to suppose that the crucial question for ontology is, 'What sorts of things exist in the world?' as opposed to, 'What must be the case in the world in order that our empirical statements be true?'" Searle, *The Social Construction of Reality,* at 25. Perhaps. But

in fact we *do* have at least implicit and often explicit answers to the former question (as Searle's own "particles and forces" ontology suggests): so asking the latter question independently is precisely what creates the possibility of an incongruity in our answers to these separate questions—or "nonsense."

31. Elizabeth S. Anderson and Richard H. Pildes, "Expressive Theories of Law: A General Restatement," 148 *U. Pa. L. Rev.* 1503, 1514 (2000).

32. Ibid. at 1517.

33. Ibid. at 1515–1516.

34. Ibid. at 1517. It seems to me that Joseph Vining has a similar notion in mind when he writes of the possibility of a legislature or court speaking with a single voice. See Vining, *The Authoritative and the Authoritarian,* at 111–112 ("But to answer that . . . a multi-member institution can have a single voice, we must assume that there *is* discussion and that statements made jointly *are* in fact joint and express the actual belief of all whose names are affixed to them.").

35. Anderson and Pildes, "Expressive Theories of Law," at 1518.

36. Ibid. at 1519.

37. Ibid. at 1523 (emphasis added).

38. See generally William N. Eskridge Jr. and Philip P. Frickey, *Cases and Materials on Legislation* 633–879 (2d ed. 1995).

39. For a recent social science analysis calling into question some of the usual conventions (such conventions of deferring to the understanding of sponsors of legislation), see Daniel B. Rodriguez and Barry R. Weingast, "The Positive Political Theory of Legislative History: New Perspectives on the 1964 Civil Rights Act and its Interpretation," *151 U. Pa. L. Rev.* 1417 (2003).

40. Edwards v. Aguillard, 48 U.S. 578, 636–637 (1987) (Scalia, J., dissenting).

41. See Frederick Schauer, "Easy Cases," 58 *S. Cal. L. Rev.* 399, 414 (1985): "The parties concerned know, without litigating and without consulting lawyers, that Ronald Reagan cannot run for a third term; that the junior Senator from Virginia, who was elected in 1982, does not have to run again in 1984 or 1986 even though the Representative from the First Congressional District does; that bills receiving less than a majority of votes in either the House or the Senate are not laws of the United States; . . . and that a twenty-nine-year-old is not going to be President of the United States."

42. In fact, this precise example provoked a spirited and entertaining exchange some years ago. See Kenney Hegland, "Goodbye to Deconstruction," 58 *S. Cal. L. Rev.* 1203, 1208–1212 (1985); Anthony D'Amato, "Pragmatic Indeterminacy," 85 *Nw. U. L. Rev.* 148, 189 n. 11 (1990); Kenney Hegland, "Goodbye to 2525," 85 *Nw. U. L. Rev.* 128, 129, 133 (1990); Kenney Hegland, "Indeterminacy: I Hardly Knew Thee," 33 *Ariz. L. Rev.* 509, 510 (1991).

43. See Hegland's essays in the previous note.

44. See Paul F. Campos, *Jurismania: The Madness of American Law* 58–61 (1998).

45. Oliver Wendell Holmes, "The Theory of Legal Interpretation," 12 *Harv. L. Rev.* 417, 417 (1899).

46. See Robert H. Bork, *The Tempting of America* 144 (1990): "If someone found a letter from George Washington to Martha telling her that what he meant by the

power to lay taxes was not what other people meant, that would not change our reading of the Constitution in the slightest. Nor would the subjective intentions of all the members of a ratifying convention alter anything."

47. See Chapter 5, at pp. 123–124.

48. See Vesan Kesavan and Michael Stokes Paulsen, The Interpretive Force of the Constitution's Secret Drafting History, 91 *Geo. L.J.* 1113, 1127–1148, (2003).

49. For a more sustained discussion, see Steven D. Smith, "Law without Mind," 88 *Mich. L. Rev.* 104 (1989).

50. Roscoe Pound, "Spurious Interpretation," 7 *Colum. L. Rev.* 379, 382–383 (1907).

51. Thus, Dan Farber and Suzanna Sherry observe that "Dworkin's conclusions track the agenda of liberal judges like William Brennan, opening Dworkin to the charge of being merely a clever rationalizer." And, "[Dworkin's] treatment of the subject is always that of an advocate presenting a brief for a preordained position." Daniel A. Farber and Suzanna Sherry, *Desperately Seeking Certainty: The Misguided Quest for Constitutional Foundations* 122, 137 (2002).

52. Llewellyn, *The Bramble Bush*, at 41–42.

## 7. Law in a Quandary

1. Richard A. Posner, "The Path Away from the Law," 110 *Harv. L. Rev.* 1039, 1040 (1997).

2. Cf. Felix Cohen, "Transcendental Nonsense and the Functional Approach," 35 *Colum. L. Rev.* 809, 833 (1935) (arguing that "[o]ur legal system is filled with supernatural concepts").

3. Harold J. Berman, *Law and Revolution: The Formation of the Western Legal Tradition* 165 (1983).

4. For an engaging narration of the change from a classical to a modern worldview with a special emphasis on Harvard and Holmes, see generally Louis Menard, *The Metaphysical Club: A Story of Ideas in America* (2001).

5. For an insightful if hilariously provocative elaboration of this theme, see Paul F. Campos, *Jurismania: The Madness of American Law* (1998).

6. See generally Thomas S. Kuhn, *The Structure of Scientific Revolutions* (3d ed. 1996).

7. Cass R. Sunstein, *Legal Reasoning and Political Conflict* 14 (1996).

8. Oliver Wendell Holmes, "Natural Law," 32 *Harv. L. Rev.* 40, 40 (1918).

9. Quoted in Ellis Sandoz, *Political Apocalypse: A Study of Dostoevsky's Grand Inquisitor* 177 n. 3 (1971).

10. A. N. Wilson, *God's Funeral* 51–52 (1999).

11. See John Stuart Mill, *Autobiography* 118–122 (Penguin 1989) (first published 1873). See also Alan Millar, "Mill on Religion," in *The Cambridge Companion to Mill* 176, 194, 200 (John Skorupski ed., 1998).

12. Sidney E. Mead, *The Lively Experiment* 60 (1963) (quoting W. E. Garrison).

13. John T. Noonan Jr., *The Lustre of our Country* 214 (1998).

14. Morton J. Horwitz, "The Bork Nomination and American Constitution History," 39 *Syracuse L. Rev.* 1029, 1033 (1988).

15. See, for example, Sanford Levinson, *Constitutional Faith* (1988); Thomas C. Grey,

"The Constitution as Scripture," 37 *Stan. L. Rev.* 1 (1984); Michael J. Perry, *The Constitution, the Courts, and Human Rights* 97–100 (1982); Robert F. Nagel, "On Complaining about the Burger Court," 84 *Colum. L. Rev.* 2068, 2081 (1984) (reviewing *The Burger Court* (Vincent Blasi ed., 1983)). See also Steven D. Smith, "Law as a Religious Enterprise: Legal Interpretation and Scriptural Interpretation," in *Law and Religion* 83 (Richard O'Dair and Andrew Lewis eds., 2001).

16. See, for example, Robert N. Bellah, *Beyond Belief: Essays on Religion in a Post-Traditionalist World* (1970).

17. Pierre Schlag, "Law as the Continuation of God by Other Means," 85 *Cal. L. Rev.* 427 (1997).

18. Ibid. at 428–437.

19. Ibid. at 439. Cf. Cohen, "Transcendental Nonsense," at 833 (describing conventional approach to law as "legal theology").

20. See, for example, Steven D. Smith, "Idolatry in Constitutional Interpretation," in Paul F. Campos et al., *Against the Law* 157 (1996).

21. Roberto M. Unger, "The Critical Legal Studies Movement," 96 *Harv. L. Rev.* 561, 674–675 (1983).

22. Duncan Kennedy, *A Critique of Adjudication (fin de siecle)* 106 (1997).

23. Ibid. at 193, 192. However, a few judges may be guilty of conscious lying. Ibid. at 202.

24. Ibid. at 200.

25. Ibid. at 199.

26. Ibid. at 191.

27. Ibid. at 194–198.

28. See, for example, ibid. at 198.

29. Ibid. at 192.

30. Ibid. at 206.

31. Ibid. at 209.

32. Daniel A. Farber and Suzanna Sherry, *Desperately Seeking Certainty: The Misguided Quest for Constitutional Foundations* 38 (2002).

33. There is still another possibility: lawyers might be in bad faith *both* in their practice and in their theorizing. They might in fact adhere to a kind of faith that they hide or disavow in their explicit theorizing; but that faith might not be one that would support the current operations of legal practice.

34. Charles Larmore, *The Morals of Modernity* 89–117 (1996).

35. Ibid. at 116.

36. Ibid. at 92–93, 96.

37. See, for example, Ronald Dworkin, "Objectivity and Truth: You'd Better Believe It," 25 *Phil. & Pub. Affairs* 87 (1996).

38. See, for example, Michael S. Moore, "Moral Reality Revisited," 90 *Mich. L. Rev.* 2424, 2493–2532 (1992).

39. Larmore, *The Morals of Modernity,* at 113.

40. Ibid. at 117, 96.

41. Michael S. Moore, "Law as a Functional Kind," in *Natural Law Theory: Contemporary Essays* 188, 196 (Robert P. George ed., 1992).

42. William Barrett, *The Death of the Soul* 78–79 (1986). Barrett adds: "The absence of such intuitions behind much of the chitchat of pseudo-intellectuals accounts for the great amount of sheer verbalism that now floods our civilization in this age of media and communication."

43. Richard A. Posner, "The Decline of Law as an Autonomous Discipline: 1962–1987," 100 *Harv. L. Rev.* 761, 762 (1987).

44. Brian Bix, *Jurisprudence: Theory and Context* 72 (2d ed. 1999).

45. David Luban, "The Warren Court and the Concept of a Right," 34 *Harv. C.R.-C.L. L. Rev.* 7, 37 (1999).

46. Ibid. at 10.

47. Patrick McKinley Brennan, "Realizing the Rule of Law in the Human Subject," 43 *B.C. L. Rev.* 227, 231 (2002).

48. Richard Posner, *The Problems of Jurisprudence* 236 (1990).

49. For contrary evidence, see the variety of essays from a number of legal scholars in *Christian Perspectives on Legal Thought* (Michael W. McConnell, Robert F. Cochran Jr., and Angela C. Carmella eds., 2001).

50. See generally E. L. Mascall, *The Christian Universe* (1966).

51. See Arthur Lovejoy, *The Great Chain of Being* 31–55 (1936).

52. One leading natural law theorist, Michael Moore, is explicit in rejecting religious belief. See Michael S. Moore, "Good without God," in *Natural Law, Liberalism, and Morality* 221 (Robert P. George ed., 1996). Another leading theorist, John Finnis, plainly embraces religious belief, but he stresses that his natural law theory does not rest on any such belief. See Thomas W. Smith, "Finnis' Questions and Answers: An Ethics of Hope or Fear?," 40 *Am. J. Juris.* 27, 29 (1995) (asserting that Finnis "believes that a major contribution of his account of ethics is its demonstration of clear and reliable moral truths about moral actions . . . that appeal to all rational persons independent of . . . religious beliefs"). However, other modern natural law thinkers, such as John Courtney Murray, have embraced the classical position with its religious metaphysics. See John Courtney Murray, *We Hold These Truths* (1960).

53. This method of indirection and repetition is consciously chosen. "If you are writing, rather than speaking intimately face to face," Vining explains, "you do not rush to bare yourself. Any writing is distillation of vacillations, resolution of doubts, linking of intermittent perceptions you know you have some days and times and have not on others." Joseph Vining, *From Newton's Sleep* 343 (1995).

54. Ibid. at 344.

55. Ibid. at 128, 130, 189.

56. Michael Polanyi, *Personal Knowledge: Towards a Post-Critical Philosophy* 267 (1958).

57. Vining, *From Newton's Sleep*, at 5. See also ibid. at 60, 224, 331.

58. See, for example, ibid. at 136, 140, 145, 176, 187, 249.

59. Ibid. at 183, 239.

60. Ibid. at 243. See also ibid. at 7–8, 182–183.

61. Ibid. at 180.

62. Ibid. at 117.

63. See, for example, ibid. at 109: "But the authority of law is not the clutch of the

past. . . . The 'dead hand of the past' is just that: dead, gone. The past cannot touch us."

64. Ibid. at 111, 239.

65. Ibid. at 180.

66. We act on "the premise . . . that there is a unity and spirit. Without spirit there is nothing in law, no reason to read or listen closely, to defer, to be deferred to." Ibid. at 74.

67. Ibid. at 200 (emphasis added). Vining adds: "As in all large matters, there is a mixture, the usual combination, of doubt and belief, made easier to live with, as usual, by strong doses of self-deception." Ibid.

68. See ibid. at 201 ("So the first and last thing we know, the ultimate object of knowledge and belief, is a person, not a principle. . . . This is what we know, what is real, what has meaning.").

69. Ibid. at 157, 222.

70. Ibid. at 128.

71. Ibid. at 353.

72. Ibid. at 220. See also the essay on "Reproduction," ibid. at 339.

73. Ibid. at 355.

74. Ibid. at 116, 128, 166, 240.

75. Ibid. at 103.

76. Ibid. at 329.

77. Ibid. at 329–330.

78. Ibid. at 160.

79. Ibid. at 110.

80. Ibid. at 208.

81. Ibid. at 264–265.

82. Ibid. at 103. See also ibid. at 179 (asserting that mind cannot be known until it is searched for, and the search must be driven by "faith").

## Epilogue

1. See Joseph Vining, *The Song Sparrow and the Child: Claims of Science and Humanity* (2004).

2. *Apology* 23d (G. M. A. Grube tr.).

3. *Gorgias* 489e.

4. *Apology* 23b, 20e.

5. *Ion* 532c (Paul Woodruff tr.).

6. Ibid.

7. Ibid. at 535e.

8. *Apology* 22c, 20e, 31d.

9. Ibid. at 29b.

# Index

Harvard University Press is a member of Green Press Initiative (greenpressinitiative.org), a nonprofit organization working to help publishers and printers increase their use of recycled paper and decrease their use of fiber derived from endangered forests. This book was printed on 100% recycled paper containing 50% post-consumer waste and processed chlorine free.